P9-DIE-430

How to Read
Nonfiction
Like a
Professor

Also by Thomas C. Foster

How to Read Literature Like a Professor
How to Read Novels Like a Professor
How to Read Poetry Like a Professor
Reading the Silver Screen
Twenty-Five Books That Shaped America

How to Read Nonfiction Like a Professor

A Smart, Irreverent Guide to
Biography, History, Journalism,
Blogs, and Everything in
Between

Thomas C. Foster

HARPER

An Imprint of HarperCollins*Publishers*

HOW TO READ NONFICTION LIKE A PROFESSOR. Copyright © 2020 by Thomas C. Foster. All rights reserved. Printed in the United States of America. No part of this book may be used or reproduced in any manner whatsoever without written permission except in the case of brief quotations embodied in critical articles and reviews. For information, address HarperCollins Publishers, 195 Broadway, New York, NY 10007.

HarperCollins books may be purchased for educational, business, or sales promotional use. For information, please email the Special Markets Department at SPsales@harpercollins.com.

FIRST EDITION

Library of Congress Cataloging-in-Publication Data has been applied for.

ISBN 978-0-06-289581-3 (pbk.)
ISBN 978-0-06-300847-2 (Library edition)

20 21 22 23 24   LSC   10 9 8 7 6 5 4 3 2 1

Contents

What's Going on Around Here?

WE LIVE IN AN age of deliberate deception. That hideous fact is a lousy place to begin a book on reading nonfiction. Can't be helped. Worse, that deception poisons our public discourse, calling everything into question. How? Consider this scenario. You walk into a bookstore and cruise the nonfiction shelves: biographies, histories, memoirs, science explainers, works of psychological or sociological insight, self-help texts, yoga instructions, essays on all manner of topics, political analyses and treatises. A dizzying array. A clerk asks if you need help. You reply that you're simply looking for something edifying to take with you on your next trip, something that will leave you more enlightened than before about some aspect of our world.

"I can help," says the clerk, "but first, I have to warn you that there are thousands of useful books here, but two of them are not your friends. They are purposely trying to mislead readers into believing things that are not true, and they are quite good at it."

"Which ones?" you ask.

"Oh, I can't tell you that. Threat of lawsuits, you know. We're required to stock them but can't criticize them for fear of dismissal."

How many books are you buying today? About the same

as if a pharmacist told you that out of all the bottles in the drugstore, two contain a single poisoned pill, and she can't tell you which ones. I don't know about you, but I've never had a headache that bad.

This is essentially the condition we find ourselves in today. Our world is a giant apothecary of information, and some of it is terrible. Worse than terrible, toxic. And much of that venom is spewed in hope not of infecting us—of making us believe that it is true, although that's a bonus for the serpents who spew it—but of poisoning everything else, of calling all information into doubt. You know the drill: you can't trust any of them, everybody's a liar, one side's as bad as the other. Any rational person, of course, knows that to be untrue. Not every book or article or opinion piece or documentary or blog post is a deliberate lie. Not every biography is written to push a political agenda. Not every scientific finding is the result of corrupt data. But how many does it take to tar the rest? A very few. And then we react not with our reason but with our emotions: you can't believe any of them, we think. And the serpents have won. They don't have to succeed, only to make sure that everyone else fails.

How Long Has It Been This Bad?

BAD NEWS THERE: IT has been ever thus. Or at least ever since democracy eliminated the wrath of kings. From the earliest days of the republic, our political scene has been awash with lies, libels, name-calling, brutishness, duels, and canings. Since duels are illegal and almost no one carries a cane with spine enough to inflict real damage with its malachite head, you'd think we might clean up our act a little bit, wouldn't you? Well, you would be wrong. The propaganda machine was in full swing in the early decades of American politics, which were also the early years of American printing. Powerful men bought newspapers, or if really desperate started them, precisely to print whatever they wanted to say about themselves or their rivals. There was no falsehood they wouldn't utter, no calumny they wouldn't invent against an enemy. A hundred years or so later, the age of *yellow journalism* was born in the circulation wars between Joseph Pulitzer's *New York World* and William Randolph Hearst's *New York Journal*. That brand of news specialized in salacious material, scare-tactic headlines unwarranted by the following story, scandalmongering, and dubious reporting.

Nor is that all. Wealthy people have always been able to hire writers to undertake saint's-life biographies that paint over the cracks in unholy façades. Corporate public relations departments have planted newspaper stories praising their firms' accomplishments and hiding their malfeasance. Big Tobacco spent millions over decades in a campaign to hide the damage smoking inflicted on the lives of its customers. For forty years, ExxonMobil hid its own studies confirming global warming while denying that burning of carbon fuels was warming up the planet. And certain tabloids displayed at grocery checkout lines specialized in stories in which the starlet of the moment was impregnated by aliens and gave birth to a three-headed fish. Although the fish part may be my exaggeration. Meanwhile, persons with vile intent have dishonored actual war heroes far braver than themselves who have had the temerity to run for high office, as the Swift Boat Veterans for Truth campaign, complete with a book and op-ed pieces, did against John Kerry in 2004 when it falsely claimed, among other malicious statements, that he had not performed the actions that won him the Bronze Star. The campaign was so nasty and so successful in diminishing someone who served honorably that it became a verb, *swiftboating*, the name taken from the type of craft he skippered.

The reliance on spin and falsehood became so pronounced in the early twenty-first century that of course satirists arose on the scene, most notably Stephen Colbert, whose onscreen über-conservative persona "Stephen Colbert" (with a French silent "t" at the end), could spin "facts" out of thin air and nonsensical explanations from the flimsiest of materials, first on *The Daily Show* and then on *The Colbert Report* (with a similarly silent "t" in "Report"). His creation was both hilarious and trenchant in skewering a certain type of political being not unknown to Fox News and MSNBC viewers and talk-radio listeners.

In this win-at-all-costs climate where hyper-partisans cannibalize even members of their own party, everything becomes tribal. Books and articles are embraced or dismissed not because of their content but because of the supposed left or right leanings of their authors. Trolls, some of whom are not even in this country but seek to stir the pot from afar, attack anyone who expresses a vaguely political opinion or disparages an anointed personage. Social media increases the *silo effect*, wherein like only talks to like, so fewer people meet across partisan or ideological lines.

Silo effect? That's what happens when people close themselves off to everyone and everything that doesn't agree with their own view. The result is that the only available view from the bottom of that silo is a tiny piece of an immense sky. Here's a working definition. The results of a February 2019 *Wall Street Journal*/NBC poll about whether likely voters believed that President Trump had told the truth about contacts with Russia were broken down by the sort of cable news viewers consumed. Fox News viewers registered positive to the question at an 84 percent clip; MSNBC fans at 21 percent, CNN viewers at a whopping 1 percent. I took the liberty of writing these results as numerals so that there would be no mistaking the story they told. The only surprise to me was that MSNBC showed a greater affirmative percentage than CNN, since MSNBC seems to skew a little more liberal than CNN. On reflection, though, it makes a sort of sense: CNN has been the constant *bête noir* of the Trump personal narrative, in consequence of which even fewer conservatives and perhaps even moderates tune in to the network. It may also be that the most liberal among us have shifted their viewing habits in that direction on the enemy-of-my-enemy theory of televiewing. The CNN viewership was also the only one of the three to register *zero* percent undecided respondents. Now that's a silo.

The thing about silos is that, minus the doors, they make pretty effective prisons. As for what becomes trapped inside, silage that can't be removed, the less said the better. That unspeakable mess, though, is not unlike what we threaten to turn our society—and ourselves—into. We are so locked into our views that we cannot see facts in front of us. We become incapable of admitting that someone with a different viewpoint might be correct about, well, anything. Worse, we begin seeing all information as either belonging to our tribe or the opposing one, begin reading everything as either ratifying or challenging our world view. And that, Dear Reader, is a terrible state of affairs. If everything becomes about winning or losing, the real loser will be the truth. And us. A friend of mine has always maintained that his favorite maxim is "A frog at the bottom of the well sees only a patch of the sky." That's not the endpoint of the Chinese fable "The Frog at the Bottom of the Well," but rather the setup. Let's hope it's not the end of our story, either.

We need to come out of our silos. Open the doors and come out into the air and the light. Hack through a wall and make a door if necessary. Expand our horizons. Understand that divergent viewpoints can be valid. That sympathetic viewpoints can be false. And that we need to be able to discern the difference.

How to Read
Nonfiction
Like a
Professor

Introduction

Why Critical Reading Matters

I SAID IN THE preface that we live in an age of deliberate deception. But we also live in what may be a golden age of nonfiction. The one statement being true doesn't make the other false; both conditions can obtain simultaneously. There will be time enough to document the range and quality of contemporary writing about the real world, so for now, let's simply say that there is a vast array of very good and even much great nonfiction writing. Which is why I also suggested that we need to be able to separate the sheep from the goats in the books and articles we read. In other words, we need to read critically, or more critically than we currently do. First, though, let's consider the nature of nonfiction and what it might mean to read critically.

Ever since I began thinking about this project, a question has dogged my steps, because I knew someone would ask: when a book has been written on a subject, why is there a second one? Why are there hundreds of books and articles on the Battle of the Little Bighorn rather than just one? Why, after the *definitive* biography of, say, Abraham Lincoln (and there have been several so deemed) do biographies keep coming? We know that the feted one is definitive; every review will have told us so. Their appearance suggests that perhaps the Big Bio did less defining than some of us thought. So why do they exist? Because at some point, human beings are involved: in the life or event or turmoil being discussed, as well as in the writing of said discussion *and* in the evaluation of that writing.

We can never know the innermost thoughts of another person. Heck, we barely know our own. In the case of the Battle of the Little Bighorn, there were three persons we would most want to hear from. The most celebrated of the three, based on bookshelves and the history of movies and television shows, George Armstrong Custer, was unavailable to file an after-action report. All we can know of General Custer's thoughts is whatever he shared with others before the battle, and history tells us that most of those thoughts were wrong. So, what about the native leaders, Lakota chiefs Sitting Bull and Crazy Horse? Sitting Bull was a holy man, a visionary, rather than a battle chief. He was not present at the battle, although he said his dreams depicted the manner of Custer's downfall and gave the war leaders a strategy to follow. Crazy Horse, who was a battle chief and is generally credited with leadership in the victory, went on the run for most of the following year. When he finally surrendered, in May 1877, he probably sealed his fate, which was to be killed four months later. So details of who decided on what course of action and why are a little thin.

And there, Dear Reader, is why we need the second book. And the third, the fourth, the two hundred and seventy-first. Nobody gets it all correct and complete. Space is limited, information nearly the opposite. What one leaves in or out is a subjective matter more than an editorial one. Maybe, just maybe, one person's bias will cancel out an earlier one's, or more complete knowledge will fill in gaps in earlier versions, and we can eventually get closer to something resembling objective truth. Which we can never achieve.

A friend of mine, upon hearing of this project, said, "When I got to college, I believed that nonfiction meant that the thing was true." Ah, we were so naive then. Well, why wouldn't she? The nonfiction writing that she—and you and I and pretty much everyone everywhere—encountered most often growing up was the textbook. And if we can't count on textbooks, whose contents we are tasked with absorbing and then handing back on tests, to be true, then where are we? Nowhere, that's where. We count on the explanations for an algebraic equation or the date of a battle to be accurate, that chlorine and sodium will indeed react in a certain way, that amphibians do indeed live their early lives where chapter three says they do. Otherwise, all is lost. We learn to trust our textbooks, if for no other reason than we need to pass the upcoming test. That strategy serves us well during our school days, but it doesn't necessarily translate well to the world of general nonfiction, where we might be best served by President Ronald Reagan's policy when dealing with the Soviet Union, "Trust, but verify." In some cases, just verify. Trust be damned.

Let's suppose that the worst thing you can do when reading nonfiction is to believe that everything you read is true. What's the second worst? *Not believing any of it.* One of the things my friend, now a professional in the world of books and publishing, learned along the way was that not every work of nonfiction can be relied on to deliver the truth, the whole truth, and that other part. One possible outcome of such a revelation is cynicism; having had our eye blackened once, we believe that every outstretched hand will clench and punch us. That every book is either false or manipulative. That there is no truth to be found. But you know what? That jaded attitude is useless. Its logical endpoint is to dispense with reading altogether. For one thing, if we decide this about printed matter, is it possible to draw any other inference regarding mass media sources, news programs and news magazines and documentaries and all the rest? To say nothing of online sources, for heaven's sake. And then where are we? Stuck with novels, I suppose. At least we expect those to jerk us around in the service of art and entertainment. It would be a boon to fiction writers, who can use all the help they can get nowadays, but not that helpful for transmitting information. What we really need is not a thumbs-up or thumbs-down on the whole nonfiction enterprise but rather a means of navigating those tricky waters so that we don't capsize or pitch up on the rocks.

Being able to rely upon what we read is critical in many ways. Before the advent of the YouTube how-to video, most of us learned to do things from instructional books and articles. From those sources you could learn everything from throwing a discus to making household repairs to rebuilding car engines to mastering the art of French cooking, as promised by the late Julia Child and her coauthors. Say, that might be a good book title. And if you can learn to make *Coulis de Tomates à la Provençale* from a book, there's pretty much nothing that can't be learned there.

Beyond how-to instruction, there is a tremendous range of knowledge we rely on nonfiction to provide. We count on journalism, particularly local newspapers, to keep civic leaders and institutions in check. When corruption—sweetheart deals in exchange for favorable policies, money for votes, campaign contributions for deep-sixing regulatory rules—at city hall or the statehouse is uncovered, who uncovers it? Damn straight. When the holder of the highest office in the land hired a bunch of thugs in an attempt to subvert an election he was basically guaranteed to win anyway, who uncovered that vicious attack on our democratic institutions, who dug down to the truth despite threats and lies at every step? Two reporters from a local newspaper. Oh, sure, we think of the *Washington Post* as a major national paper and Bob Woodward and Carl Bernstein as stars in the journalistic firmament, but before Watergate they were just two young, and not very highly regarded, reporters at a local paper—whose locale just happened to contain the White House. The ability of journalists to investigate governmental wrongdoing rests on a foundation of trust: we have to be able to trust that they are giving the news to us straight, all truth and no fantasy, and they have to earn that trust with every story they write, every article they publish. That is why newspapers and magazines have traditionally insisted on multiple sources for facts in articles; the more explosive the story, the greater the need for solid facts. And it is why they are quick to admit mistakes and issue corrections. No human endeavor can be perfect, but for journalism to matter, it must come mighty close.

Nor is it just governmental wrongdoing that we count on *The Daily Herald-Star-Examiner* to apprise us of. Who broke open the story of sexual abuse in the Catholic Church? The *Boston Globe*, specifically a team called Spotlight, investigative reporters working together on stories of sufficient scope that they take months to uncover and publish. When they were finished, their list of pedophile priests had grown from one to thirteen to eighty-seven, just in greater Boston. Numerous priests were removed from clerical duty, several were tried and convicted of abuse of minors, lawsuits were filed against the Archdiocese, and Cardinal Bernard Law, who had overseen the cover-ups for years, was forced by the weight of public opinion to resign his position. Throughout the process, the Spotlight team had to fight church and city red tape to open sealed documents and unearth carefully hidden evidence, while also fending off community resistance to the truth being revealed. It was attacked for making up stories or trading in false tales peddled by "disturbed" individuals. Yet they persisted, and their efforts were rewarded with the 2003 Pulitzer Prize for Public Service. And that, friends, is what journalism can do and why we need courageous nonfiction.

I recently read an article that reported the death of local newspapers—a process that has been going on for years—will mean that fewer instances of official malfeasance will be uncovered, which will be a national calamity. And so it will.

Every week brings us new reasons that we need professional journalists and investigative freelancers. The latest as I write is the misbehavior by Boeing in hiding the defects in its 737 MAX 8 jet, which caused two disastrous crashes in 2018 and 2019, one in Indonesia and the second in Ethiopia. The previous year, it was the horrific stories of Dr. Larry Nassar's sexual abuse of girls and young women, mostly athletes, under the guise of treatment as a team doctor for USA Gymnastics and Michigan State University. Before that, it was the Flint water crisis, a series of bad decisions and shoddy processes that led to terrible water for residents of the city and lead poisoning for its children. That human-caused disaster also, however, involved the heroic efforts of a committed physician, Dr. Mona Hanna-Attisha, to reveal the problem despite efforts to discredit her by state and local officials. Dr. Hanna-Attisha later augmented the reporting on the crisis with her own 2019 book, *What the Eyes Don't See*. With all of these stories, the common thread is that none of the institutions involved willingly shared information about criminality or malfeasance. Reporters (and their lawyers) have to take journalistic sledgehammers to the stonewalling by companies and educational institutions and governments, because no entity cheerfully gives up incriminating evidence. This process of prying the information loose from unwilling hands is expensive, time-consuming, and not for the faint of heart.

The business of nonfiction, however, is not all gloom and doom. It can inspire, as did *The Boys in the Boat*, about the 1936 University of Washington rowing team that won the premier event and spoiled Hitler's Olympics narrative as much as their brethren on the track, or *Seabiscuit*, about a cast-off horse, cast-off trainer, and cast-off jockey who came together to create the Thoroughbred sensation of the Great Depression. It can entertain and amuse, as do David Sedaris's autobiographical essay-memoirs. It can pull back the curtain on moviemaking or rock and roll stardom, reveal the depths to which the human mind can sink or the heights to which it can ascend, unravel the mysteries of the universe or the inexplicable behavior of social organizations, explain the inner workings of the atom or the structure of ancient civilizations, expose horrific crimes from last week or a thousand years ago. In other words, it can offer us almost any knowledge the world has to offer. That's all swell. It's just that . . .

. . . we can't always trust what nonfiction itself offers.

The same form that can unmask a hoax can also perpetrate

one. And has, with some regularity. If it can illuminate the work-ings of disease and its treatment, it can also be used to promote quackery and distract sufferers from legitimate information. It has equal facility to expose the sins of industry and to hide them or recast them as virtues. And here's the real problem: if we only read surfaces, we won't be able to tell the difference between the righteous and the right-around-the-bend.

There's a solution here: we can learn to read past the surface. To discern motive, to evaluate evidence, to analyze arguments, to avoid being hoodwinked. Such a reading program can give us greater appreciation of valid, and valuable, nonfiction while help-ing us to sweep the chaff away from the wheat.

I say it's high time we got started. How about you?

1

The Structure of Nonfiction Information

How We Find Out What We're Reading

I'M GOING TO ASK you here to think like a writer for a little bit. Not what you signed up for, I know, but it will be worth it. Besides, you don't have to *actually* write anything. And let's talk here about longer-form nonfiction: magazine articles and books. The daily newspaper reporter is moving so fast that she rarely has time (or space) to concern herself with these matters. And what are we talking about? Salesmanship. Advertisements for yourself, or at least for your work. The first job of every writer on page one is to get the reader to page two, and then from two to three and so on. How do we do that?

By not sucking?

That would help. That's why the *hook*, that rhetorical or narrative gambit, is there at the front, something to win readers' goodwill and buy a little space to lay out the essentials of the work to follow. And how do writers manage that laying out of essentials?

The four Ps. Like the Five Ws of journalism, but fewer and with a different letter. Not Who, What, When, Where, and Why, but Problem, Promise, Program, and Platform. Not as catchy, but no less essential. These terms come up in writing book proposals and first chapters, but they also apply in magazine articles and books. Let's see what they mean.

☞ Problem: the prime cause that pushes the writer to commit this piece of nonfiction. You're establishing need here. If your article is on new and bizarre ways to use up zucchini in season, you want to establish that zucchini overpopulation is a menace to society, so we need all the help we can in eradicating this scourge. In *How to Read Poetry Like a Professor*, I made the claim that a great many readers fear poetry because they believe they can't understand it or the weird rules and terminology that accompany it. If you're writing a biography, the problem may simply be a lack of information: here is someone you never heard of, but that's been your loss because he's terrific and has much to teach us. Or the problem may be that there have been dozens of biographies of this famous person from the past, but the approaches have been inadequate to the task, or this newly revealed information changes everything. The nature of the problem matters less than your sales job about its importance for readers.

☞ Promise: in essence, "I can fix that for you." For the zucchini article, your promise is that these five new recipes will change readers' lives and rock their world. Heck, their kids won't even notice there's zucchini in there. In *Poetry*, my promise was that I would take the terror out of poetry reading and actually make it fun by demystifying the form (avoiding *genre*, because that's part of the mystification). And also that they wouldn't notice the zucchini.

- Program: how the writer will achieve the promise. In the case of the magazine article, the program *is* the article, so next to zero space (a precious commodity) is given over to that. For the book writer, this is a big deal, how we go from promise to fulfillment. It goes, roughly, by examining this and then attaching it to that, we will achieve our aims. The historian or biographer will discuss methods and approach, the ways in which this specimen will differ from those earlier ones that, while laudable, couldn't quite achieve what this one will. For *Poetry*, I said that we would work first of all on simply getting the surface meaning of a new poem, from there working on figurative language and images and all those devices that make us uneasy as beginning (or returning) readers, and then we would examine the "grammar," the specialized set of rules by which poetry operates, by looking at a wide variety of poems from the very old to the quite new.

- Platform: your justification for stepping up on your soapbox. Who are you to tell us something new, anyway? Some people opt for expertise. In my "Like a Professor" books, I use the fact that I am, indeed, a professor with considerable experience teaching beginning literature students. A person writing a dog training book will probably allude to his forty years as a dog trainer, with numerous wins and placements to his credit. You haven't been creating award-winning recipes for forty years? That's okay, there are other platforms. Maybe you have talked to expert cooks, gleaned tips that you then parlayed into new takes on old recipes or entirely new ones. The dog training book author may not be an expert at all but has interviewed fifteen of them to find the commonalities among their approaches. Or you can bluff your way through: "You don't know me from Adam, but when you taste these recipes, you'll be glad you read the article." Obviously, this approach has its greatest appeal on shorter pieces. It's hard to coax someone to read four hundred pages by saying, just wait till the end.

Why, then, did I ask you to think like a writer? So you can be a better informed reader. I believe it is best to know what strategies are being employed so that you can be more fully aware of a written work's structure. You already have a sense, when you read a first chapter, of where the book is going to go. Isn't it better to know why you have that sense, turning it from a vague feeling into concrete knowledge? That's what I thought.

Structural Design

When we discuss fiction, we frequently use the term *narrative strategy*, by which we mean the design plan wherein the writer arranges and releases information to the reader. Every writer has to have a plan, even if he claims not to have one. The plan usually comes ahead of the writing, but not always. Even so, the strategy becomes apparent in the eventual organization of that information. A writer such as William Faulkner can say that he merely trots around behind his characters with a notebook, writing down what they do and say, but a point comes in the writing process when revision and rewriting replace drafting, and it is there that the novelist isn't trotting anywhere. Rather, he's stuck at his desk sweating details large and small, and some of those details involve whether the narrative strategy is working as it stands or needs some rearrangement.

Something similar happens in nonfiction, too. In fact, sometimes it isn't merely like narrative design, it *is* narrative design. That's because some nonfiction is narrative in nature—some, but not all. Some is expository, some argumentative, some informational, and much a combination of one or more of these types of writing. So rather than gum up the works with a term borrowed from another genre that only sometimes applies in this one, let's go with a more generic term, *structural design*. As we read a work of nonfiction, we want to notice not only what that design is, but how the writer achieves it.

As an example, let's take two of the most successful sports books of this century, Laura Hillenbrand's *Seabiscuit: An American Legend* (2001) and Daniel James Brown's *The Boys in the Boat: Nine Americans and Their Epic Quest for Gold at the 1936 Berlin Olympics (2013)*. At first glimpse, they might not seem to have a great deal to do with each other. One is about a horse, the other about a group of boys turning into men one stroke of the oar at a time. Stripping away the surface difference, however, we see that they share a lot of similarities. Each is a multiparty tale in which the backgrounds, successes and failures, and ambitions of the parties matter immensely to the outcome for the participants and therefore to readers' understanding. Each story is set against the background of the era, the Great Depression and, in the latter, the rise of Adolf Hitler's Nazi Party. And each has a cast of hard-luck characters. Seabiscuit, jockey Red Pollard, trainer Tom Smith, and owner Charles S. Howard all struggle to overcome setbacks and personal failings. Smith, for instance, was down to one horse when Howard, on a blind recommendation, hired him to train the temperamental stallion who despite blazing speed seemed to invent ways to lose races. And Pollard, who had his own long list of races lost (and few won), was a brawler and a heavy drinker before reforming himself as part of the task of managing his difficult mount.

Those boys in the boat, eight rowers and a coxswain, came from hardscrabble backgrounds, the most severe adolescence belonging to Joe Rantz, abandoned by his father and stepmother at age twelve and left to make his way in the woods of the Northwest. Additionally, a story about rowing must focus on the coach and any other central figures. In this case the coach was Al Ulbrickson, a hugely talented rower in his own right but a frustrated coach who found his Washington Huskies always lagging behind the powerhouse University of California Golden Bears, while the seminal figure was shell-building genius George Yeoman Pocock, who doubled as a father-confessor and Zen master of the boathouse. He, too, had his own backstory of difficulties and setbacks. And looming over everything is the desperation of the Great Depression and the gathering geopolitical clouds in Europe.

In narratives of such widely varying figures, it is hardly surprising that the authors choose strategies that lean toward the kaleidoscopic, shifting from character to character and event to event with each new chapter, and sometimes even within chapters. After a scene-setting preface (Hillenbrand) or prologue (Brown)—the differences between those terms being largely one

of personal preference—the authors use early chapters to intro-
duce the key personnel and situations in their stories. Hillenbrand
begins not with Seabiscuit himself but with chapters on the
self-made, automobile-dealing millionaire Howard, followed by
taciturn trainer Smith, and then the feisty jockey Pollard. Only
once she has her human livestock safely in the stable, as it were,
does she introduce the horse. For his part, Brown also devotes
his first chapter to management, to Coach Ulbrickson, then gives
one to the earliest days of Joe Rantz, followed by a third devoted
chiefly to the enigmatic Pocock, before returning in chapter four
to Rantz and his backwoods marooning. In each book, once we
reach the end of the fourth chapter, the narrative die has been
cast, and the telling will follow the now-established pattern.

It's worth noting that such a structure is not inevitable, not
dictated by the material. There would be other ways to organize
the information. One could easily, for instance, keep the focus
on the main character, whether equine or human, so that every
chapter is about Seabiscuit or Joe, with other characters being
relegated to second-tier importance as they elbow their way into
chapters that follow a single-minded storyline. Handled this way,
the books become straight biographies of single beings. Noth-
ing innately wrong with that. In the case of *Seabiscuit*, the title
wouldn't even need changing. Brown, on the other hand, might
have needed to rename his *The Boy in the Boat and the Eight Oth-
ers Who Helped Him to Glory*, which is somewhat less satisfying.
Or accurate. Neither, however, would be the book we have. Or
anything nearly as interesting. The point is, a steady through-line
narrative would significantly change the focus and the *telos* of the
work. "Telos" comes from Greek and means "goal" or "endpoint."
In this case, think of the change in structural design effectively

moving the goalposts. The actual structure has a lot of advantages for these books reaching their desired endpoints. The shifting focuses allow for development of multiple characters, while the largely single focus within chapters keeps that development from being chaotic or overly diffused.

In the case of *The Boys in the Boat*, the structural design has one added benefit: it avoids reader burnout. Joe's story is sufficiently harrowing in its perils-of-Pauline details that lingering there extensively could prove gloomier than some of us could bear. Brown is wise enough to take readers up to the point of pain, then end the chapter and move on to another topic before continuing that story. This angle applies chiefly to his childhood, but since that occupies the first part of the book, which is also when people decide whether or not to continue reading, it carries outsized importance.

But what about a book with a different subject entirely, one that doesn't rely on narrative of a group? Maybe a self-help book? I'm not sure if David Brooks's *The Road to Character* (2015) exactly fits the genre, but it has to do with self-improvement. He takes as his starting point the admission that he has plenty of room to improve, declaring that "I was born with a natural disposition toward shallowness," and calling himself "a narcissistic blowhard," hardly surprising for a newspaper "pundit and columnist." What he seeks, then, are examples of other people who have managed to surmount their own natural dispositions to become better versions of themselves. What sort of structural design strategy will carry his search forward and interest readers? That's the question.

He opens the book with an introduction that states the main

problem: human duality. Taking his terms from Rabbi Joseph Soloveitchik's 1965 book, *The Lonely Man of Faith*, he calls these two sides "Adam I" and "Adam II." Adam I is busy, ego-driven, successful perhaps, but self-involved. He embodies what Brooks calls "resumé virtues," those achievement items like high grades or test scores, sales figures, professional accomplishments—not bad in themselves (taken in moderation, one supposes), but hardly expressing the whole of human possibility. Adam II, by contrast, is characterized by mastery over the self, or perhaps over the ego, and his strengths are "eulogy virtues," things like kindness, compassion, honesty, faithfulness that we hope will be spoken of at our funerals. From there he launches into the book proper with a first chapter that elaborates on the dichotomy he has set up between the two Adams, along with plenty of examples from recent decades that indicate why we need to cultivate Adam II. What follows from that is a series of eight chapters, each focusing on one or at most two persons—the journalist and social activist Dorothy Day, President Dwight Eisenhower, General George Marshall, writers George Eliot and Samuel Johnson, and quarterbacks Johnny Unitas and Joe Namath—demonstrating the weaknesses of character that each struggled to overcome. Each chapter is a narrative in its own right that demonstrates what one might call (although Brooks does not) the Deadly Sin that held the person back or the Cardinal Virtue that helped him or her surmount the character deficit. The final chapter is both a summation and a fifteen-point recap for those who might have had difficulty gleaning the lessons from the foregoing chapters. On that, readers may be forgiven; Brooks is reticent about pushing his lessons, sometimes to the point of obscurity. In general, however, he makes his case fairly clearly. And his final list, if not absolutely necessary, will be welcomed by many readers simply for bringing his numerous conclusions together in one place.

The beauty of this book is that we need not wonder about the structural design; Brooks lays it out for us at the end of the introduction. In a section called "The Plan," no less. Oh, if only every book were so, right? Actually, most are, if not quite as baldly stated as this one. Authors for the most part do not wish for readers to be confused or to feel lost, so if we read with just a little bit of care, we generally understand where the book is headed by the end of the introduction and completely by the conclusion of the first chapter.

Some books have a very straightforward structural design. Stephen E. Ambrose's *Undaunted Courage: Meriwether Lewis, Thomas Jefferson, and the Opening of the American West* (1996) follows Meriwether Lewis from birth to death in chronological order, bringing Jefferson into view only when his presence explains how Lewis became the front half of "and Clark" and what that remarkable tandem achieved. We are not surprised by such a strategy; it is the natural state of historical biography, and he or she who would tell a life in some other order will have to offer a certain amount of justification to readers. It can certainly be managed otherwise, but the writer needs a pretty compelling reason.

The point of these examples is that every writer has a plan for his or her book, and we will understand the book—and often something about the writer—better by noting that plan, by observing the strategy by which the information is delivered to readers. We'll get back to the specifics of structure in a bit. For now, it's enough to know that every book, every article, every column has one, even the ones that purport to have none. Chaos can be structural, right?

2

The Ecology of the Nonfiction Biosphere

Or, Who Writes What, When

LET'S SAY, STRICTLY FOR the sake of argument, that you want to read a work of nonfiction. We know that, in the real world, you may not have a lot of choice, that the purpose may be driven not by desire but by compulsion. You have a school assignment. Or a work assignment. Or a need to keep up with (or begin to have) basic knowledge in a field. Sometimes, you really don't have a choice. But humor me and pretend that you do and that your choice is to read that item. Which can also be true even if you're being forced to do it. You might, say, want to do well in the course or get a promotion or not look like an idiot when you speak before the school board. There are lots of reasons to want to read something even when the impetus is not your own desire.

Here's the good news: every form of human communication has a basic grammar, a set of rules of the road that will govern how information is offered to readers. So if you understand that grammar, that set of rules and practices, you can make your way down that road a little faster. Swell so far, right? It's just that . . .

You have to know the form to know the grammar. Part of that identification is fairly easy: if you see a broadsheet format in multiple sections, that's probably a newspaper. But not all parts of the morning paper are the same; news articles follow different rules from features, which are in turn different from opinion/editorial content. Happily, the third of those occupies a separate part of the paper—usually the last page or two of the front section—and the first two sometimes have separate sections. We'll discuss that further in a while, but on with the problem! Magazines, like newspapers, appear at regular, defined intervals (normally weekly or monthly rather than daily), but they have sets of rules of their own. I say "sets" because magazines also publish a variety of forms in their pages. And books have a host of grammars. Is the book you just picked off the shelf history, biography, how-to, self-help, memoir, essay, current affairs, nonfiction narrative, journalism, New Journalism, travel, arts, true crime, psychology, spirituality, or philosophy? There will be many points of overlap, but they will all follow their own rules and policies.

Take, oh, history versus New Journalism or what is now often called participatory journalism, the sort of writing pioneered by Hunter S. Thompson, Tom Wolfe, Joan Didion, and John McPhee. In both sorts of writing there will be an emphasis on accuracy; that is, the writer is obliged to report what was actually said and done, while avoiding putting words in anyone's mouth or inventing actions in a sort of what-if speculation. Whether the trip is undertaken by Lewis and Clark in Ambrose's *Undaunted Courage* or Ken Kesey and his Merry Pranksters in Tom Wolfe's *The Electric Kool-Aid Acid Test* (1968), readers want to know that the text is accurately reporting what went on back in the mists of time. Or just last year. So there's one similarity. Another is that in both genres, writers should reward readers by being somewhat interesting. This expectation would not be inevitably valid, by the way, for academic histories—or books in a lot of other academic fields from mathematics to sociology to, yes, literary criticism. Academic readers, prompted by professional concerns, will often put up with boring or downright bad writing if the insights or new information are sufficiently compelling. More's the pity: they are afforded ample opportunities to practice such forgiveness. Lay readers, on the other hand, should not be expected to suffer unduly just to acquire a little information. My experience is that they are pretty good sports about minor suffering, but they have their limits.

This distinction raises an "interesting" question: how engaging is engaging enough? For Ambrose, it seems, the material is so compelling that he has only to stand to one side. We're talking *Alice in Wonderland* with grizzly bears. This new world was a fantasy land. With the threat of sudden, violent death. Get out of the way; let the story tell itself. Don't clutter it up with excess analysis. Don't get between the reader and the explorers' astonishment and elation and terror. Don't try to be the star of the show. Ambrose's claim to authority is the mass of scholarship that lies behind his narrative. He need not press an argument that he is an authority; the better strategy is to let that mountain of learning speak for itself. Wolfe has a different problem: there is no mass of scholarship precisely because the phenomenon in *Electric Kool-Aid* is so new. This is First Contact with Aliens. The only way to intimate any sort of expertise or authority is to get on the inside, to worm his way into the unworldly culture. A relatively transparent narrative approach will never do. Instead, Wolfe makes his narrative persona the star of the show: preening, smart-alecky, hip, clever, judgmental, ironic, linguistically ostentatious, simultaneously involved and detached. By making his narrative filter manifest, he becomes a tour guide or maybe a carnival barker for this collection of oddities. He wants us to be taken with *Electric Kool-Aid*'s main cast—Kesey and his crew—but not to be taken in by them. His stratagem has the paradoxical effect of seeming to bring us inside the group while at the same time inoculating us against the most damaging excesses to be found there.

We'll go into requirements for specific nonfiction genres in more detail a bit later. For now, we need only remember that the rules aren't set based on the physical form, the *codex*, but by the type of contents that form presents.

Types of Writing in Your Morning Paper

One of the things we need to learn as readers is how to manage our expectations. By "manage," I don't mean "reduce." Rather, if we're going to get the most from our reading, we need to learn which expectations are appropriate for which types of writing. Remember those sections of the newspaper? Let's go back there and see what we can see. A newspaper is a diverse neighborhood. Lots of different sorts of writing coexist in close proximity. True, the comics page and the editorial page are isolated in their own quarters, not quite walled off but nearly so. More like chain link than cinder block, but behind barriers nonetheless. Whether this is to protect those two places or the rest of the paper from contagion via close contact is hard to say. What other writing do we find in those pages? *Hard news* stories, the just-the-facts-ma'am, who-what-when-where-why meat and potatoes of news gathering. *Features* are often longer (unless news items are large-scale exposés) and softer as to subject matter and reportorial stance. They may range from human interest tales, oddball topics, remembrances of businesses long gone or prospects for those just opening, beautiful-home stories, the kinds of pieces usually cast as *soft news*. Most can be said to lie along a continuum between hard news reporting and public relations news releases. The home beautiful articles, for instance, are sometimes glorified real estate listings, complete in recent years with asking prices for the properties. Ongoing *columns* are another category (or maybe several categories). We may think of recurring columns as synonymous with op-ed pieces by syndicated or in-house writers, because many of those are (a) columns and (b) recurring, but there are many other types. Certain columnists take human interest features as their beat. These columns are sometimes concurrent with *ombudsperson* type items. That is, the columnist will take reader input about being wronged by companies or government, ferret out the most truthful version she can find, and try to set things right by acting as intermediary between the parties or by playing the public scold to shame the wrongdoers into doing a little bit more right. The columnist will assume the mantle of Avenging Angel on, say, Monday, Wednesday, and Friday, interspersed with Seeker of Interesting Neighbors on Sunday, Tuesday, and Thursday. Or she may do something entirely personal, something like my-life-in-the-community reflection pieces in which she contemplates nature, her family, her dogs, and maybe the night sky. That's okay, though: being an Avenging Angel is tough work.

Is that all papers have to offer? Not at all. They offer *reviews* (books, movies, television shows, dance and theater performances) and *previews* (upcoming programs on television). They carry specialized *advice columns*, usually by national figures, on relationship problems or questions about finance. They provide, perhaps less often than formerly, the previous day's stock market numbers, for which there may or may not be accompanying analyses. There are *travel pieces*, which may be reviews or features, designed to lure us at least in imagination to far-off places. And there are *letters* from readers, wherein we meet some of the more thoughtful and, occasionally, less securely hinged neighbors.

A fully functioning newspaper, aside from rapidly becoming a rare commodity, is an astonishing compilation not only of writing but of *types* of writing.

Where is the one place in the paper where all of these categories find a home? The Sports section. The front page or two will usually be taken up with straight reporting, hard news for sports fans. The purest form of hard reporting in the sports pages is the *box score*, a specialized reading challenge. To the uninitiated, a box score is a jumble of names and numbers signifying nothing. To the cognoscenti, on the other hand, it is a way to reconstruct a ball game from a list of abstractions. Sadly, one of the victims of reduced income and squeezed space in contemporary papers is precisely that box score. It may be a minor loss in an age when all of the information can be found somewhere online, but the beauty of the traditional model is that all of these things appeared in a single section of the dailies. But that's not all. There will often be sports features, particularly in the Sunday edition, and most papers still employ local columnists and import syndicated columnists for commentary on national stories. And those columns will have more than a little opinion in them. Indeed, for sheer contentiousness, the Editorial page has nothing on Sports. It's the section that can stand as a microcosm for the entire paper.

Why does it matter what kinds of writing appear in a newspaper? Because each of them demands a slightly different reading strategy. In part, it's about pace. I mentioned a bit ago that features are more leisurely and ease their way into their material. In a straight news piece, the famous Five Ws—who, what, when, where, and why—are frontloaded, more often than not in the first paragraph. Some folks append an H, how, to those five elements, or even substitute "how" for "why," but I think "how" is what the rest of the article is about. The *lede* (or, *lead* in some journalistic quarters) paragraph is the thumbnail of the event being described in the article; the rest is explanation, filling in the blank spots until a complete picture emerges. If you read a feature with the same expectations for rate of revelation, you are bound to be disappointed. The lede in a feature is often a tease. It may be a hint of difficulties to come ("As Larry Davidson sat at the traffic light, he could little imagine the life change coming his way") or a picture of an endpoint ("Back at his workbench, Larry Davidson is happy to once again handle his drawknives and chisels"). Actually, if you published those two together, readers could probably assemble the story for themselves, but that would defeat the purpose of a feature. You cannot, however, figure out the facts of the story from the lede alone—at least, not in a soft news story.

It's hard to keep these various types of newspaper writing sorted. Even the pros have difficulty sometimes. In discussing a hugely viral fake news item from 2016, Professors Cailin O'Connor and James Owen Weatherall in their otherwise terrific *The

Misinformation Age (2019) compare it to an "article" in the *Washington Post* that, by comparison with the phony tale, was shared over one hundred thousand times fewer, even though it was the most shared among legitimate media pieces. Just one problem: the article in question was actually a column by *Post* opinion writer Paul Waldman. They further identify the piece as "nakedly partisan," "hardly 'news' at all in the standard sense." Of course not. By definition, a column is not a news item; it is an opinion piece, here as is customary identified as such and printed on the opinion page. We wouldn't criticize a news article for lacking an opinion, would we? I so hope you said no.

Wait a minute. You keep acting like newspapers are critical to a good life. But they've been dying for a while now, and life goes on. Just how critical are they?

I suppose that's up to us, and sadly, a lot of us have voted. Newspapers used to be a good deal longer than they are now. Gradually, through the final third of the twentieth century, many—not all—readers lost interest in the in-depth articles, the long exposés, and just the sheer length of the morning (or afternoon) *Daily-Journal-Tribune-Herald-Globe-World-State-County-Times-News*. Along about that time, in 1982, either responding to or anticipating declining interest, the Gannett Company published a new sort of national newspaper, *USA Today*. Articles were shorter, punchier, largely stripped of context, more focused on graphics and photos, nearly as much color as the Sunday funnies, and written in simpler language than the flagship dailies such as the *New York Times* or *Boston Globe*. Readers could breeze right through it. It became the lightning-round first rough draft of history. As you can guess, the new creature provoked strong reaction. The critics, who were legion, hated it, called it McPaper or "television you can wrap fish in," and suggesting that the fish-wrapping was its highest best use. They also predicted that *USA Today* would lead to the demise of the daily newspaper. Others hailed it as a breath of fresh air in a stale news environment that hadn't kept up with the times or taken readers' wishes into account. As you can also guess, it caught on with the public. Although it, too, has experienced readership decline, its daily subscription sales as of late 2017 were just under a million daily. Add to that the number of local Gannett papers that include a section from the mother ship as well as the various mobile device apps and searchable content, and the daily total climbs much higher, possibly as much as seven million. My own local paper has long since ceased to carry national or international content from traditional wire services in favor of *USA Today* content and has more recently dropped syndicated columnists and national sports stories in favor of Gannett-originated writing. The changes cannot be called improvements, and the paper has continued to shrink. It does, however, still publish every day, something not a lot of journals can claim.

Because of the ceaseless work of journalists, newspapers (or some electronic version thereof) will continue to occupy an *essential niche* in the nonfiction environment. We still want hard news, personal interest features, game results, movie reviews, articles on music trends, obituaries, police blotter reports. And where else are you going to get those in one place? Social media? Not very likely. Sure, Facebook will have lots of stories on the death of a disgraced politician or a movie star in her prime, but not the one for your aunt Mabel or your neighbor's father. Moreover, we, or at least some of us, would prefer those reviews, those backstage stories, that analysis be written by someone who actually knows something. Including how to write. The quality of a great deal of online information is simply dreadful, and sometimes far from true, however passionately presented. So that's why I would suggest that those niches are in fact essential.

Okay, then, but why do we need all these different forms of publication? You know, newspapers and blogs and magazines and books. I mean, what's the point?

That's easy: time. The thing of which there is never enough. That heals all wounds or possibly wounds all heels.

Time? You sure?

Absolutely. Don't forget the maxim that "journalism is the first rough draft of history," often attributed to Philip L. Graham of the *Washington Post* (whose death allowed his widow, Katharine, to succeed him as publisher and be played by Meryl Streep in *The Post*). The reality is that Alan Barth, also of the *Post*, had said the same thing in a book review in *The New Republic* in 1943, and he may not have been the first. In any case, the bromide has rattled around long enough in the culture to be pretty widespread by now. What does that mean? Chiefly, that the news is the first indication most of us have that something large or small has happened. In the old days, a major event—a sudden death, say, or an explosion at a factory—that took place in the morning would be in a large city paper's evening edition. You can tell that was the old days by the fact that papers had multiple editions when needed. Nowadays, it would be in *tomorrow's* edition, which is still pretty fast. The name of the journalistic game is speed, at which papers excel. What they sacrifice in the headlong rush to publish is context. Between late afternoon, when our putative event takes place, and around eleven o'clock that night when the editors put the paper to bed (an old expression meaning, send it downstairs to the printers and pressmen), there is precious little time to establish context. That's okay, though: there will be other days on which the writers can provide more background, more insights, more context.

Which is also the job of magazines. Even a weekly magazine can't possibly compete with the dailies for speed of reporting. And a monthly magazine? Forget it. So what do we need those for? Other kinds of stories. Many monthlies have never been interested in news or current affairs reporting, because by the time an issue appears, news is old and stale. Even news in a weekly is likely to be several days old at best, and in the age of the twenty-four-hour news cycle, several days might as well be years. What, then, can a magazine provide if not news? Perspective. Analysis. Context. Those things take time. Obviously, the perspective gained through three or four weeks is hardly that of three or four decades, but it is enough perspective that we can think of it as a second draft of history: a little less rough, a little more fleshed out, a little more shapely. *Time, Newsweek, The New Republic, The New Yorker, The Atlantic, Harper's, Life, Look*—those are among the classic weekly and monthly magazines with an interest in current affairs. The first two are full-on news magazines. Others take news coverage as part of their mission. Several rely on a good deal of commentary. They all provide greater context and perspective than is possible in daily journalism. A couple, *Life* and *Look*, were famous for the addition of lots of photographs to the public record. All of them, whatever their publication schedule, shared with papers the unforgiving deadlines that sometimes cause incomplete stories to be dropped at the last moment or cut off at the knees to publish what has been constructed thus far. Better, more complete, more contextualized. But not complete.

Nor are magazines interested only in current event and political coverage as their contribution to the historical record. Many periodicals come under the heading of *specialty* journalism. These are magazines devoted to every sort of human activity, from cooking to model trains to landscaping to fly-fishing. But only one of those activities per journal, which is what the "specialty" term suggests; they stick absolutely to their special field of interest. Anyone looking for political reporting in *Martha Stewart Living* or the *Pointing Dog Journal* will find they have made a wrong turn in their search. Others, like several of those I listed above, are *general interest* magazines, meaning that they publish a variety of types of stories on many different subjects. In *The New Yorker*, an article on the opening of the latest Broadway show may reside next to one on the environmental hazards of copper mining. Not everyone will approach those two stories with the same enthusiasm, which is one reason that general interest magazines have dwindled from the most common type in the middle of the last century to a mere handful. At the same time, this eclectic approach holds appeal precisely for the surprises it offers. Few readers expected, upon opening the April 27, 1987 issue of *The New Yorker*, that they would be attracted by an examination of the history of dynamite, much less a two-parter that stretched into the following week's issue, yet that is what Bryan Di Salvatore's fascinating "Vehement Fire" offered them.

So here's a question: if journalism is the first rough draft of history, where does the final draft find a home?

In histories.

{ Building Blocks of Argument }

Claims, Grounds, Warrants

THE FIELD OF NONFICTION has just as many, and very likely more, genres than does fiction. Instead of horror, detective, historical romance, psychological realism, and so forth, it gives us biography, history, how-to, political analysis, sociology, art history, and a whole lot more. But with the exception of *reportage* (the reporting of events in the truest form possible)—and that is limited largely to daily newspapers and a smattering of weekly magazines whose numbers continue to diminish—the actual form of all of these is *argument*, the attempt to convince readers or listeners that the writers' angle is the correct one. Comparatively few biographers have the luxury of writing the only life of their subject. So each succeeding one sets out the same argument: this version is superior to all preceding versions in ways *X*, *Y*, and *Z*. The most common argument for superiority is completist: recently discovered information (a trove of letters not previously known, documents previously held in trust but now available to the public, synthesis of all the competing prior biographies of the subject) makes it possible for me to be more thorough, more detailed, and a whole lot longer. There is a much smaller subset whose argument is the opposite: these massive bios have gotten out of hand, so here is one that gives you the facts without all the palaver. Usually there is a swell of competing biographies when a new hoard of documents is opened to scholars. There was a biographical stampede not unlike the Oklahoma land rush when the Ernest Hemingway Collection became available at the John F. Kennedy Presidential Library and Museum in Boston in the mid-1970s. Suddenly a wealth of new material presented itself for examination, and the race was on. And almost as suddenly, Carlos Baker's definitive biography, *Ernest Hemingway: A Life Story*, was a good deal less definitive. Now each new Life of Hem could draw on this wealth of previously unknown or unconfirmed details, which was swell. But they also had to make the case as to why *this* life was better than the last, better than any of the others, and certainly better than poor old Baker.

This sort of thing happens in other fields as well, but our thoughts here are for argument as a form, and for reading same. Those can range from sidebar claims in an otherwise nonargumentative work to editorials and opinions in papers and magazines to whole books making a fairly global set of claims. The success of argument, whatever the scale, rests on *proof*, on making your points and then making them stick not just for those who agree with you but for those who would disagree.

I'm not crazy about specialized terms. Jargon is just so . . . jargony. Well, sometimes it can't be helped, and this is one of those times. There are three words that we can't live without in discussing argument: *claims*, *grounds*, and *warrants*. Hey, don't blame me, these are from philosopher Stephen Toulmin's *The Uses of Argument* (1958), a book that changed the way we talk, and maybe think, about argument—and not only by hanging three new terms around our necks. A *claim* is sometimes called a "conclusion" or even a "thesis" (and a thesis statement in a deductive essay is typically a type of claim), but we might best think of it as an assertion. If someone tells you that she is an American citizen, then that is her claim, and, were there any real need, it would be up to her to prove it. A *ground* is a fact, piece of data, or other evidence that will be used to buttress the claim. In this case, our friend's ground is that she was born in Guam. But on their own a claim and a ground are just two strangers standing next to each other at a dance; if you want them to go steady, you have to pin them together. That act of pinning is called a *warrant*. The question that the warrant needs to address is the one that may have occurred to you: why Guam? So here's her answer: "Guam is an American territory, and the fourteenth amendment to the Constitution guarantees birthright citizenship for all persons born in the United States, including its incorporated territories." Now the claim and the ground have a real relationship compliments of the warrant.

At its most basic level, a warrant is simply the act of logically connecting an assertion (the claim) with its supporting evidence (the ground): the supporting evidence I'm using to support my assertion provides that support because of X and Y, and here's how it does that. In that sense, a great deal of writing is like court arguments. If you as the attorney make an assertion and present evidence to support it, you're only partway there; without tying those two things together with ropes of logic and reason, all is lost.

There are three areas where an argument can go sideways. You may have heard of them: the claim, the ground, and the warrant. The claim can be lacking in real support or badly stated or inept in some other way. The ground can be false. False facts are never good, but they do happen. Unlike the claim, the ground can be fact-checked because it's—what?—presented as a fact. If our friend's ground is that she was born in American Samoa, we can quickly discover that while it is a territory, it is not one of the territories where birthright citizenship is offered. The warrant, for its part, can be flawed, illogical, mistaken. In forty years of teaching college students about writing, I saw every way warrants can go wrong, as well as a thousand times as many ways they can go right.

This discussion barely scratches the claims-department surface. Toulmin, being a philosopher, has a number of other terms: *backing, qualifier, rebuttal* among them, but we'd really rather not get lost in the argumentative weeds, and these are the big three for our purposes. So next time you're reading or watching or listening to an argument, keep them in mind. They'll show you what's true and help you filter out a good deal of nonsense.

3

The Power of the Prologue

That Funny Thing Up Front

WHAT'S ALL THIS BUSINESS that happens before a book begins? I mean, forewords, prefaces, introductions, and prologues—who needs 'em? And why are there so many? To the first question, you do, fellow reader. And so do I. And to the second, they are multiple because of different functions. First, the easy one: "introduction" doesn't mean anything except "up front." It can be part of an article or book, labeled or not, written by the author or someone else, be part of the text of the book proper (that is, it will appear in every edition ever) or an appendage specific only to the edition at hand. If you're like me, you may have spent much of your early academic career skipping intros by outsiders to get to the meaty part. That would be a mistake, but it rarely proves fatal.

From here, things get more specific, if not clearer to the civilian. Here's the interesting thing: forewords, prefaces, and prologues are all the same thing etymologically, the "first word." A foreword, whose origins are likely the German translation of the Latin "preface," is front matter written by someone other than the author. Often, these forewords are appended to later editions of works, as when Famous Critic A writes a new foreword to Famous Novel B for a classroom edition of the novel. Forewords of this sort are fairly short; if they turn into fifty-page behemoths, they usually also turn into "introductions." These instances differ from prologues and prefaces by not actually being part of the narrative or argument that is the author's text. They are explainers, offering context or salient points to help readers on their way. A preface, from Latin and meaning something like "spoken before," is front matter by the author to a book of nonfiction or fiction, narrative or otherwise. A prologue, from the Greek for—you guessed it—"the before word," is most commonly prefatory material (see how hard this is?) for a fiction or nonfiction narrative. The differences between these last two are in the angels-dancing-on-pinheads category, so fine that mere mortals can't distinguish. How, then, do you know if something written by the author is a preface or prologue? Easy: they tell you. The item will almost always bear a title, so just go with it.

So what does a prologue do? It gets you ready for what comes next. The original of the type was in the plays of Euripides, where the playwright's representative (originally, likely the playwright himself) would come onstage and explain the backstory and setup. How to work in the contextual exposition—easy in fiction—has always bedeviled drama. Let's face it, explaining stuff is boring. Euripides, one of the first playwrights, tried the obvious thing: just stand there and talk so you don't have a lame first act. Starting with his near-contemporary Sophocles, writers tried to have a crisis in the first act so that our interest would be piqued enough that we would put up with the boring bits, as in the ghost business at the outset of *Hamlet*.

Swell. Plays. But nonfiction books are all exposition, so what's the point of a piece of exposition up front? Do we really have to explain the explaining?

Actually, the prologue in a piece of nonfiction is sometimes narrative, not expository. And the purpose of that anecdote is a lot like the purpose of the prologue in a Euripides play: to set the stage, offer background, tell the audience how we got to this point. It may tell us who's who in the story to come, or why this story matters, or why we will find reading it rewarding. Most of all, it will suggest why we should read on.

Consider *The Boys in the Boat*, Daniel James Brown's unlikely bestseller. In his prologue, Brown tells us how the book came to be, how a visit to an elderly neighbor he had never met, a man dying of congestive heart failure who in his youth had been one of nine young men—eight rowers and a coxswain—who pulled their way to glory in the 1936 Berlin Olympics, turned into a series of interviews and subsequent research that sought to place their achievement in its historical, sociological, and personal context. The quick story Brown tells focuses on the rowing, of course, with its camaraderie and suffering and sacrifice, but also on the remarkable physical feats of the old man, Joe Rantz, who among other things turned standing cedar trees up on a mountain into nearly half a mile of split rail fence around a pasture down in the valley below. By himself. In his mid-seventies. In something under two and a half pages of text, Brown hints at the dimensions of the story, the incredible hardships that Joe had to overcome in childhood and adolescence, the capacity for hard work that he displayed throughout his life, the huge emotional investment in "the boat" that, even after all these years, could bring him to tears, and the race against time the author faced to get all the information he could before it disappeared forever.

Read on? How could we refuse?

Not every prologue works this way. And despite Brown's example, they may not all be called "prologue." I incline toward "preface" myself, for no particular reason except habit, although it may also be because I intuited vaguely that "prologue" was more suited to narratives, which my books manifestly are not. Here are some ways that different authors handle the issue:

- In *A Higher Loyalty*, James Comey called his prologue/preface an "author's note."
- By contrast, in *Fire and Fury*, Michael Wolff's "author's note" fulfills the traditional role of that item, sitting before any other prefatory material and explaining how he went about writing the present volume. He then begins the book proper with "Prologue: Ailes and Bannon," which focuses on an election night party in 2016 attended by then–Fox News head Roger Ailes and, belatedly, campaign strategist Steve Bannon.
- David Brooks, in his excellent *The Road to Character* (2015), calls his prologue "Introduction: Adam II," arguing that a new being, unmoored from traditional notions of character, stands as a sort of New Man (or Woman) to challenge the old model, which he traces back to that guy in the Garden.
- Margot Lee Shetterly, in *Hidden Figures* (2016), her book on the "computers," the black women who handled the

calculations—by hand—for the first American space flights, uses her prologue, so titled, to tell us that the work grew from a comment her father made that Margot's former Sunday school teacher, now quite elderly, had been one of those numbers whizzes. For African American female mathematicians, shut out of traditional math-related jobs by both race and gender, these positions were literally the opportunities of a lifetime. From that comment and a talk later that day with Kathaleen Land, the computer in question, Shetterly got the idea for the book.

➽ Stephen E. Ambrose's *Undaunted Courage*, perhaps the definitive telling of the Lewis and Clark expedition's story, employs an "Introduction," which tells not about that journey but about a chance encounter with another inspiration, his aunt Lois Ambrose's set of the journals of Lewis and Clark, which she gave him to read, leading to his narrative of the ultimate roadless trip.

➽ Ron Powers's book about murders carried out by adolescent boys in his hometown, Hannibal, Missouri, *Tom and Huck Don't Live Here Anymore* (2001), came about when he heard stories of horrific events in the seemingly idyllic childhood home of the man who would become Mark Twain. His "Prologue" details how he went from passive recipient of information to active researcher and writer.

➽ Two very different writers, David McCullough in *1776* and Tom Wolfe in *The Electric Kool-Aid Acid Test*, eschew the prologue form entirely, instead launching us straight into the meat of the text. In McCullough's case, any prefatory note might have seemed like special pleading for a work that is, in essence, a biography of a year. And in Wolfe's radical experiment in reporting from inside the story, what he called *New Journalism*, nothing he could have offered would have prepared readers for what was to come.

Is that the entire list of options? I'm sure not. But what all of these (aside from the last two, which are opt-outs) have in common is that they are brief, somewhere between a squib and a chapter, and that they try to provide a glimpse into some aspect of what's to come. That may mean any combination of who, what, why, and how, with maybe a touch of when and where. But mostly, it's a come-on, a letter of seduction to prospective readers.

The writer of a prologue is under twin obligations, first to write something that will entice and tantalize, and second to make sure the rest of the book lives up to the promissory note that draws us in. In exchange, readers are under an obligation to give that prologue the attention it deserves. We do well to remember that the prologue—or preface or personal note or whatever the author chooses to call it—is not an afterthought tacked onto the front of the book; it is a planned part of the book itself, acting as a springboard on which readers can dive into the rest of the text.

4

The Parts You Don't Read

ADMIT IT: WHEN YOU "read" a book you don't read all of it. You know it's true. In fact, you may not even know the names of those parts. Which is strange, since they're almost always labeled. No need to be ashamed; everybody does it. I used to feel sorry for those poor professors who wrote long, detailed introductions or forewords to chunky novels that showed up in my undergrad classes—all that effort going to waste. Look, if a novel is six hundred pages, the last thing a student wants to see is another fifty at the outset that doesn't advance the story and may bog down completely for those who haven't already read what follows. We all skipped that and headed straight for "Call me Ishmael." In later years, I learned that those pages were of use for instructors about to teach those books, and they seemed to be written with them in mind, not the first-timers.

We need to recognize, however, that in nonfiction books those items at the front and back (called *front matter* and *back matter*— who knew?) actually serve a purpose, and that that purpose is to help us out. So, let's resolve not to simply skip these elements just so we can get to the fun stuff. And let's start by giving them names.

Front Matter

Just for the record, everything before page one of the text, the point where the book proper begins, is counted with roman numerals, in lower case. Back matter, by contrast, continues the numbering of the body text, meaning that it employs numerals we can actually read. It would be just too confusing to jump back to roman form, almost as confusing as saying that arabic numerals are the familiar ones and roman the aliens. But there it is.

TITLE PAGE—Just what it sounds like: the full title and subtitle, along with the author's name and that of the publisher/imprint.

COPYRIGHT PAGE—Usually the reverse or *verso* side of the title page, this is the home for publication particulars, including date of publication, publisher's address, and number of edition or printing, and, finally, the Library of Congress publication data. This page is critical to students (and others) who may be writing a piece that will use the book at hand. **Never leave a potential source without recording this information**; failure to do so virtually guarantees misery down the line (say, the night before the deadline). I speak from vast personal experience.

DEDICATION—The one entirely optional item in all of

this, although most books do display a dedication to someone, be it family member or revered colleague.

FOREWORD—This is the one item not written by the author. By convention, "foreword" indicates a part of a book written, concurrent with or, more commonly, well after initial publication by a second party. That writer may be another novelist in the case of works of fiction, a scholar in the case of an academic book or established classic, or a fellow journalist when appropriate. Not every book has or needs a foreword, but they can provide insights not available to the author herself.

TABLE OF CONTENTS—Our roadmap to the book that follows. Typically, the *TOC*, as it's known in the trade, offers chapter titles (or numbers) and the page numbers on which those chapters begin. It also includes all other designated items in the book, such as the sections we're discussing here.

Back Matter

APPENDIX—Another name for this could be "Stuff too detailed to include in the text without bogging down readers' progress." But that's a little wordy. It's from the Latin *appendere*, meaning to "hang upon," and relates to "appendages" for arms and legs, which are hung upon the torso. And because it's from Latin, the plural is *appendices*. It is tacked on at the end for things like side arguments that would digress from the main point or charts or graphs best looked at separately. The text will usually offer helpful directions such as "See Appendix B." Whether or not you see it is up to you, but it's probably a good idea.

Notes—You know all those funny little numbers that sit above the line (called *superscript* numbers)? They are the questions that have their corresponding answers in this section. A note number in the text means that this information was borrowed. The numbered notes in Notes tell us from whom it was borrowed. These notes are most commonly arranged by chapters so that we don't arrive via continuous numbering at a three-digit superscript numeral. There are also such things as *content notes*, which are sidebar discussions that don't quite fit into the main argument. They can range from the tediously pedantic, where the writer is just showing off knowledge, to the genuinely interesting, when they become mini-essays on something almost related to the main topic. I've read articles and books where the content notes were more engaging than the text itself. Those content notes sometimes appear (based on the organizational logic of the writer and editor) at the bottom of the page so that (a) they appear on the page where they make the most sense and (b) we don't miss them when we skip the Notes section.

This is tempting, I know, but we really shouldn't ignore the information in this section. Notes tell us about sources. If the notes indicate that more than half of the details come from The Heritage Foundation and the Cato Institute, we can ascertain that the slant of the text is likely toward the right; if The Carter Center and the Center for American Progress, then leftward. That assumes, of course, that the author is not spending all of her time picking fights with the other side. Neither invalidates the work at hand, but an overreliance on highly politicized sources may indicate an approach that is something less than balanced, so it is worth knowing if we wish to be informed readers.

BIBLIOGRAPHY—The actual list of sources, arranged alphabetically by author, that went into the writing of this book. Full details—not just title and subtitle but publisher, place of publication, and year of publication—appear here. Organization is the key to usefulness: we can work our way through the listings to trends in the research behind the book.

INDEX—The best thing a book has besides the text itself. From Latin *index*, which is handy, meaning "forefinger" or by extension "one who points out." The plural is *indices*; sorry, can't be helped. Ideally, an index identifies every mention of a person, event, place, or concept and on which page each mention appears. I say "ideally," because sometimes things get missed by the compiler (I was a terrible compiler, which makes me an expert on this point). And because it lists every mention, even those in any appendices, it has to come at the very end.

Why is it so handy? Because you can go there and find out exactly which pages you need for your course paper or your personal edification. This is very useful when you want to know some specific thing *in* a book but don't need to read the entire thing. We don't need to read every page of every book we consult. Or have the time. There's no shame in that. Reading for information is a utilitarian enterprise: we want to find what is useful to us in our current activity without flooding our brain with information that might be useful to someone else or even us at some other time but that is useless at this moment. In an attempt to assist us in locating that useful information, an index will often break down mentions into categories: not merely every mention of a person but separate categories for, say, his married life, his career, his intellectual legacy. This specificity is more likely the case for major figures or topics. Because Daniel James Brown's *Boys in the Boat* filters his story of the 1936 University of Washington rowing team through one rower, Joe Rantz, he has many more mentions than any other figure in the story. Since he is mentioned on so many pages, lumping them all together would be less than ideal, so those mentions are broken down into categories such as "athleticism of," "musical interests of," "personality of," all arranged alphabetically under his name. So if you want to know about Joe's personality, you discover that you need only look up twenty-two passages rather than hundreds. Peripheral figures in this tale will have fewer mentions and those indexed items are lumped together. No one would argue that coxswain Bobby Moch was peripheral to the boat's success, but he is peripheral to the tale Brown chooses to tell, which is about one boy's struggles to overcome personal hardship and achieve success, and the way those struggles are representative of the team and indeed the era. So while Rantz's listings run to a page and a half with names for different types of information, Moch's, which all run together uncategorized, take up about a column inch and a half.

Stephen E. Ambrose's *Undaunted Courage: Meriwether Lewis, Thomas Jefferson, and the Opening of the American West* focuses, as its subtitle suggests, on the Lewis half of "Lewis and Clark." William Clark is very much present, but it is his younger coleader whom we follow most. The index listings for Lewis singly (as opposed to when he is half of the team) fill an entire page. Of those, mentions of his journals occur on sixty pages. Here is where we can engineer a more precise search. Looking at every one of those sixty pages can still be time-consuming, particularly if you're like me and are easily distracted by intriguing details. If we cross-list those mentions with chapter titles, we can refine our likely results. Let's say we want to find out what Lewis thought about the Mandans at whose village the expedition spent the winter and whose corn likely saved their lives. If we flip to the table of contents, we see that there are three chapters on his time with the Mandans, and that those chapters cover pages 176 to 210. Heading back to the index, we discover that only three of those entries in the journals appear on the relevant pages. A word of warning here: there could be mentions elsewhere, and our quick-search system might miss those. If our search of these three indexed mentions doesn't yield results, we might expand to either the Lewis category, "Indian diplomacy of," or the separate listings under "Mandan Indians." As it happens, we find gold with the second indexed listing on page 200, where he both praises and plans to "manage" the chief of the upper Mandan village, Black

Cat: "This man possesses more integrity, firmness, inteligence, and perspicuety of mind than any indian I have met with in this quarter, and I think that with a little management he may be made a usefull agent in furthering the views of our government" [*sic*]. And we managed to find it without reading the other 483 pages.

Sometimes an index holds tantalizing clues in the form of letters attached to the page numbers. The item under Lewis "burial, place of," directs readers to "476n." The note in question gives us the location and appearance of his resting place. In other works we may find an abbreviation or whole word in the index. In my now-ancient *History of American Art* by Daniel M. Mendelowitz (1960), black-and-white photos are identified not by page number but by "Fig." for figure, followed by a number, as in "Fig. 42." One then simply needs to thumb through the text to find the designated image or, better still, discover if there is a figures list included in the front matter. Because there are comparatively few full-page color plates of paintings, those are indicated by plate number *and* the page on which they appear. Thomas Eakins's "The Gross Clinic," for instance, appears in the index as "Plate 15, p. 309."

Names matter, people. The thing matters more, but the name also matters. Lest you think I'm just being pedantic here, I can't tell you the number of times students came up to me to ask about the "table of contents" when they meant the index, or when I referred them to the "index" and they turned to the front of the book. That would be the opposite end.

Finally, let us consider titles a bit more fully. You may regard this as burying the lede, but I've held off for a reason. To lump them in with other parts you don't read would be unfair, since almost everyone reads the title of a book or article before starting in. In fact, article titles are the reason most of us can find the Table of Contents in a magazine: we go there to see what stories look like appealing places to start. What I mean, rather, is that titles are often *under-read*; that is, we take them at face value and don't consider what they have to tell us. The reality is that they often serve as important signposts for the book or article to follow. And by "title," I mean the subtitle as well. I mentioned earlier that Ambrose's *Undaunted Courage* gives valuable guidance for our expectations in its subtitle: the book will be more attuned to Meriwether Lewis than to his fellow captain, William Clark. In the January 14, 2019 edition of *The New Yorker*, Malcolm Gladwell has an article titled "Unwatched Pot: Do We Know Enough about Marijuana?" One could argue that the subtitle leaves the matter up in the air, but your own experience tells you otherwise, that there is an overwhelming likelihood that the answer is "No." I have not made a comprehensive study of questions in titles, but my sense is that the likelihood of a negative finding stands at about 70 percent. Maybe higher. I would suggest that there are two reasons for this. First, there's not much percentage for a journalist to write a piece that says everything is just swell. The *grammar* of journalism as regards titles indicates that a Yes/No question in a title or subtitle will usually be answered in the negative. Unless, that is, the conventional wisdom says that it is not at all swell. And second, the conventions of reportage argue against declarative statements in titles. To appear to know the answer before writing the article looks like bad form. If we change Gladwell's subtitle to a pronouncement, "We Just Don't Know Enough," savvy readers may well expect not reportage but opinion. Gladwell is inviting us along on a voyage of discovery, not confronting us with an op-ed, so the interrogative form better fits his intent.

There are exceptions, of course, and this pattern is far from a rule. As I said before, if prevailing wisdom leans toward a negative answer to the question, then the article will likely reply in the affirmative. And the one place that affirmative answers routinely pop up is when the word "really" is introduced into the question. "Is President [insert current model here] Really That Arrogant?" You betcha.

One caveat here: writers for newspapers and magazines rarely have the luxury of writing their own headlines. Those often fail to express nuances in the articles, but this is one time that the author is probably blameless. Book writers generally get to own their titles and therefore have to stand by them.

The point here is that titles are meant to be helpful to readers, to clue us in on the content to follow. No one in the publishing process intends to make nonfiction more obscure, and every part of the article or book is available to help readers access and understand the writing at hand. It is merely prudent, then, that we make use of those instruments wherever they fall in the publication.

5

It May Just Be Me, But...

Reading Bias

AS YOU WELL KNOW, *you* are a fair-minded person, able to over-come any preexisting biases or prejudices that you might have. Which you don't. Have biases, that is. You can examine any situation objectively, no matter how passionately you might feel about the issue at hand. On the whole, there has never been a more evenhanded, open-minded, square-dealing person than yourself. Well, guess what: me, too! I can listen to both sides of any argument, weigh them carefully, and pick the winner on the basis of merit. And here's the thing: writers are that way, too. They see clearly, analyze objectively, present fairly, never cut corners, never jump to conclusions. How do we know? They tell us. Now, the other guy . . .

Enough of that nonsense. I was beginning to get the shakes from truth withdrawal. I'm not dispassionate and objective. Nor is David McCullough, or Bob Woodward or David Brooks or, well, anyone. Including you. We try, most of us, most of the time. But we'll never escape who we are. A lot of what we think is, if not hard-wired in us, so entrenched that it might as well be. We can struggle to overcome it or succumb to it, but it's a fact of our existence.

Disclaimers

This one isn't foolproof (what is?), but you want to know one way of sniffing out bias? See what the writer says he isn't biased against. I can't tell you how many times I have read (or heard on television or radio), "I don't dislike soccer." What follows is invariably a catalog of all the things wrong with soccer as a spectator sport or even a mildly human pursuit, at least from the writer's or speaker's perspective. And if the above statement is immediately followed by, "No, I really don't," what comes next will be really bad. Two "really"s? It's the devil's spawn. I decided some years ago to take special pains, whenever that disclaimer appeared, to notice if the rest of the article did something other than trash soccer. I'm still waiting.

I was thinking about this while reading conservative columnist David Brooks's *The Road to Character* (2015). Near the end of his book, having thoroughly trashed American culture since roughly 1960, which by no means excludes the world of online self-promotion, he offers this astonishing disclaimer: "I'm not a big believer that social media have had a ruinous effect on the culture, as many technophobes fear." Any guesses how long it takes the "but" to appear? Wrong. There's a sentence in between. Is Mr. Brooks trying to deceive us? Deluding himself? I don't think so. Rather, I get the sense that he really does feel that he's made peace with the Internet Age, recognizing that it arrived, took up residence, and shows no signs of decamping anytime soon, so he might as well make the best of it. He just has reservations about what sort of "best" might be made.

Quotes, Etc.

ONE WAY OF DETERMINING the leanings of a writer is to examine whom he quotes and whether the context around those quotes is approving or derisive. Nearly everyone who writes nonfiction will have occasion to cite, quote, or paraphrase *someone*. It may be true that no man (or woman) is an island; it is absolutely true with writers. And the people to whom we are beholden, who have played the role of models or ideals or irritants in our lives, are likely to show up in our texts from time to time.

Those borrowings, however, aren't cost-free. When a writer uses other people's words, he's under a set of obligations. One is to credit the person whose words he uses. This duty is to both the person quoted or paraphrased and to readers. Students (and former students) will recognize this obligation as lying behind the rules about citation and plagiarism, which can be summarized as a matter of intellectual property: people deserve recognition for what they write, and any attempt to limit that right is theft. But it goes beyond that "academic" position. Even if they are speaking—in an interview, for instance—they are entitled to their words being credited to them, including not being credited if they request that. In news articles especially, we see someone quoted but not identified. They may have any of a thousand reasons why they want their name kept out, in which case their name becomes something like "a highly placed source." Such lack of attribution does not necessarily indicate that the writer made up the statement, despite what detractors of the news (who may have their own reasons to discredit the reporter or the media in general) may claim. A witness to gangland activity may, quite reasonably, not want to die. An employee might wish to still be employed but believe that the truth needs to come out. Another may not want to open himself up to prosecution. Or he may not want to acknowledge publicly that he knows the person being reported on. The speaker's reasons are as various as speakers and cover a wide range of legitimacy behind those reasons. If you are a reporter, however, your job is not to question those reasons; if you give your word to the source to keep their identity secret, you must do so.

A step beyond the unidentified speaker is information "on background." In this case, the writer offers neither the identity of the speaker nor the specific words used. It may not be the most emotionally satisfying way to receive information, but if the information is genuine, would you rather have that or nothing? Who speaks on background? A surprising number of political figures. How many times have we read or heard, "an administration official, speaking on background" in the course of a story? Lots. It's a way to release general information without getting down into the weeds. Corporate figures do it, too. Here's a difference, although it won't hold up in all circumstances: speakers on background tend to be official sources who aren't ready to be quoted (and whose statements likely have approval from higher-ups), while speakers who are quoted but not named tend to be leaking information that someone (possibly that same higher management) doesn't want released. In all of these cases, the reporter follows the wishes of the source *unless she informs the source ahead of time that she will not do so.* In such cases, the source is unlikely to cooperate.

You want to see how this works in practice? Early on in *All the President's Men* (1974), the tale of unraveling the Watergate break-in orchestrated by Richard Nixon's re-election campaign, when Bob Woodward and Carl Bernstein are trying to figure out who this character, E. Howard Hunt, was who had attached himself to Charles Colson's staff at the White House, Woodward makes a call to "a young presidential aide he had once met socially." During their hour-long conversation, Woodward promised that the aide's name would not be attached to the article, and the aide told him that Hunt had been ordered by someone to investigate Senator Edward Kennedy's personal life. While he would not or could not identify the source of the order, he strongly intimated that Colson had known about the assignment. And this in the midst of a cover-up that would become legendary for its fog of misinformation. There you go—no attribution, no direct statements, all background, but no less true for all that.

And on the subject of quotes, there's the small matter of accuracy. If you have never had to transcribe another person's statements, you have no idea how difficult that can be. People don't always carry their thoughts through in a straight line. They ramble. They backtrack or sidetrack. They produce jumbles of speech known as "word salads" in the manner of a well-known leader of the free world. Try untangling one of those sometime. Well, you know what? You must. People deserve to have their words conveyed correctly. That doesn't mean what they meant to say but what they actually said. If they misstated, that can be emended later; if they were misquoted, that's writerly malfeasance. Of course, voice recordings make that easier. Reporters (and others) used to carry tape recorders; now they just whip out their smartphones.

Fair(ish) Treatment

Beyond accuracy, sometimes the media best serve the public interest by allowing a speaker to correct something said earlier, even if that something was perfectly quoted. One afternoon in the summer of 2018, President Trump said of Russian interference in the 2016 election, "I don't see any reason why it would be Russia." The statement was of a piece with the tenor of his entire discussion of the Russia probe that afternoon, and the response was predictable: how could he go against his entire intelligence establishment, who were united in saying that it definitely *was* Russia, and so on. The next day, he offered a revision of his earlier sentence, saying that he meant to say, "I don't see any reason why it *wouldn't* be Russia," explaining that he was using "sort of a double negative." He went on to say things that suggested he didn't really mean that at all, as when he said, as he has often done, that it "could be others, you never know." His first statement was not an instance of misreporting, given that the whole world could hear him actually say it. But he got to come out the next day and rework the problematic sentence. News people didn't refuse him a forum for retraction. Readers and listeners could decide for themselves which version was more likely. Which they did, along the usual fault lines. That's fair.

What's not fair is to change a speaker's words by oneself.

In examining the sides of a discussion, does the writer offer balance not only of space but of analysis? Okay, you're right, almost nobody offers true balance. But do they come close? Or is the opposing view presented as a straw man, set up only to be knocked down? You see it all the time in online comments, so-and-so backs Speaker of the House Nancy Pelosi, so she's essentially not merely a Democrat but a Socialist, practically a Communist who desires to take away our freedom. While such-and-such backs President Trump, so he really supports white supremacists (who sometimes express favorable opinions of the president) and therefore a neo-Nazi who desires to take our freedom away. From all appearances, our freedom is a delicate flower ceaselessly imperiled by all sorts of jackbooted knaves. Now, comment writers are not professional journalists, and they are held to a low standard of veracity, but we do see folks who write for a living get carried away with rhetorical guilt-by-association from time to time. It ain't pretty. Certain newspaper opinion columnists make character assassination their stock-in-trade. Cal Thomas generally portrays liberals as devils incarnate or at least as persons led astray by a devil. I believe they must be related to the conservatives whom Paul Krugman knows; each group is reduced to caricature by the respective columnists.

Rhetorical Tilt

WE CAN LEARN A lot about a writer's leaning by observing the slant of the words she uses. This is related to the fairness business above but is getting down to the microlevel. What kinds of words does she attach to the people or views she admires? To the ones she resists? Just yesterday I came across an op-ed in my local newspaper about an upcoming vote in the state on an antigerrymandering bill. For those of you who don't live and die politics

(I mostly die, or at least groan a lot, but that's another story), gerrymandering is the process, long practiced by both parties and recently perfected via big data, of drawing congressional and state legislative districts to resemble Rorschach test images. The goal isn't to create weird shapes for their own sake but to make some votes (the district-drawing party) count more than others (the out-of-power party). For the moment, we're less concerned with maps than with rhetorical flourishes. The writer's blurb after the column says that he "is not associated in any manner with the ballot initiative." Sounds like the soul of impartiality, no? But if we get down in the weeds a bit, we find that the supporters of the initiative aren't even present. Rather, the key sentence about them is couched in the neutrality of the passive voice, "An initiative has been proposed . . . and has received enough valid signatures, etc." But the opponents are abundantly active: "Those invested in the political status quo have claimed," and so on. "Invested," "status quo," and "claimed" are all charged words. You can hear the weight in them: "claimed," for instance, carries at least a slight taint of "wrongly" or "unfairly" that tries to push in unless the word is modified quickly.

Since I find myself in general agreement with the writer that gerrymandering tends to undermine the first principle of democracies that majorities are supposed to win power, I am inclined to look beyond his tilting the rhetorical scale. Others who see the practice as the fruits of fairly won elections (even those that have resulted from heavily gerrymandered districts) will likely find the words unfairly charged. That's readerly bias in both cases. Which accentuates or cancels out writerly bias on a case-by-case basis.

Here's the thing about bias, though: within limits, it doesn't mean that the writer is wrong or that the article or book has no merit. Nor does it mean that the bias you find in her makes her worse than the bias you may or may not acknowledge in yourself. Discovering the nature of a writer's bias will, however, let readers see where she's coming from and heading to, so that they can question (*interrogate* is the in-vogue term these days) the intent and the methods by which she pursues her case.

Care for an example of how to acknowledge your bias? If you're going to write about the role of psychedelic drugs in modern psychiatry, you'd better be prepared for questions. Among them, the preeminent concern will be something like, "What in heaven's name is wrong with you?" There will inevitably be a presumption that the writer is some sort of druggie seeking to justify his own interests. Or else someone with a financial interest in resurrecting a long-buried idea. This is precisely the situation of Michael Pollan, best known for his writing on food, in his 2018 book, *How to Change Your Mind: What the New Science of Psychedelics Teaches Us about Consciousness, Dying, Addiction, Depression, and Transcendence.* Pollan, it should be noted, is something of a professional skeptic. He writes about food, diet, restaurants, gardening, and his own misadventures in construction with a raised eyebrow that questions the current enterprise. In his *In Defense of Food* (2008), for instance, he explores how food myths embraced in the late twentieth century about such elements as whether dietary fat and cholesterol correlate as strongly as believed with cardiovascular disease and how "nutritionism" has turned Western attitudes toward food consumption into an increasingly wary and uneasy relationship. In much of his work he doubts his own reactions as much as those he challenges.

Such an approach serves him well in this book. Of the 2006 article detailing a study that found that a dose of psilocybin could prompt mystical experiences, he writes that it "piqued my curiosity but also my skepticism" about the value of psychedelics. The interest came from the fact that there were serious, academic researchers who for some reason were willing to risk damage to their reputations in order to reexamine the potential benefits of hallucinogens, this time weighing them against the hazards. Such was not the case a half-century earlier when LSD hucksters like Timothy Leary and the "acid tests" of Ken Kesey's Merry Pranksters brought the entire class of drugs—and those who studied them—into disrepute.

Pollan further tells us that he had no youthful experience of any psychedelic drugs, having been born a touch late (1955) for the flowering of LSD experimentation but right on time to receive all the antipsychedelics messages the society began putting out in the late sixties. The allure, moreover, of a drug-prompted mystical experience would seem lost on someone who confesses that he was unsure that "he has ever had a single 'spiritually significant' experience," a philosophically materialistic person who never considered himself "as a spiritual, much less mystical, person." He does, however, note that he understands that there may well be limits to the "scientific-materialist perspective." In other words, he knows what he thinks but suspects that what he thinks may not be everything that is thinkable. He announces that he will attack the questions raised by this new-old science with openness but also doubt toward all parts of the story, including his own role.

One place that this reserving of judgment proves useful is in his own exploration of the experience of the drugs in question. There is no way to know what a trip on LSD or psilocybin is like except by taking one. We can read all we want, but an experience so completely internal resists mere description, even by those who have undergone it. Yet Pollan does not wish to seem (or be) a drug-addled enthusiast seeking to justify his own life choices.

So, then, bias: be we ever so honest with ourselves and our readers, none of us can ever be wholly aware of our slants in this direction or that. Those can only be seen from the outside. The best we can hope to do is be honest about where we think our bias lies and work against it where we need to. After all, we're not fooling anyone but ourselves; it's not as if readers won't notice. Especially if they don't share our viewpoints.

6

Source Code

Where Do Writers Get That Stuff?

EVERY ARTICLE, COLUMN, OR book that makes a claim has certain obligations. To readers. To logic. To its own integrity. And chiefly to offer proof. What constitutes proof? Many different things. The writer's personal experience is one form: I was there, and this is what happened. A related category is *professional expertise*: I know this area of inquiry in a way few people on earth do. Good in certain situations, although not in all. *Statistics* can work, if used properly. *Eyewitness testimony,* in which case multiple eyewitnesses are good. *Expert sources* are the gold standard.

Here's the problem: what's an expert source? How can we tell if a source is likely to be golden?

We find ourselves in a strange time. The proliferation of online sources, including blogs (with or without expertise) and social media noise can make it difficult to separate sense from nonsense.

Worse, it can have a leveling effect, making everything seem like nonsense. This has long been a strategy for certain *agents provocateurs*, Russian political operatives in particular: produce enough terrible material so that all material begins to look terrible. If you can seem to turn the whole world into a cesspool, even roses seem to stink. But it also happens by the very nature of online discussion: all posts seem to carry equal weight.

Here's an example. Women academics are frequently subjected to attacks on their claim to special knowledge. Strangely, trolls seem especially angered if the women attach their titles or credentials—Professor, Doctor, PhD—to their names. Abuse comes in the form of challenges to authority: you don't know anything more than everybody else, you just spent however many years being indoctrinated and told what to think whereas we can think for ourselves; you hate men (this one almost always shows up in the troll-iverse). It can happen to male professors as well; I once made a disparaging comment about a terrible novelist whose work bewitches the conservative, adolescent male mind, and the trolls arrived to suggest that I wasn't smart enough to understand this particular writer. It was amusing on one level, knowing that none of them had read my work, which would have told them I had written on Joyce and Faulkner and T. S. Eliot and loads of truly difficult writers. But it was also distressing as a symptom, that having an opinion, no matter how ill-informed, was all that expertise amounted to. I got off lightly, though; I had to *do* something to arouse the abuse. A woman in my situation would merely have had to stake a claim to authority to receive a much greater volume of nastiness. Why? Because her hard-won knowledge and insight is threatening in some quarters. Because she earned something that someone else lacks or fears or feels intimidated by.

Still, that's what it means to have expertise, that someone has put in a huge amount of study in a field, or worked for years in one area of specialized knowledge or experience. An army general need not have a PhD in military affairs to be justly considered an expert. Her combination of study (no one comes straight from middle school into the officer track) and years in rank tell us she knows a lot about her field. Be a little wary though; the letters before or after a name don't tell the whole story. I hold a PhD, which means I can call myself "Dr. Foster," but if I start handing out medical advice, you should move away quickly. Expertise only exists in a narrow band of human understanding, and mine is strictly literary.

If personal expertise—knowledge, experience, length of practice—is one source of reliable information, it is not the only one. We also look to trustworthy sources outside one's experience. And most of the history of the world is beyond anyone's experience. There is not a person alive today, for instance, with an entirely reliable personal memory of baseball great Ty Cobb's playing days. He had a long career, but it ended in 1928, so the youngest person to have seen Cobb slide into second base with his sharpened spikes aimed at his opponent's knee, assuming that ten years old is about the earliest that such memories are remotely solid, would be a hundred years old as I write this. And for information we can take to the bank, I would prefer someone a bit older than ten. Wouldn't you? To know anything for certain, we need a different sort of account. You could seek out contemporaneous news accounts, see what was written in the Detroit papers on a given day in July 1921, but that sounds a whole lot like work. The newspaper files themselves, assuming your library even carries them, would be off limits because of the fragility of antique newsprint. That leaves microfilm or -fiche, the first of which comes as a roll and the latter as small flat sheets with a great many windows. Their job is to capture images of no longer accessible documents in a tiny format that requires a machine to read them. If you've never spent days on end searching microforms, trust me when I say that you won't like it. Some periodicals have been digitized and more eventually will be, but the searching for original reports is still a tedious process. So if *primary sources*, which is what the first drafts of history are, prove difficult or impossible to access, what are your options?

In the case of a historical figure, a biography is a good place to begin. This next bit may seem counterintuitive, but those biographies closest to the time their subjects lived are not top choices. They can be fun, especially if the subject, like Cobb, lived in the day of overheated rhetoric in the sports pages, an age when Grantland Rice could dub the starting backfield of the 1924 Fighting Irish the "Four Horsemen of Notre Dame" while asserting that they formed "the crest" of a "cyclone" that swept Army "over the precipice." The article in question is justly famous, but it's also a bit purple for contemporary tastes. In that environment, biographies also tended to be worshipful, something in the manner of Lives of the Saints that the Church created for centuries, usually with little or no factual basis for claims of those lives. Hagiography may be inspiring for the faithful, but it also tends to exist in a fact-free zone. The lives of those less saintly, say politicians or muckraking journalists, may suffer in the opposite condition, as a writer with an ax to grind vilifies the subject based more on political affiliation or current prejudices than on objective analysis. With a figure as divisive as Cobb, it is unsurprising that his first biographer, a sportswriter named Al Stump, did his level best to blacken his name, vilifying him as a racist with very violent tendencies. Nearly all of Stump's claims have been discredited. While this is an extreme example, it is in the nature of human beings to be led astray to some degree when looking at the world they know intimately, making every early biography at least a little suspect.

The corrective to that problem is time. Actually, time and subsequent additions to the historical record. The further away we get from a person's life or career, the more evidence becomes available. In the case of Ty Cobb, the decades have shown that he was neither as violent nor as bigoted as claimed, and in fact his views on race, which we would still not deem enlightened, did mature and soften in his later years. Most important, the passage of time allows every biographer of a famous person to stand on the shoulders, if not of giants, at least of a succession of other biographers. The same thing happens with histories, of course. We learn things from each new recounting of a war or famine or highway system. Alas, that phenomenon also has the tendency to make them vast. There is not a biographer who lived around the time of Alexander Hamilton who would have been capable of achieving the perspective and wealth of knowledge of Ron Chernow in his magisterial *Alexander Hamilton* (2004). At the same time, neither would they have composed the 818 pages of Chernow's tome. *Magisterial* denotes a work that is commanding, imposing, with more than a hint that it achieves those qualities by being really long. Even so, this biography is compelling enough to have made Hamilton cool again with the help of Lin-Manuel Miranda, who relied on it for his Broadway smash musical.

Can We Trust Anyone Here?

One of the destabilizing activities that Russian hackers undertook during the 2016 elections was to put out so much bad information that it called into question the validity of *all* information from all sources. During and after the campaign, you could hear the same refrains—"One side's as bad as the other"; "You can't trust any of them"; "It's all just opinion"—from colleagues and family members and folks sitting in the next booth at the restaurant.

But we had been headed that way for a good while before then. With the rise of the internet, a curious thing happened. We can call it the Great Leveling of Information. In a land without gatekeepers, purveyors of bad information have equal access to the new "publishing" world. An article by a leading authority in a field and published in a *peer-reviewed* periodical carries no more weight with many readers than a blog written by a twelve-year-old or a deliberate lie by someone meaning to undercut that leading authority. Indeed, there came to be a good deal of resentment of expertise, including decrying experts as "elites," as if that meant they had no right to claim mastery of a subject area. What lies behind that sentiment is a belief that no one knows more than the speaker, and that opinions are all equal, so why should anyone listen to experts? When I had my troll attack, my education was derided as meaningless or worse: all I had experienced in my pursuit of advanced degrees, they claimed, was Maoist-style brainwashing that took away my ability to think for myself. Untutored trolls had it all over me in the free-thinking department. Which is pretty funny if you actually saw how wackily uncontrollable grad students were in the mid-seventies. And continue to be in every decade since.

This charge tends to take root when words are the stock-in-trade. You will notice that such complaints die away when the subject is, say, brain surgery; no one really believes that the local mechanic is just as knowledgeable as the neurosurgeon. For that matter, the all-ideas-are-equal crowd rarely thinks someone is an expert mechanic because he once rode in a car. Still, that's where we are with information and analysis. We'll come back to online sources and social media later on. For now, let's merely note that the rise of the internet has coincided with a loss of respect for expertise and with even greater difficulty in recognizing it when we encounter it.

Have Source, Will Travel

AMONG NONFICTION WRITERS, ONLY the memoirist is exempt from the requirement to have rock-solid sources, since presumably her source knows what she's talking about. Even then, any claims made outside the scope of personal experience need documenting. Hillary Clinton is the foremost authority on her experience. One may dispute her presentation of facts about her time as First Lady, senator, or secretary of state, but no one on earth besides herself knows what she thought and felt about the events she chooses to describe. Same with James Comey in his memoir. His critics may, and have, argued against the externals of his case as he describes them, but he's on solid ground when discussing his motivations and reasoning. One may doubt his presentation of his thinking, but doubt is not proof; without evidence—emails, journal entries, conversations reported by second parties—to the contrary, it is impossible to say that his assertions are untrue.

For the rest of us, however, the weight of proof must lie outside ourselves. We have to bring the knowledge of others to bear in our writing.

Eyewitness Testimony

One of those forms of knowledge, as we mentioned earlier, is information from persons who experienced the events or figures in the story. Biographers, for instance, seek sources who knew the subject of their new project. A staple for many years in venues such as the *New York Review of Books*, *New York Times*, and *The New Yorker* is the biographical request, a small blurb asking anyone with information and a willingness to share to contact the writer. It typically goes something like this: "For a biography on [insert noteworthy subject here], anyone with reminiscences and information about her is asked to contact [insert writer's name here] at [address or post office box]." Journalists now achieve this crowd-sourcing through social media requests for information. Obviously, this approach won't work for Ron Chernow writing about Hamilton or Ulysses S. Grant. In that case, the writer has to rely on letters, journals, articles, interviews, anything in the written record by persons who personally knew the subject. I recently read an article about W. H. Auden by Hannah Arendt, herself a writer and thinker of renown, based in part on her personal acquaintance with the poet. Much of the article could have been written by anyone who knew Auden's work (and had Arendt's mind, which shortens the list a good bit), but there are also details that are available only because she knew him personally. Those bits can be gold for the writer of the poet's life.

Most journalism relies to a very large degree on personal testimony: who was there, what did they see, what are they willing to tell? This part doesn't change whether the story is about the opening of a local bakery, the anniversary of the Kent State shootings, or the transgressions of the Nixon administration. In fact, it doesn't change even if the telling is experimental and out-of-kilter. The New Journalists—Tom Wolfe, Joan Didion, Hunter S. Thompson, and the rest—were certainly new, but first and foremost they were *journalists*. The "new" part had only to do with the manner of the telling, such as using techniques from fiction, including some of the more experimental techniques for rendering characters' consciousness. None of that obviated the need for finding out what people in the story had experienced. In fact, it could be argued that this movement or moment or whatever it has been is even more reliant on getting the story from those who were present. When Wolfe, for instance, writes those jazzy imitations of characters' manner of speech, early critics often saw that as parody or ridicule. It can be more properly understood as a version of "free indirect speech," a technique invented by Gustave Flaubert and practiced by that other Woolf, Virginia. This technique is not so much a form of stream of consciousness as an attempt to capture the thoughts of the character in the language the character would use if she had enough access to her deep consciousness to be able to articulate those thoughts. A journalist has to get pretty close to his subject to be able to do that credibly. Wolfe does.

The Writer as Witness

SLIGHTLY DIFFERENT FROM THE eyewitness testimony is journalism that reports what it sees. We're quite accustomed to this from daily newspapers, where basketball games, city council meetings, and street protests, among so many other events, receive direct coverage from reporters on the scene. My first paying job as a writer was covering the high school football and basketball games for the town's weekly paper. Games were on Fridays, and sometimes Saturdays for the latter, and the first order of business was to attend games and take notes. Then there was a Sunday evening call with the head coach (for reactions, statistics, and general insights) and a frantic period of writing to make the Monday noon deadline. Pay was by the column inch, and the impoverished reporter was determined to produce a lot of inches. The prime directive here, of course, was to be at the games and *report* what actually happened. All coaching conversations in the world are useless without that foundation. And so it is with all forms of direct reporting: being there makes all the difference. Being able to convey speakers' tones of voice or the height of the flames at the blaze downtown or the number of protesters and the content of their placards brings an immediacy that brings the article to life. **Detail drives the story.** Detail alone is not enough—we need context, background, explanation as well—but it is essential.

Here's the odd thing about reportorial presence: it recedes in fairly direct proportion to the time between the event and the publication date. Newspapers have the most articles where the reporter—our representative—has actually witnessed the events being described. Weekly newsmagazines tend to have somewhat fewer, monthlies fewer still. Books? Unless they are writing about the experience *as* experience, which usually involves a first-person viewpoint, books have very little immediacy. Why does this trend exist? Because it expresses **the economy of information**. Primary information has high value, but only in the first stage of reporting. Within a day or two of a major event, the facts are usually known and widely distributed. That's what daily papers (and later radio and television news) have always excelled at: grabbing the facts as currently known and getting them out to the public. If we know the day after the robbery that the Dillinger gang got away with $859 and a guard took a bullet in the shoulder, who's going to pay for a magazine that comes out three and a half weeks later to tell us the same thing? What magazines do instead is flesh out the basic knowledge structure that first appeared in the papers. They will mention the basic facts as first known, naturally, but move on to larger questions. How soon was the FBI on the case? How did this job fit or diverge from the gang's *modus operandi*? Can this scourge be stopped? How? When? That's what monthly periodicals have traditionally added to the information flow. By the time books begin to come out, questions of how and when will likely have been answered, complete with the Woman in Red and the police ambush outside the movie theater. The job of book writers is not so much origination of knowledge as its synthesis: bringing all the disparate threads together to create a narrative or expository tapestry that is sturdy and satisfying. They seek to convey not news but understanding.

To be clear, writers at all stages of this hierarchy act as witnesses. Newspaper reporters provide firsthand and quick-take secondhand information, depending upon whether they are reporting what they see or what they are told by persons who were present or by officials such as police officers and firefighters who were on the scene shortly afterward. Magazine writers build on that initial knowledge and add to it by finding more witnesses, hearing from officials (think, medical examiners and fire marshals) who have collected more evidence than was available in the early days, and reading statements from various agencies on their findings. Book writers can and do take everything known at the point of beginning their own work, to which they can add their own research and analysis. They may find that early reports played up one element at the expense of others of ultimately greater value or that government entities withheld information that changes our understanding of events. Not infrequently, new intelligence comes to light that changes everything.

New information struck like a lightning bolt in the Pike County, Ohio, murders. On the night of April 21–22, 2016, eight members of the Rhoden family were shot in their beds (in four different houses), execution style, by persons unknown. Investigators had no solid leads and no suspects for a long time, a situation exacerbated by the refusal of potential witnesses in or around the case to provide any assistance, whether out of reluctance to get involved, a need to protect the perpetrators, or fear for their lives. The silence surrounding the case led, as it will, to all sorts of speculation, up to and including involvement by drug cartels. Eventually, four members of the Wagner family were arrested and charged with aggravated murder, two others with perjury and obstruction of justice. Those arrests took place on November 17, 2018, more than two and a half years later. That space of time approaches eternity in the world of daily journalism, and as of this writing, it is far from over. At their arraignments, all four principal defendants entered not guilty pleas, and the court cases could drag on. When the mystery is finally resolved for good and all, books will begin to appear. Book writers dislike stories without endings, unless of course they write the sort of books that speculate on endings. Reporters—in this case principally but by no means exclusively from the *Pike County News Watchman, Cincinnati Enquirer, Columbus Dispatch,* and *Dayton Daily News*—who covered the events and the criminal investigation throughout, have no such luxury, forced by time constraints to work with the facts as known at any given moment. They are, however, present at each stage of investigations and report as new information flows out, whether in a trickle or a cascade. Positioned as they are, this constant presence is why the first books to appear on a sensational murder or a matter of public corruption are frequently by those who have covered the story from its outset.

Data

LIES, DAMNED LIES, AND statistics. You've heard it before, and probably a lot. Mark Twain attributed it to Benjamin Disraeli, although the phrase never appears in any of his writings, and the first published uses yet found postdate the great statesman's death by a number of years. In any case, *somebody* said it, at some point, in the later nineteenth century. And a great many people have picked up on it down the decades. It does not mean, although it is sometimes taken thus, that statistics are always false, only that they can be made to *seem* to say things they don't actually support. You can add to that the fact that most of us are utterly mystified by our first brushes with statistics as an area of study.

The terminology is befuddling, the conclusions can seem counterintuitive, and we often dislike the results. There is only one statistic that is beyond dispute: the mortality rate, everywhere in the world and at all times (so far), is one. Frankly, we're not all that crazy about that one, either.

But people do manipulate numbers all the time for their own interests, even if those interests are in confusing debate. Climate skeptics leapt at the chance to trumpet the "fact" that 2017 represented the biggest single-year drop in global temperature average ever. Therefore, global warming is a hoax. But here are the other facts that they "overlooked" in their triumphal assertions:

1.   That drop was from the hottest year ever recorded.
2.   2017 was the hottest year ever without an El Niño event.
3.   Even with the drop 2017 was the third warmest ever, after the two preceding years. In other words, if you remove 2015 and 2016, it is the hottest year ever measured.

We can debate till the cows come home what motivations drive those who seize upon a single data point as disproving a decades-long trend, but following the money, as we will see later, will demonstrate that coal and oil money is behind many of the loudest climate deniers.

Sometimes discrepancies are a little fuzzier, if no less puzzling. In February 2019, *Forbes*, through its online Forbes.com news site, reported an average of $28,650 in student debt for 2017 graduates, basing that number on statistics compiled by The Institute for College Access & Success (TICAS). Wikipedia, citing an article from the same *Forbes* reporter, Zack Friedman, from June 2018, informs us that the total student loan debt for 2016 grads was $38,390, although the number he states in his piece is $37,172. His source in this instance is an outfit called Make Lemonade, one of whose business interests is student loan refinancing. Neither number works mathematically: dividing total student debt ($1.52 trillion) by total debtors (44.2 million) only gets us to $34,389. More to the point, what are the chances that the average student loan burden *dropped* by nine or ten thousand in one year? Even if he misstated the year, how could it have gone up by that amount when sources cited in the Wikipedia article state that the rate of increase has been dropping in recent years, having only gone up by $600 from the previous year? There are a lot of numbers here, and they mostly don't add up. At the very least, Friedman could have used a hard-nosed, old-time editor who made him question the accuracy of his sources. Or at a minimum, do the math. Or maybe not rely solely on an operation that profits from the topic on which it released the data. Bottom line: unless you know the source, its motivations, and its methodology, statistics alone can be pretty unreliable.

So yes, you can lie with numbers. Like other evidence, they can be misrepresented, taken out of context, subjected to all manner of falsification. You already knew that. Even so, it is nevertheless true that numbers, facts, the broad category we call "evidence" remains an invaluable tool in proving one's point. There are such things as facts that exist independent of our beliefs and prejudices, that are not subject to our will. If the prosecution in a murder case presents a gun with the suspect's fingerprints on it and a ballistics match to the fatal bullet, it simply won't do for jurors to say, "I don't believe it. He seems like such a nice guy." Nor will it do for us as readers, as citizens, as thoughtful human beings, to reject objective facts out of hand because of preconceived notions. Nor to accept falsehoods and "fun facts" because they comport with those notions.

"Fun facts"? Yes, indeed. We are flooded these days by what presidential advisor Kellyanne Conway dubbed "alternative facts." She said this apropos of then White House press secretary Sean Spicer's claim of crowd size at Donald Trump's inauguration, which was supported with pictures the White House published, ostensibly of the crowds at Donald Trump's inauguration. Those turned out to be from Barack Obama's inauguration. Various spokespersons for the administration along with the president himself continued to support the claim even after it was thoroughly debunked. Trump supporters inclined toward blaming the media, his favorite whipping boy, rather than the initial falsehoods themselves. This is one incident, from one day, from one small if highly visible part of the information universe, but it goes on all the time, in many quarters. We'll return to these matters in a bit, but for now, I offer it only as an instance of the way falsehoods insinuate themselves into our social conversation and how attractive they prove to be for adherents to a cause more interested in the cause than the truth.

7

All in How You Look at Things

Structure and Meaning

WHEN WE TALK ABOUT fiction and poetry in literary discussions, we want to know how the current piece is arranged. What is the starting point? Does it move beginning to end or back and forth or in some sort of curlicue? Does it begin with the ending? The beginning? Some other key moment? In other words, how is it structured? That's what we do with works that are essentially fictive in nature. So here's the question to consider: why should nonfiction be any different?

Because it's not made up? Because the stuff in it really happened?

No need for that to matter. Yes, the events—births, deaths, marriages, discoveries, criminal trials, and all the rest—did actually happen. That doesn't mean they don't have to be arranged.

But they happened in a specific order. You know, chronology.

In fact, I do know chronology. But I also know structure. One is a timeline of events. The other is a framework over which those events get stretched. Participants will experience something, a basketball game, say, as moving from beginning through middle to end, opening tip-off to final buzzer. Each one will experience it slightly differently based on his or her own subjectivity—things like team affiliation and how well they like certain players—but in general they will agree that the Blue Demons beat the Red Devils on two late free throws, and that the turning point was when the Red Devils' star forward fouled out with four minutes to go. The newspaper article in tomorrow's paper, on the other hand, may not be at all interested in the chronology of the game, choosing to focus on the psychology or the drama. We can be sure, for instance, that the lede will not be the tip-off (it almost never is), and it wouldn't be terrible to think it will instead focus on something much closer to the end: "Kevin Hamlin looked at the rim and tried to calm himself for the first of two free throws with nine seconds remaining. The sophomore, pressed into service by foul trouble and injuries to the Blue Demons' backcourt, focused on the process—two bounces of the ball, an easy breath, bent knees, and a smooth release. As he completed the follow-through, the rim hardly seemed to matter anymore, and the ball barely rippled the net, nor did the second one, ensuring the Demons first place in the conference." What follows may show almost no interest in the order of events but cling to the drama inherent in the rivalry or the story of an unlikely hero. The dismissal of the opposing star with five fouls may be the next thing mentioned or may not show up until the end of the piece. The difference between the game itself and the story of the game is the structure imposed on telling that story. The question is always, how can I tell this in the most effective way possible? How can I convey the intensity and struggle and keep readers hooked?

John McPhee may or may not be our greatest living writer of nonfiction (hint: he is), but he is almost certainly our greatest thinker about writing nonfiction. Of necessity. He has taught one seminar in nonfiction writing two out of each three years since 1974 at his alma mater, Princeton University. His collected class rosters read like a Who's Who of contemporary American journalism, although there were also plenty who went on to success in business, the arts, and other lesser endeavors. In 2017 he published *Draft No. 4: On the Writing Process*, which is virtually that class, now called Creative Nonfiction. So what part of that process obsesses the master of writing?

Structure.

For that obsession, he credits (or blames, depending on your viewpoint) his favorite high school English teacher, Mrs. McKee, who required a "structural outline" for every piece. She did not insist on roman numerals but accepted any honest effort at describing the shape of the writing. Every writer has to impose some organizational rationale on every piece of writing, and there are two ways to get there: outline the structure beforehand or wait till afterward and wrestle an octopus. That's what teachers are attempting to do when they force students to shake hands with the *five-paragraph theme*. There are multiple iterations of this wily beast, but they share certain elements: put the thesis statement *here* (or else *there*), make each body paragraph have a main point and some supporting evidence, and place something at the end that makes the bloody thing feel finished. This is not the formula for good writing, but it is a method of imposing order on the disorderly adolescent mind, a way of teaching structure to fourteen-year-olds. Well, guess what—forty-year-olds also have disorderly minds. And sixty. And eighty-seven, as McPhee is at the time of this writing. The nature of the order thus exacted is up to the writer, but it is required for the writer, as a means of disciplining thoughts that incline toward dishevelment if not derangement, and for readers, to bring them maximum *something*: pleasure, understanding, fulfillment, insight.

Here's the thing writers (and readers who would understand them) need to remember: **Chronology does not equal structure**. Structure cannot ignore and certainly must not *falsify* the actual sequence of events, but it need not be a slave to it, either. To illustrate this point, McPhee tells the story of writing his book on Alaska, *Coming into the Country* (1977). His method is to create and store a very large number of note cards on which pieces of an eventual book are first committed to writing. He then arranges them in patterns on a work table until he finds the organizational design that will serve him best. For this book, he knew early on that he didn't want that design to depend on the sequence of his own journey in the state. That would make the results about him more than about his subject, a situation that never appeals to him.

With the first section of *Coming into the Country*, "The Encircled River," which describes a canoe-and-kayak trip from Alaska's Brooks Range to the tiny hamlet of Kiana, he encountered a seemingly insurmountable problem: the climax occurred on day one of the nine-day trek. While he and other members of the five-man group took a long hike around the base of a mountain, they encountered a massive grizzly bear feasting on blueberry bushes. As in, whole bushes loaded with fruit. The experience was exhilarating and alarming in equal measure, since the big bears are notoriously unpredictable. This is in a sense the perfect Alaskan moment. To tell the story in straight chronological detail would be disastrous to the narrative; it's all downhill from there. And he can't falsify when the bear sighting took place, as he says in *Draft No. 4*, because this is nonfiction and facts are facts. The solution? Don't stick to chronology, at least in a front-to-back straight line. He begins on day five shortly after, we later learn, a second bear sighting. Not so huge or scary, but big enough and magical enough: the young bear is playing with a salmon it has killed, tossing it in the air again and again. When it senses the humans floating by, it moves off into the underbrush.

So why begin and end where he does? For one thing, it allows him to begin midstream, as it were, and avoid all that tiresome business of arrival and shifting gear and such. We're thrown right into the trip because these guys are already on it, dirty and sweaty and somewhat beaten up. But also because he can set up a narrative cycle, which corresponds to the cyclical nature of everything arctic, as he sees it. And because he can end with a bear—not *the* bear, to be sure, but a bear—which holds the promise of becoming that one of near-mythic proportion that he sees on day one. Here's how he structures this narrative. He begins on day five, which he places at nine o'clock if we imagine a clockface. He goes over the top for days five through nine (put this one at three o'clock) and then flashes back to day one. We have been taught to expect that flashbacks end and flash forward to the "now" of the story. As McPhee explains in *Draft No. 4*, however, that's not the plan; he will stay in the flashback until the section ends. That allows him to put the huge bear at the midpoint on his narrative dial, and then walk us through the first four days so that the young bear comes right at the end, as he completes the cycle. It works: the young bear, standing for all that is wild and foreign to our puny human experience, is a fitting culmination to this story.

Okay, but why nine and three o'clock, and not twelve and six?

He doesn't say, but I think it has to do with visual aesthetics. Lateral opposites feel (which is to say, look) more balanced than the polar kind.

Structure—the design of the piece—is always something to consider as you read nonfiction just as much as with a short story or a novel. **The structure of a piece of writing affects its meaning.** Which means it pays for us to notice. In any story with a timeline, there are three places to begin: the beginning, the end, and anywhere in between. Doesn't exactly narrow the field, does it? Each of those options presents a different set of questions. If we begin at the beginning, for instance, the questions revolve around the big one: where is this thing going? At the end: how did we get here? In between: how did we get here, where is it going, and why did we start here and not somewhere else? Just about every manual on short story writing will tell you to begin *in media res*, Latin for in the middle of things, but at a point as near as possible to the end. Often, the actual beginning—of events, not of the story—never appears, or else it resides in a quick reference or two to something that in the *now* of the story lies back there in the mists of time. Even if those mists are only fifteen minutes old. Why do they tell you that? Chiefly to keep beginners from bogging down in exposition, the swamp that eats reader interest.

Nonfiction articles often start the same way, at some moment before the very end (although they start there sometimes, too) but fairly close to it. Why is that? For some of the same reasons.

The first-year player standing at home plate or the free-throw line in the biggest moment of the year is dynamic and filled with drama. So is the defendant rising before the judge for a verdict. The moment also contains a complete backstory, which is where the article will likely spend most of its time, and will also jet forward into the finale. The near-the-end opening can work and has done times without number. That said, articles also have begun at the beginning, at the end, and at points earlier in the middle. With success. The only rule here is that the resulting piece needs to succeed, and that is often down to the skill of the writer, not to a fixed policy.

And what about books? Same thing. The question is, what can you, as the writer, make work in this instance? Let's take two books about the Trump White House in 2018. In *Fire and Fury*, Michael Wolff begins with the end of the beginning in a prologue dealing with Fox News chief (and founder) Roger Ailes, and Trump's campaign strategist Steve Bannon at a dinner two weeks before inauguration day. He then launches into the tale of taking over at the beginning, with a first chapter called "Election Day." Here he wants to strike two themes. First, that Ailes and Bannon saw themselves (and acted) as puppet masters, that the candidate, now president-elect, had to be stage-managed into success, protected against his political naivete and worst instincts while strengthened in certain leanings toward hypernationalism. And second, that as we see in chapter one, the incoming administration was unprepared to assume the awesome responsibility of running the country, unprepared in many cases even for the victory they had just achieved. He's writing a gang-that-couldn't-shoot-straight narrative, and the prologue and opening chapter signal that intention.

Bob Woodward's *Fear*, on the other hand, begins a good bit later, nine months into the administration. His prologue seizes on a single moment, when Gary Cohn, director of the Council of Economic Advisers, allegedly pilfered a draft letter withdrawing the United States from its free-trade agreement with South Korea (known as KORUS) from the Resolute Desk in the Oval Office. Cohn and others believed breaking the agreement would be financially and politically ruinous. By contrast, President Trump had announced his opposition to all existing trade deals, largely based on a misunderstanding of the effect trade deficits have on the American economy. Woodward then launches the narrative proper in the first chapter by diving back to the very beginning, maybe even before the beginning, to a meeting Trump had with Bannon and former House investigator and longtime conservative activist David Bossie in 2010, when they vetted him as a potential candidate and offered advice they were sure he would never take. Only then does he move forward to the chronological beginning of his story of the Trump presidency, to the day following Trump accepting the Republican nomination. Yes, there is a lot of beginning before *that* beginning, but not for the narrative Woodward is constructing. And why does he land there? Because he wants to focus on an emblematic crisis, a *New York Times* story about the inability of Trump's handlers to get the candidate to "control his tongue." Bannon again shows up, frantic to not be seen as the architect of certain disaster as he talks to anyone who will listen, but chiefly to Robert Mercer, whose arch-conservative ambitions run as deep as his pockets, a man who has devoted millions and millions of dollars not merely to Republican causes but to the right wing of the right wing. From that point on, Woodward will move back and forth among the many passengers and supposed conductors on the Trump train, but he will generally stick to a chronological approach. His goal is to not confuse readers.

In opening as he does, Woodward strikes his own themes, first that everyone who comes into Trump's orbit supposes they can control him, and second, that he very much needs controlling. Wolff's tale is one of a dysfunctional administration; Woodward's of an administration made dysfunctional by the erratic behavior of its chief executive. Wolff believes that the president was surrounded by crisis actors, Woodward that he turns everyone around him into such.

How late does Woodward begin his narrative? In terms of chronology, the moment of Cohn's decision ultimately arrives on page 265 (of 357).

A book can even begin long after the events related in it, as works by Daniel James Brown and Margot Lee Shetterly prove. Brown's *The Boys in the Boat* (2013) begins many years after the heroics at the Berlin Olympics with the author making the acquaintance of the aging (and ailing) Joe Rantz, the last living member of that elite group, and perhaps the one with the most compelling personal story. Shetterly opens *Hidden Figures* with a meeting in her childhood with one of the "human computers," the black, female mathematicians who ran calculations for the early US space program. Unlike Brown's meeting, Shetterly's initial contact, Kathaleen Land, vanishes from the book but provides a pathway into other contacts and the research that led to her book. Aside from that difference, the two works share many similarities: a wide-ranging cast of characters whose backstories are filled with challenges and obstacles, the interlacing of momentous achievements (individual races or rocket launches) and external circumstances, whether the Depression and the rise of

Hitler or the Jim Crow South and entrenched racial prejudice, and cuts between chapters on different characters and events in ways that insist on readers balancing the various elements of the story.

Having said all this, I should note that some books do, indeed, begin at the beginning. One particular area of nonfiction that is obliged to chronology is the life story. We really do need to follow the life (most of the time) in the order in which it was lived. Some biographers and autobiographers can bounce around between an endpoint and events surrounding it and earlier phases of that life, but they have to be really adept to keep us from bewilderment. That does not inevitably mean, however, that they start at point A, but some do. Stephen E. Ambrose begins his *Undaunted Courage: Meriwether Lewis, Thomas Jefferson, and the Opening of the American West* with the birth and youth of the title explorer, whose development is critical to arriving at a point where the Corps of Discovery can begin its expedition. True, the book is not a typical biography, concerning itself with the most important journey in American history, but it never takes its eye off Lewis as the primary focus. The trip itself is similarly managed in chronological order as befits its subject. And if following a person's life is best handled by sticking to the timeline, can that be any less true of the life of a year? In recent decades there have been a number of books that focused on a single year, the best known of which may be David McCullough's *1776* (2005), which he begins in the fall of 1775, after the Battles of Lexington and Concord had precipitated the Siege of Boston, which was ongoing despite the colonials' effort to dislodge the British in the Battle of Bunker Hill. Indeed, British troops would not be forced to withdraw from Boston until the Fortification of Dorchester Heights the following March. McCullough, relying on a tremendous number of contemporaneous documents, marches readers into and through the eponymous year and all the way to Washington's famous Delaware crossing and the Battle of Trenton on December 26.

As you have no doubt suspected, straight chronology is not the only way to manage structure even in a life story. In *Alexander Hamilton*, which served as the basis for Lin-Manuel Miranda's Broadway smash, *Hamilton*, Ron Chernow brackets the chronological treatment of the life with prologue and epilogue that focus on Elizabeth Schuyler (Eliza) Hamilton in great old age, first forty-six years after her husband's death in the Aaron Burr duel and again at her own death four years later, at age ninety. This structure imparts an automatic long view, a sort of preview of our own distance of two centuries from the death of the great man.

All this focus on histories and biographies is all well and good, but what about books not limited by the march of historical events? Books like, say, this one?

Let's start by saying that there are comparatively few books written that owe nothing to the passage of time. Even works on science, at least the physical sciences but I think the life sciences as well, have to account for the way that discovery builds on discovery, newer thought on previous thought whether in agreement or opposition, theory upon theory. One major exception can be the how-to and self-help genres. But it is certainly possible to write about science with a minimal adherence to chronology. Take Michael Pollan's *How to Change Your Mind: What the New Science of Psychedelics Teaches Us about Consciousness, Dying, Addiction,*

Depression, and Transcendence (2018), which, despite the "How to" at the beginning, is emphatically not a do-it-yourself guide but a review of the new science, as the massively long subtitle makes clear. Having said that, though, we must admit that it starts out as if it will be a chronological study of the history of psychedelics. The prologue begins with the initial discovery of LSD in 1943 by Swiss chemist Albert Hofmann and the discovery by the West in 1955 of a drug long known (in its mushroom form) in indigenous New World cultures, psilocybin. Then, just when we think we see how this will go, the focus switches to Pollan himself, to his comparative ignorance of all things psychedelic, including its history. The first chapter, by contrast, begins not back at the beginning but with what he calls the "renaissance" in psychedelic study in clinical settings, research that stopped cold in the 1960s in response the counterculture's enthusiastic embrace of any mind-altering substance. This rebirth had to wait for the new century and, with it, new findings in neuroscience.

This structure of the new-discovery text, as with most other genres, varies from writer to writer and work to work. Malcolm Gladwell, the contemporary master of new social science discoveries, has a formula he follows in his books. He begins with an anecdote that comes to a surprising conclusion and in turn leads to an insight into human consciousness and behavior. From there, he walks through the psychological, sociological, and economic research and theories that help explain the phenomenon in his opening, with abundant examples to illustrate his major points. In his second book, *Blink: The Power of Thinking Without Thinking* (2005), that anecdote involves a statue, claimed to be ancient Greek, that was purchased by the still-young Getty Museum. Its scientists performed all manner of tests, taking considerable time and expense in the process, the outcome in almost every case being to ratify the seller's claim to authenticity. When art experts came to look at the statue—a young, nude male figure known as a *kouros*—the story was quite the opposite. The experts declared the kouros a fake, and the average time to reach that decision was measured in seconds. Of course, they turned out to be right. Gladwell uses this example to introduce the theory of *thin-slicing*, the ability of the unconscious to recognize patterns at a glance based on highly specialized experience. He builds out from this explanation to related concepts and examples, both of successes and of horrible failures, as in the 1999 police killing of the entirely innocent Amadou Diallo in the Bronx, when a case of mistaken identity led to forty-one shots fired, almost half of which hit the victim. While there are warnings about the dangers of "thinking without thinking," readers generally tend to remember the strengths of the approach and the positive examples. Gladwell's structure won't work for every book, even for every book attempting something similar to his. But he has clearly found an approach to parceling out information that works for him.

The bottom line in all this? Structure matters. And not just because it determines what you read when. It matters because it changes meaning. If the writer presents two timelines in alternating chapters, present following past, that will produce a very different understanding than if she presents the entire past and then moves to the present. If another begins with one bear encounter and ends with another, and neither of those is the beginning or the end of the journey, he's telling us something by that choice. If the narrative is circular, that will feel different than if it were linear. If a science book moves from discovery to discovery, how will that alter our perceptions from those we would have had if he moved from scientist to scientist? Or if he began with the most recent discovery and moved steadily backward? Hey, it happens. And if structure matters, it behooves us to notice how any given piece is put together.

Fake News and "Fake News"

ONCE UPON A TIME, we knew, or thought we knew, that the news was true. Responsible journalists strove to tell the truth, and mostly they did. When they were wrong, they owned up to their error, as when Walter Cronkite, as near to the voice of God as ever appeared on the nightly news, came back from Vietnam convinced that he had been lied to by the Johnson administration and in particular by Secretary of Defense Robert McNamara about the war and its prosecution, and that he had been complicit in spreading those lies. His broadcast recanting his earlier position was a bombshell that shook the nation's belief in itself and its government. Journalists' willingness to admit mistakes is part of why most readers and viewers and listeners have been inclined to trust the media. Until lately.

In the years just prior to the 2016 election, social media became incredibly powerful but also incredibly compromised. It served to spread a great deal of information, and people in increasing numbers said they looked to Facebook or Twitter for their news sources. Alas, it also spread vast amounts of disinformation, much of it purposely designed to deceive. So consider this question: if you rely on a single type of material for your news, and if much of that material is false, either due to sloppiness or malice, how accurate is your "news"?

That's what I thought.

Throughout 2016 and the early months of 2017, those bogus sources of information acquired a name: *fake news*. What nearly everyone understood the term to mean is what its users intended it to mean, that a news story was intended to deceive. For decades, the phrase, if used at all, was applied to grocery checkout tabloids like the *National Enquirer*. The *Enquirer*, it should be remembered, paid to bury stories (called catch-and-kill in the in-house parlance) on Trump while finding liver cancer and two strokes supposedly plaguing Hillary Clinton in the absence of any medical opinions or, evidently, any source at all beyond fertile imagination. The term found new life, according to the BBC, in the summer of 2016 when Craig Silverman, the media editor for BuzzFeed, the internet media and news company, noticed that a tremendous number of utterly false stories having to do with the American presidential election were emanating from a single town in the Republic of Macedonia. This seemed odd since Veles is a fair distance from any point in the United States and has a population under 45,000 souls. To have more than 140 websites dedicated to creating fake news that would go viral and dominate news cycles seemed at least peculiar and more likely sinister. That BuzzFeed would notice is hardly surprising; it was created a decade earlier as a sort of laboratory to track viral online content. And this stuff was viral with a vengeance. The content, almost all utterly false, skewed right but also had a certain amount of pro-left nonsense, a curious sort of propaganda in that it appeared to have no dog in this political fight, unless sowing confusion can be said to be canine in nature. And the various sides latched onto the fakery aimed toward their sensibilities as onto holy writ. The warring tribes seemed to have discovered their self-justifying myths. If one has decided that the other side is un-American if not inhuman, then a story that claims—out of thin air—that, say, the FBI agent who supposedly leaked the Hillary Clinton emails was found dead in an apparent murder-suicide, well, that's just too good to be false. Nor was the disinformation campaign blindly sent everywhere; some was targeted with fair precision. A study by Oxford professor Philip N. Howard found that fully half of all Twitter material aimed at voters was junk or fake news, meaning that no more than half was from genuine news sources. So throughout the summer and fall, the internet was filled with fake news and with more sober voices calling it out as "fake news."

Seems like we got that all sorted out, doesn't it? If only.

In December 2016 defeated candidate Clinton gave a speech in which she said that the cascade of "fake news" (using the term in its accepted sense) was threatening our democracy. Many listeners and commentators took that to mean she believed she had lost the election because of fake news. She didn't quite claim that directly, and her chief concerns seem to have been the danger to a Washington, DC, pizza parlor that was spread by, among others, an alt-Right community on the social media platform Reddit (this sort of herd of like-minded individuals is known as a subreddit) and that became known as *Pizzagate*. The story claimed that there was a child sex ring involving Secretary Clinton and other major Dems in the basement of the Comet Ping-Pong pizza restaurant. The trivial fact that Comet Ping-Pong lacked a basement proved no impediment to the fertile minds of conspiracy theorists. This all seems preposterous on its face, but right-wing social media lit up and one adherent traveled hundreds of miles with a gun, then opened fire in the restaurant (firing wildly and managing not to hit anyone) while announcing that he was there to get to the bottom of things. That sorry saga was what Clinton had in mind when she referred to lives being endangered by all the fake news stories, but a great many people interpreted her comments as meaning only that she disliked these stories because they cost her the election.

One of those interpreters, evidently, was President-Elect Donald Trump, who seemed to believe that what Secretary Clinton meant was that news she disliked she deemed fake. And he ran with that. In January 2017, in a remarkable act of linguistic jiu-jitsu, he flipped the term to mean not what everyone else had meant previously but solely that whatever news he didn't like was "fake." And what he mostly didn't like was mainstream media (MSM in the parlance of the cognoscenti). He first used the term against CNN White House reporter Jim Acosta, telling him, "You're fake news." From there, he has kept up the steady drumbeat about his private "fake news" sources in every speech and at every rally and in a very large number of tweets, thereby effectively changing the meaning of the term from what had formerly been understood to simply "that which displeases Trump." His maneuver proved a godsend for dictators and strongmen around the world since it gave them a handy way to dismiss all negative coverage (very useful for the corrupt and murderous among world leaders). And he has used the term on an almost daily basis—along with derisive terms like "failing," "phony," and "hack"—ever since to deride respected news sources from the *New York Times* and *Washington Post* to National Public Radio and CBS, where Cronkite publicly renounced the government's lies all those years earlier.

Instead, he favors the *National Enquirer*, whose parent company over the years has paid hundreds of thousands of dollars in kill fees to bury stories unfavorable to Trump, whom they regard as the goose that lays golden "news" eggs, and Fox News, which does virtually no actual news gathering, relying much more on opinion shows, many of which traffic in conspiracy theories and demonstrably false stories from shady sources, not least of those being the *Enquirer*. From its inception, Fox News has set itself up as an alternative to mainstream news media, following founder Roger Ailes's distaste for what he perceived as the liberal bias of much of the coverage found there. As a result, the Fox slant is decidedly and, to its credit, overtly right-wing (nothing hidden there), but it frequently allows that partisanship to make truth a casualty. Fox is a fact-checker's paradise. It made use, for instance, of Pizzagate stories, although usually by laying authority off to some purveyor like InfoWars further upstream in the conspiracy theory watershed.

One upshot of presidential behavior is that any public figure can now feel free to try a "fake news" defense, at least in the court of public opinion. Such stratagems work better among right-leaning audiences, but even then, the outcomes are uncertain. While Trump has had marvelous luck, others accused of misdeeds, like ousted Alabama Supreme Court Justice Roy Moore, have lost elections despite living in overwhelmingly Republican states. It's harder to hide behind claims of fake news when the accusations involve underage girls rather than porn stars and *Playboy* models.

One of the standard tactics, from Richard Nixon forward, is to dismiss all reporting based on anonymous sources as false. Such denials are more likely to be untrue than the reports they deny, assuming the reports come from reputable news outlets. If not, well . . . During the 2016 Trump campaign, Bob Woodward tells us in his excellent *Fear*, Steve Bannon roared out during a meeting about Trump's disgraceful *Access Hollywood* videotape, where he claimed to be able to sexually assault women with impunity because of his fame and money, that all deep background stories are complete "lies and bullshit." Here, we can assume, Bannon was speaking from experience: as CEO of the website Breitbart News, he would have had extensive experience in managing made-up stories, such as articles claiming that the Obama administration and Hillary Clinton supported ISIS, and attributing them to "unnamed sources." But let's look at the historical record a moment. Nixon and his various hatchet men claimed that the deep background Watergate stories by Woodward and Carl Bernstein in the *Washington Post* were falsehoods. They went on making that claim right up to the moment they headed off to prison or, for the great man himself, to the helicopter taking him to the political wilderness. But then, Woodward and Bernstein published *All the President's Men*, in which a number of witnesses who previously had spoken on deep background allowed themselves to be identified, and the country discovered that these people really did know whereof they spoke. Most significantly, thirty years later, Mark Felt, who had been the number two man at the FBI, came forward to reveal that he had been Deep Throat, the most famous unnamed source in history, which Woodward corroborated, and any shred of doubt about the truth of that reporting vanished forever.

These repeated attacks on the press, often by politicians caught with their hands in cookie jars or other places they didn't belong, are why major news outlets like the *Post* insist on rigorous vetting of sources, multiple sources for any important information, and absolute adherence to the truth as best it can be known. And why they punish journalistic fraud so severely. A newspaper or magazine or television program is only as good as its reputation. Without that, audience trust is utterly lost.

Look, we're never going to agree on the veracity of information. Liberals will always suspect the *National Review*, conservatives *The Nation*. Traditionally, however, that has to do with their editorial positions, not the quality of their reporting. That mistrust is simply how things are going to be. But there should be some things that all rational people can agree on: that some sources routinely traffic in falsehoods, that others make mistakes but own up to them, that certain bad actors (often from outside the country) deliberately plant untrue material in the public consciousness, and that we all have to put in some work to dig out informational treasures and throw out the trash. Most of all, we have to admit that our prejudices are not the same as rational judgment and as such need to be held up for inspection.

As a coda to this discussion, on April 18, 2019, Department of Justice special counsel Robert Mueller published the report of his team's investigation of Russian interference in the 2016 general election and possible Trump campaign/administration staff involvement. The report found that the Russians, as everyone understood by that point, had attempted in a variety of ways to interfere in the election on Trump's behalf, but while there was a good bit of contact between various persons in the Trump circle and Russian actors, some of whom may have been agents of the government, that contact did not rise to the very high bar required for charges of conspiracy to be brought. On the matter of President Trump's possible obstruction of justice, the report said that he couldn't be prosecuted, chiefly because of a DOJ policy against indicting sitting presidents, but that the evidence would not allow Mueller to declare him innocent. Both of those decisions immediately became the subjects of wild spin from both sides of the political aisle. For our purposes, however, the big news was that nearly all of the stories about life inside the campaign and then the White House that had been reported by major news sources—the *Times*, the *Post*, NPR, *The New Yorker*, and ABC, NBC, CBS, and PBS—and condemned by Trump and his allies with the now-tired epithet *fake news*, were corroborated in sworn testimony by members of the campaign staff and administration. While the report does not mention those news outlets, in case after case, from

- the story that Trump told White House counsel Don McGahn to pressure Deputy Attorney General Rod Rosenstein to fire Mueller and, when McGahn refused, to deny that Trump had told him to;
- to reports of the meeting involving Paul Manafort, Donald Trump Jr. and Jared Kushner with a dubious Russian figure, Natalia Veselnitskaya, who promised dirt on the Clinton campaign, although various members of the American contingent repeatedly lied about the purpose of the meeting;
- to clandestine meetings with Sergey Kislyak by future attorney general Jeff Sessions, Kushner, and Michael Flynn,

the news stories are confirmed in the report. So much for "fake news." Now, can we for crying out loud retire the term?

Traditional
Nonfiction
Sources

8

Bringing the News

Reading Journalism

IN A SENSE, HARD news journalism is, by design, easy to read. It is written at a ninth- to eleventh-grade level (depending on the paper). As anyone who has ever encountered day one of an Introduction to Newswriting course knows, there are Five Ws required for any piece of writing: Who, What, When, Where, and Why. And their place is clearly stated: as close to the front of the piece as the writer can manage. Which means in the first paragraph. Real newspaper practice, like everything humans undertake, can be rather more complex, but placing five essential pieces in the lede paragraph is the ideal. In a perfect world, readers know everything they really need to know by paragraph two; the rest is just detail and context.

That's the theory, anyway. And it mostly works. Most news stories about fires and car wrecks and City Hall doings, along with virtually all sports stories and your local human-interest columnist's efforts, will grade out right in that range on what's called the *Flesch-Kincaid Grade Level* scale. The contents, though, as opposed to the prose, may be anything but easy reading. Things get more complex in the realm of investigative journalism. And that's not the fault of the writers. Let's consider two investigative efforts, one from an entire news staff at a local paper and the other by two guys who stumbled onto the most important story in American political history.

Journalism at Full Speed

Way, way back there I laid out the various kinds of writing to be found in a newspaper—reporting, opinion, advice, analysis, profile, human-interest, exposé, and so on. You may be wondering, why do we need all these different forms in a daily (or weekly) paper? Because every single one fills an essential niche in the journalistic ecosystem. Because we can't live without them. As luck would have it, I live next to a gigantic university with an equally large problem. The collision of massive institution and major crisis illustrates the function of daily newspapers in their communities. In September 2016, stories began coming out, first as a trickle and then a stream and eventually a cascade, that USA Gymnastics team doctor Larry Nassar, a physician and faculty member at Michigan State University, had, under the guise of therapeutic treatment, sexually abused hundreds of girls and young women, a great many of them elite athletes. Armed with what seemed specialized knowledge and buttressed by scholarly articles (by him), he deceived employers and athletes alike into believing that his "treatments" were not only healing but necessary. He was abetted in this campaign of evil by his dean, William Strampel, who was later revealed to have a history of sexual harassment and abuse of his own, and by the coaches and advisors at USA Gymnastics (USAG), MSU, and various other gymnastics facilities. He was praised for the miracles he claimed to work in getting gymnasts back on the mats and equipment after injury. And part of the secret of his success was the youth and gullibility of his victims, who were being told by every authority figure in their lives that his treatments were vital to their success and that any qualms they might have reflected badly upon themselves rather than upon him. Even when the mothers of very young athletes were in the examining room with Nassar, he allayed their fears regarding the treatments. At least one local police force investigated claims against him, only to come away convinced that he was performing legitimate medical procedures. Their sources for that conclusion were the toxic two, Nassar himself and his boss, Strampel. By cunning and charisma (and a bit of luck), he had contrived the perfect recipe for longevity as a sex abuser.

But it couldn't last. Someone, eventually, would have the courage to break through the wall of official silence. In this case, that someone was Rachael Denhollander, a former gymnast who reported to MSU Police that Nassar had abused her years before, then filed a Title IX complaint with the university and shared her story with the *Indianapolis Star*. That story put the first crack in the dam. As recently as 2014, when the first Title IX complaint was filed by a former cheerleader, Amanda Thomashow, MSU's Title IX officer found problems but those were not sufficient to move the case forward to law enforcement. Nor did that office share the complete findings with Ms. Thomashow, who has said she felt "so small, and useless and disposable." Now, however,

Ms. Denhollander had enlisted not only the Title IX Office but also the press, and the *Star* was not susceptible to the Nassar guile.

And this is where the Fourth Estate comes into play. From the moment the Denhollander case hit the pages of the *Star*, the *Lansing State Journal* mobilized its entire staff to cover the scandal. From the late summer of 2016 through the convictions and sentencings of Nassar (and beyond), the *State Journal* ran pieces in every section of the paper except the comics pages. Of course there were hard news stories, malfeasance in this or that office, testimony from the trials, new disclosures of Nassar's misdeeds, and eventually, exposés on when and how MSU or USAG dropped the ball. And there were features, profiles on many of the brave women who came forward to add their stories to first one or two existing accusations and then to what seemed poised to become an unending list. Also profiled were various parties involved in the trial, including Judge Rosemarie Aquilina, an army reservist and longtime family law specialist who also writes mystery novels. Seemingly custom-made for a trial already guaranteed to be a spectacle, she commanded further interest not only through her sometimes-acid comments but also when she decided to allow survivors and parents of victims of Nassar's abuse to make victim statements during the sentencing; the number grew from an expected two dozen or so who would speak over a couple of days to one hundred fifty women who would occupy the spotlight for two weeks. There were editorials and op-eds about the case, the role that the university played in what had happened, and the price that should be paid by campus administrators. Eventually several, including President Lou Anna K. Simon and Athletic Director Mark Hollis, would lose their jobs and find their legacies in tatters. Those resignations and firings prompted retrospective features on the principals as well as postmortems on the events and actions—and more commonly, inaction—that led to the departures. Nor was all the printer's ink confined to the first section. This was a sports story as well as a criminal one. So *State Journal* sports writers and columnists found themselves tasked with more than the customary stories about this week's games or analyses of coaching brilliance or blunders.

One upshot of all of these disparate pieces of writing, some in unfamiliar sections of the paper, was that readers had to notice what genre a particular article belonged to. Names didn't help much: columnists had occasion to write investigative stories, reporters to compose opinion pieces or profiles when their special knowledge demanded that. This is not difficult, of course, but we do have to adjust our expectations to match the generic requirements. The greater demand on both journalists and readers was endurance. These stories kept pouring forth for more than a year and a half. They were legion. Shakespeare knew what he was doing when he had Claudius say in *Hamlet* that "when sorrows come, they come not single spies, but in battalions." And maybe when he gave such a line to the villain.

That such effort would be devoted to the larger story was natural. It was, after all, the paper's hometown school that had fallen from grace, and many otherwise celebrated individuals fell with it. A friend of mine, in Hong Kong for a conference, had only to say he was from Michigan to get a response to the effect that, Michigan was where *that* university was. That sort of thing will happen when a world-famous sports doctor turns out to be a sexual predator abetted for whatever reason by the powers that be. But it was more than that. The victims were ours, too, in enough cases to make the whole thing personal. And one of those young women was Jordyn Wieber, a gymnastics World Champion and Olympic Gold Medalist who grew up within a dozen miles of campus. She gave one of the later victim statements in Judge Aquilina's courtroom. Locals may have felt bruised by the relentless torrent of articles, far too much of it involving new revelations of criminality and betrayal of trust, but it was as nothing compared with what those many young women had gone through. With so much desolation and outrage, what else could a daily newspaper do but become the voice of the community? There are times when a normally sleepy small-town newspaper must become that Avenging Angel. And this is the greatness of a free press: there will come a time when no individual can cover a story so vast, so bewildering in its many parts, so appalling. In that moment, sorrows are not the only things that must come in battalions. And only a daily paper has the journalistic firepower to cover such a parade of evils.

And Full Contact

In the field of investigative reporting, there is one title that stands above all others. We should probably have a look. We might as well get this out of the way right now: *no one* says, "Follow the money." Not Woodward or Bernstein or Deep Throat or anyone else in the book. It sticks with us because (a) that's what our intrepid reporters wind up doing, and (b) William Goldman, who wrote the screenplay adaptation, knew just how to phrase it and just where to plant it as a line we'll never forget. But for our current purposes, we shall try. We're talking here about *All the President's Men*, which is a book of investigative journalism, and not *All the President's Men*, the movie thriller made from said book.

I've been worrying about that line for a few decades now; I mean, next we may find out that Butch and Sundance never said, "Who are those guys?" Same screenwriter, so how can we be sure?

Before proceeding, I think we may want to do a little genre reassignment surgery. While it is true that the book is based on Bob Woodward and Carl Bernstein's *Washington Post* investigative reporting on Watergate, which ultimately brought down Richard Nixon's presidency, it is much more than a repeat or transcription of those earlier stories. In fact, the book wasn't really their idea. The story goes that Robert Redford, who would play Woodward in the film, wanted to buy the rights to the story, but in order to do that he needed a *thing* whose rights he could purchase. A book is a thing, you know. And what he really wanted was a buddy film of two dogged, smart newsmen running down the biggest scoop in the world. Not Paul Newman this time—they'd already been down that road a couple of times—but someone closer to his own age. But there was a stipulation: for this to work as a buddy film, the, um, buddies needed to actually appear as central figures, the people we're following. Moviegoers weren't going to pay for a buddy film on, say, Watergate conspirators H. R. Haldeman and E. Howard Hunt. Too many initials. Besides, movies that end with the heroes in prison are downers. That meant Woodward and Bernstein had to write the book the way the whole thing must have felt to them, that they were the stars of this pursuit of wraiths and shadows. So they did. Which leads back to the genre question. The original stories were entirely about the crimes and the cover-up. That would be the textbook example of investigative journalism. The book, on the other hand, would be about two driven, if flawed, individuals chasing hell-bent-for-leather after a story. Which is about investigative journalists, not quite the same thing. The movie is easy: almost everyone calls it a "political thriller." Does that work for the book? Maybe, although it sounds overwrought for a work of nonfiction. We can call it, perhaps, a "memoir of investigation journalism," but that, besides being unwieldy, sounds so tepid that no one would consider reading it. An "investigative thriller"? Possibly. "Participatory journalism" or "New Journalism"? It is, on one level, but that undercuts the hard-news angle and smacks rather too much of the mugging of Hunter S. Thompson and Tom Wolfe or the preciousness of Joan Didion. Most sources punt and call it "Nonfiction."

Not exactly descriptive, is it? I've come to think of it as a postmodern work that defies older typologies. The work is aware, some might say hyperaware, of its status as a made object; that is, it is not merely the story of official misdeeds but rather the tale of compiling that story. Not so much a who-done-it as a how-we-found-out-who-done-it. For that reason, I have settled on *meta-journalism* as my genre classification, although "genre" might be a misnomer, given that the number of works in the category is one. For *All the President's Men* is *sui generis*, which is fancy Latin for not fitting into any category. First of all, there were two writers, which remains uncommon, and then they take a form, journalistic reporting, which is virtually always told from the outside, and turn it inside out. Almost no reportage has ever been handled like that—not before and rarely since. For one thing, if you attempt it, you're likely to be damned in reviews as having produced "a low-rent/cut-rate/tepid/pallid *All the President's Men*," and I'm pretty sure you wouldn't want that. And for another, most reporting isn't that interesting. It's done by phone or by ringing doorbells and it's a dull grind. If gathering the story were the entirety of journalism, I'm pretty sure most reporters would quit the first month. Writing the story, seeing it in print, that's the big payoff. It makes the drudgery worthwhile. And if it is drudgery to the people who perform it, why, oh, why would anyone want to read about it? Woodward and Bernstein's tale is interesting because the difficulty of gathering information forced them into the role of detectives in a mystery novel. Universally resistant witnesses unwilling to talk to them, the need to badger prospective sources to give up what they knew, clandestine meetings in parking garages, and the knowledge that life-and-death consequences were not out of the question give the book the air of a thriller. True, *Spotlight* (2015), the story of the *Boston Globe* team of investigative journalists unmasking the Boston diocese sexual abuse scandal, makes use of the same narrative approach, but that is a movie from an original screenplay that's based on the original *Globe* exposés. Same with *The Post* (2017), which recounts the *Washington Post* efforts to publish the Pentagon Papers over the Nixon administration's efforts to quash them. Interestingly enough, Josh Singer was half of the screenwriting team in each film, suggesting he has carved out a successful but limited niche.

All of which leads to another question: if the two writers are the stars of the show, and if the story is going to still be about Watergate and its aftermath, how on earth do you tell it? If you are just writing the straightforward exposé about the crimes of an administration, that's easy: third-person, past tense, objective but not quite omniscient point of view. That is, you can't report thoughts or conversations unless you've been told by a person involved or, in Nixon's case, by secret audio recordings most remembered for a certain eighteen-minute gap in them, but you can detail the actions from a semi-divine perspective. It's done all the time. If you're writing about your own, singular exploits, also easy: first person, told from the inside, probably past tense. But what if the first person turns out to be first persons? And the exploits are only part of a bigger story that sits there demanding to be told. There could be so many uses of "I" that readers could get really tired of the egotism of it all. Not to mention that there is the question of which "I" is I? Would that be I, Carl or I, Bob? The solution is simple, elegant, and successful: they have names, so use them. Bernstein is "Bernstein" and Woodward "Woodward" throughout in just the manner that they refer to other characters as "Mitchell," "Hunt," or "Dean."

The strategy serves them well: the authors are able to maintain command of facts—actions, conversations, documents—while also revealing their frustrations, uncertainties, suppositions, and occasional missteps in pursuit of those facts. What readers receive is the story of just how precarious gathering the truth of Watergate had been, as well as the truth itself. Here is an early encounter between Woodward and "Deep Throat," the code name given to his secret source by the *Post*'s managing editor, Howard Simons:

> The day after the indictments came down, Woodward broke the rule about telephone contact. Deep Throat sounded nervous, but as the draft of the story was read to him, it said that federal investigators had received information from Nixon campaign workers that high officials in the Committee for the Re-election of the President

had been involved in the funding of the Watergate operation.

"Too soft," Deep Throat said. "You can go much stronger."

The Bookkeeper [another source, also unnamed] had been right about the money in [former secretary of commerce, now treasurer of the CREP, Maurice] Stans's safe. It had financed the Watergate bugging and "*other intelligence-gathering activities,*" he said. John Mitchell's assistants were only "*among those*" who had controlled the fund. He would not say if the former Attorney General had had prior knowledge of the bugging attempt.

That code name has itself become a cultural marker; taken from the title of a wildly successful 1972 pornographic movie, it reveals both its historical moment and the hard-charging, boys'-club callousness of American journalism in that moment. In part, the name sprang from the source refusing to ever be quoted and his grudging willingness to reveal information only on "deep background," a not-infrequent situation in political reporting. Beyond that, this passage is an excellent example of the strains on Woodward's source. Even the telephone, which could have been bugged, was perilous. Meetings in a parking garage (indicated by the location of a small red hazard flag on Woodward's balcony) were safer from prying ears. Wherever and however contact took place, though, Deep Throat had his boundaries: he would go so far but no further with revelations, as with his reluctance to directly implicate Mitchell, presumably because either he didn't know or that knowledge was so restricted that giving it would expose the identity of the leaker. We eventually came to know his name as Mark Felt, but only after thirty-one years of Woodward keeping faith with his promise of silence.

The two reporters worked in a web of secrecy, shielding identities so that even other secret sources had no idea who else was feeding them intelligence. Certainly coworkers and superiors were kept in the dark. The knowledge-loop encompassed only two persons, and in at least one matter, just one. Does that invalidate the stories in the *Post*, or the ones in *All the President's Men*? Not at all. President Nixon and his supporters attempted to make that charge, that the sources were invented, that the facts revealed under cover of darkness were false, but history has borne out nearly every claim and charge in the book, and more time may reveal support for the rest. Other targets of other exposés have also attempted to discredit those journalistic stories as fairy tales because some sources remain unnamed, and more than one administration has tried to unmask sources (usually for reasons that have nothing to do with Truth), even to the point of jailing the reporters.

In the end, however, journalism almost always wins out. Why? Professionalism. Most reporters would never consider single-sourced facts. Yes, it can be a shortcut to a scoop, but in the long run it is a sure path to unemployment. Those who rely on single sources for facts will eventually be caught out, publishing stories that turn out to be false. At one point, Woodward and Bernstein are alarmed when a source, Hugh Sloan, suggests that he had "deduced" a conclusion that on the previous interview they had taken as a factual statement. Worse, Sloan was their backup source for someone whose information had seemed a lot less solid than his. To have two shaky sources could topple the entire edifice they had been building; one faulty cornerstone can prove more than adequate to wreck a structure—or a career. As the interview proceeds, however, it becomes obvious that his "deduction" is based on a long string of hard evidence and that their concerns have been for naught. This sort of professional ethics is not an inherent trait in newspapermen. Or anyone else. It has to be learned and, once learned, reinforced by a higher power. In this case, the higher powers were Managing Editor Howard Simons and Executive Editor Ben Bradlee, men who brooked no nonsense where the reputation of the paper was concerned. Early on in the investigation, both demanded multiple sourcing for each story, with three being better than two and two being better than nothing, which is how they regarded single-sourced stories.

This story carries another moral having to do with a question of ethics, in this case, the use of unnamed sources. Sloan, as the authors tell us in a note, went unnamed in all of the reporting for the *Post* and only consented to have his name published for the book. And only then did they use it, proving that not only were they good to their word but that unnamed sources do not equate with fake news. Sloan, as it turns out, while being absolved of complicity in the break-in, was warned by prosecutors in the case to make no public statements. He could only be used for background and unnamed confirmation.

The story of Watergate is almost hopelessly tangled. The Nixon administration and re-election committee tried to make it impossible to follow and nearly succeeded. That strategy produces its own difficulties. Anyone who tried to follow the original reporting on Watergate knows that it has as many characters as a Russian novel, the only saving grace being that the characters lack those patronymic middle names like Sergeivich or Ivanovich.

And they don't all have either Masha or Pasha as a nickname. Be thankful, I suppose, for small favors. I can't speak for others, but I never read one of those doorstop novels without having to make a list of the characters while cursing the novelist for failing to create a page or two of *Dramatis Personae*. Woodward and Bernstein anticipate this difficulty and provide a Cast of Characters. It runs to three pages. That favor turns out to be quite large.

All the President's Men's impact, and here I include also the *Washington Post* reporting that formed its basis, on culture—and on journalism—was seismic. To unmask corruption and deliberate damage to our constitutional system at the highest level of government, and not merely by a handful of overenthusiastic hirelings as that government had maintained, shook the country's confidence in itself as nothing short of an outright defeat in war could. That paranoia and isolation could so warp the mind and actions of the most powerful man in the world that he would risk his accomplishments, his legacy, his very presidency in order to win an election that was already all but in the bag was inconceivable. Until two young reporters showed that it wasn't. The thing is, though, that when you cause earthquakes, you're going to get shaken yourself. The attacks on Woodward and Bernstein, as well as on the newspaper that employed them, were sustained and vicious, the more so the closer they got to the truth. They were lied to and lied about, threatened with jail time, threatened with lawsuits, called every name in the book ("traitors" being a prominent epithet) and a few that are not repeatable. The administration maintained long past the point of believability that the reporters were making up stories because they used unnamed sources for deep background. Even years after publication, after convictions, after resignation, after a torrent of confessions and apologies, a significant minority of the American electorate refused to believe them. History, however, has borne out their findings.

The most important thing that the book taught subsequent journalists and readers of investigative journalism was the thing they were accused of not doing: *show your work.* It reminded exposé writers that the work they do is important, so much so that it is incumbent on them not to take shortcuts, not to fiddle with the truth, not to take witness statements on faith, not to got sloppy with the facts, not to be lazy. Ever. Did everyone learn those lessons? Of course not. Even Woodward, speaking of the publication of *Fear* (2018), his exposé of the Trump White House, said that it marked a return to doing things the hard way, that perhaps some of his reporting during the intervening years had gotten lazy, had not relied as much on burning shoe leather and knocking on unwelcoming doors at ten at night, but that he had returned to first principles for this one. Quite an admission by arguably the most consequential investigative journalist of our era.

In fact, this is where the cyclical nature of history gets strange: we find ourselves in an uncomfortably familiar place. Woodward's new book, *Fear*, about the chaos surrounding another presidential runaway train, has just appeared as I write this. No major crimes in this book, simply a staggering catalog of incompetence, attempts to control or calm the commander in chief (and occasionally to outright subvert him), and a West Wing that resembles nothing so much as a sieve through which juicy gossip and major policy arguments simply pour. Like Nixon, President Trump, having declined to speak to Woodward for the book, accused him even before the book was out of writing "fiction," of hiding his lies behind a refusal to name sources who wished to remain anonymous. And Trump has something Nixon never had: a ready army of apologists on conservative talk radio and Fox News Network, some of whom seem never to have forgiven Woodward for partnering with Bernstein. Even if they weren't alive then. But Woodward has something he didn't have in those days: a track record, much of which rests on that very partnership so reviled by the Right.

In this case as in that earlier, more famous one, his practice is his defense. He and Bernstein used unnamed sources but didn't quote anyone who remained anonymous, or if they did, they explained their reasons for doing so. They demonstrated the lengths—sometimes literal, as when they flew to California or Florida in search of a detail, an unlikely interview, or even a nod or wink—they went to in order to corroborate leads. They got three and four sources before taking a story to press. This was not always easy for two young, ambitious, and often frustrated journalists, but they had Simon and Bradlee to keep them up to the mark. They knew that a conspiracy is built on lies but that an attempt to unmask it can collapse because of a single falsehood. And the book, unlike the *Post* articles on which it was built, shows their constant struggles to avoid anything false or slipshod.

The effort was worth it: *All the President's Men* is a book like none before it. It showed just how far good reporters have to go to build a story. It unmasked official misdeeds, declared that no one was beyond the reach of the law or the prying eyes of journalists on a mission, shattered our illusions of the nature of American democracy. It became arguably the most important nonfiction book of the twentieth century.

9

Living the News

Participatory Journalism and Creative Nonfiction

FOR MOST OF OUR nonfiction reading, we make one basic assumption: the author remains detached from the material she presents. I don't mean that she doesn't have an opinion or strong feelings about her subject matter. Everyone has those, writers included, and sometimes those opinions are strong. Nevertheless, we expect a certain amount of objectivity in our nonfiction. The genre demands a degree of evenhandedness. How do I know this? Because of the number of reviews I have read over the years that use the term "evenhanded" approvingly. We don't really want a biographer to have a thumb on the scale. And that goes for the preponderance of nonfiction works.

Except when it doesn't.

There is a class of nonfiction writing in which the subjectivity of the writer is part of the story. We might call this class "Heisenbergian" nonfiction, but I doubt it would catch on. Werner

Heisenberg, you may recall, gave us the *Uncertainty Principle*, which states, among other things, that the results of an experiment (we're talking the atomic level here) are colored by the position of the observer. The writers of this sort of prose begin by admitting that the observer in this particular field of endeavor is *never* neutral—not really—and from there move to a position that acknowledges and even celebrates the subjectivity of the author. There are two sorts of writing that fall under this heading of *subjective nonfiction*: participatory journalism (which breaks down into what was dubbed "New Journalism" and more broadly immersive journalism) and creative nonfiction.

"New Journalism"

THERE WAS A TIME when a reporter inserting himself into a story was anathema. Or a news anchor. When Walter Cronkite said at the end of every broadcast, "And that's the way it is," you could be bloody well sure that *it* was just that way. News articles were written as if from on high, an Olympian view with as little personality as possible. That was not, however, exactly the ethos for the rock-n-roll era. The birth of the New Journalism came roughly a year after the Beatles' first appearance in America, its heyday running more or less from "yeah, yeah, yeah" to the snarls and screams of the Sex Pistols. There's nothing causal going on here, it being hard to imagine Truman Capote or Tom Wolfe rocking out to Led Zeppelin and The Clash. Rather, both are symptoms of a historical moment of resistance to accepted norms and constraints. Why should musicians want to break barriers and writers be satisfied with the status quo? In any case, a group of writers with an abundance of personality began inserting themselves into the stories they wrote. The effect was stunning. Readers felt they had never seen anything quite like this.

The actual approach was, if fairly new, not entirely novel. James Agee, for example, had moved along this road toward more personal reporting in writing about Southern sharecroppers in *Let Us Now Praise Famous Men* (1941). As a system, no matter how ragged, though, this movement was revolutionary. Truman Capote, in what may well be the first instance of the New Journalism, inserted himself into the action in *In Cold Blood* (1965) as "Capote." He went on to decree that, in what he called the "Nonfiction Novel," use of the first person should be avoided. Well, ain't that just the way? You get a brand-new, shiny literary form, all full of possibilities and freedom, and the first thing somebody wants to do is start imposing rules and limitations. Norman Mailer both followed and subverted that edict in *The Armies of the Night* (1968), his account of the 1967 anti–Vietnam War protests at the Pentagon, calling himself "Mailer" while also taking a star turn upon the stage. Capote, by the way, knew he was being mocked, and the event produced an enmity between the two that lasted until Capote's death. Hunter S. Thompson's *Hell's Angels* had appeared in 1967 and Tom Wolfe's *The Electric Kool-Aid Acid Test* would appear a mere three months after Mailer's book. Taken together, they form the four holy books of the New Journalism.

Woodward and Bernstein, by contrast, are not writing New Journalism; they are pursuing journalism in its traditional sense. The difference? In some ways, it involves the impulse toward art; of these other four writers, only Thompson has shaky *bona fides* as a fiction writer (the line between autobiography and fiction being very unstable), although Wolfe came to novels later than either Capote or Mailer. All four are concerned in their work with artistic impulse of their narratives. Reading *All the President's Men* cover to cover, however, one will not identify any concern with the artistic possibilities of the book. These are reporters going about their work, even when their work has become part of the story. The other difference between the two types of writing: the New Journalists all work their way inside the subject of their reportage while reveling in their subjectivity. Wolfe, for instance, all but vanishes into the story he is telling, so that some people, such as Jay Cantor in his review in *The Harvard Crimson*, see him as essentially a cheerleader for Ken Kesey and the Merry Pranksters' drug-fueled mayhem. Woodward and Bernstein, by contrast, remain stubbornly outside and objective; they have no interest in becoming part of the sleaze-pool that was the Nixon political apparatus. Still, like New Journalists, they exploit the devices of fiction—point of view, use of scenes, reliance on dialogue, use of telling details—to make their point. What they achieve is not art so much as a very high level of craft, which is to say that their work is a triumph not of vision but of technique, by which they can manage two tracks of information: the story and its revelation.

Not that these participatory journalists are doing the same thing, any more than *The Sun Also Rises* and *Ulysses*, both ostensibly modernist novels, can be said to have the same ends or methods. The one constant is that the reporter—and here we must include Jimmy Breslin, Joan Didion, Gay Talese, Terry Southern, and numerous others—records his or her presence as an observer/participant in the events of the story.

We might as well start with the one who is least like, well, anybody. Hunter S. Thompson crashed the party with *Hell's Angels*

(1967), but his most famous paragraph is the opening of *Fear and Loathing in Las Vegas* (1971):

> We were somewhere around Barstow on the edge of the desert when the drugs began to take hold. I remember saying something like "I feel a bit lightheaded; maybe you should drive. . . ." And suddenly there was a terrible roar all around us and the sky was full of what looked like huge bats, all swooping and screeching and diving around the car, which was going about a hundred miles an hour with the top down to Las Vegas.

It takes precisely one sentence to realize that this experience, this writing, is not going to be normal. The book is a drug-fueled romp through the scene in Vegas: loud, profane, crude, hilarious. That part is certain, but not everything is. For instance, what is it? It started out as a magazine assignment (*Sports Illustrated* initially hired him to provide a two-hundred-fifty-word caption and photo for the Mint 400 motorcycle race), but that largely melted away in the, er, research process. The main character is called "Raoul Duke," but when that person is shown a photo of himself, he identifies it as Hunter Thompson. There is much that is true in the book but much that is fictionalized. For a while, it was seen as an extreme example of gonzo journalism, a term a colleague provided to Thompson that he quickly embraced. More recently, a mild consensus has formed that it is a novel, a *roman à clef* or novel in which a thin veneer of fiction has been cast over real-life personages.

And there lies the problem, or perhaps problems, with Hunter Thompson. His "journalism" is so gonzo that it veers away from reality with considerable regularity, yet other elements are grounded in truth of one sort or another. That's item A. Item B is that his brand of New Journalism centers on his own consciousness and experience. External events fade into the background, giving way to his madcap adventures. Whether or not his book is nonfiction or novel, we should probably place Thompson at one pole of the immersive journalism continuum. No one could get further out than he did.

Toward the opposite pole, if not all the way there, is Tom Wolfe. He may not exactly be Emerson's transparent eyeball—he wears suits, after all, and seems physically present in the action—but he does his best to merge with the scenes he describes. What Wolfe does with prose in *The Electric Kool-Aid Acid Test* is remarkable. No journalist before him had tried quite so assiduously to capture the inner lives of his subjects. Indeed, a first principle of journalism is that we can only know surfaces, what people do and how they behave. From that, we may infer interior lives, but no writer can burrow into the mind of another except in fiction. Wolfe's response? Maybe, but we can figure out a lot from how they sound. And he does, indeed, figure out a great deal.

The book begins with Wolfe's introductory, jouncy ride into the San Francisco world of the Merry Pranksters in a Day-Glo painted pickup truck with shot suspension. His fellow travelers are a kid called Cool Breeze, who has some legal troubles (a recurring theme) and a black peaked hat best suited to the well-dressed gnome; a Mexican-American young woman, Black Maria; and Lois Jennings, the girlfriend and later wife of Stewart Brand, who is driving and who will become known for the counterculture magazine *Whole Earth Catalog* (1968–72) and then for various visionary activities in the realm of electronics. The passengers are all riding in the pickup's bed. Lois is firing a cap pistol that looks exactly like a Colt .45, picking off "marshmallows," their term for ordinary people. Black Maria has just told Wolfe that he seems too "solid" to be a Pisces. This kicks off a set piece of Wolfean free association:

> But I know she means stolid. I am beginning to feel stolid. Back in New York City, Black Maria, I tell you, I am even known as something of a dude. But somehow a blue silk blazer with a big tie with clowns on it and . . . a . . . pair of shiny lowcut black shoes don't set them all to doing the Varsity Rag in the head world of San Francisco. Lois picks off the marshmallows one by one; Cool Breeze ascends into the innards of his gnome's hat; Black Maria, a Scorpio herself, rummages through the Zodiac; Stewart Brand winds it through the streets, paillettes explode— and this is nothing special, just the usual, the usual in the head world of San Francisco, just a little routine messing up the mind of the citizenry en route, nothing more than psyche food for beautiful people, while giving some guy from New York a lift to the Warehouse to wait for the Chief, Ken Kesey, who is getting out of jail.

This is not Wolfe's native style. Rather, he is attempting to render the emotional and psychic realities of his subjects. I described this earlier as a version of Flaubert's "free indirect speech," a mediated (by a narrator) version of the character's thoughts; we can think of that as the way a character would speak about herself if she had the ability to step outside herself and bring her inner consciousness along. In this case, that freely indirect rendering is a group effort—a little bit Cool Breeze, a little bit Black Maria, a little bit Lois Jennings, but probably not Brand since he is alone in the cab and has not yet conversed with Wolfe.

We don't have to wonder if this is Wolfe's intention: he tells us it is in an author's note at the end of the book. "I have tried," he says, "not only to tell what the Pranksters did but to re-create the mental atmosphere or subjective reality of it. I don't think their adventure can be understood without that." Indeed, in 1968, when the first edition appeared, the reality of the "head world," as he calls it, of the Pranksters was as remote as the moon, on which humans had not yet set foot. To merely record their actions in standard journalistic prose would have been to present them as space aliens, although it could be argued that presenting them in their own private language merely situates them in a different version of space. This examination of closed social groups—the Hell's Angels, the Pranksters, the Apollo astronauts, presidential campaigns, groups of Wise Guys—turns out to be something at which the New Journalists prove to be quite adept. Their methods seem well suited to ferreting out what is scary or amusing or strange or shocking—in short, what is fascinating—about their subjects.

Problem Child

A LITTLE WHILE AGO, I mentioned that a number of writers get lumped together under the rubric "New Journalism." One of that number is Joan Didion, whose relationship to that movement seems especially tenuous. In fact, her relationship to any label seems problematic. Like the New Journalists, she places herself and her reporting inside the stories she tells. And much of her work has indeed appeared in "journals": *Life, Esquire, The Saturday Evening Post, The New York Review of Books, Holiday, Vogue.* What she was doing in those early years, moreover, was distinctly new, so both parts of the name are covered, yet her work seems to fit uncomfortably, if at all, beside that of Capote and Wolfe and Thompson. While she employs certain techniques of fiction in her work, they seem to add up to something less than the sustained narratives of those other writers. Much of her work, in fact, gets classified as essay, although that moniker also seems to fall short. And critical responses sometimes attack her for not pushing any of the genre buttons cleanly. In her 1980 review, "Joan Didion: Only Disconnect," Barbara Grizzuti Harrison called her a "neurasthenic Cher," reliant on "a bag of tricks" for her effects and writing only, whatever the ostensible subject, about herself. This review itself became a source of controversy and a point of annoyance for Didion for decades after its appearance.

That review appeared in the wake of Didion's 1979 *The White Album*, a collection of journalistic essays from and about the late 1960s. The title work, which kicks off the book, was named by *Publishers Weekly* in 2013 as one of the ten most important essays since 1950. But here's the thing about that designation: if it is an essay, it isn't one that Ralph Waldo Emerson or Joseph Addison and Richard Steele would recognize. Handled in a disjointed, pointillist style, the piece moves dizzyingly from figure to figure and moment to moment to capture the gestalt of California circa 1968–69, from The Doors' third album to the Tate-LaBianca murders with side trips to Black Panther Huey Newton in jail awaiting trial and San Francisco State University, site of demonstrations in support of Newton, and to fellow Panther Eldridge

Cleaver's apartment and to Charles Manson "family" member Linda Kasabian at a women's correctional facility where she was held in protective custody ahead of her testimony against other members involved in the Tate-LaBianca murders to a party at Didion's where Janis Joplin showed up, brought by unknown persons to, well, a lot of places, sometimes for only moments. All of this is related in Didion's peculiar, Hemingway-esque flat-affect prose, as if she has been leveled out by Valium or whatever her preferred antianxiety drug may have been at the moment. This is the quality that Grizzuti Harrison calls "neurasthenic" and that English novelist Martin Amis more charitably describes as "listless." How much of this is Didion and how much a part of her strategy to depict the anxiety, paranoia, and sense of impending doom in the California she knew then is hard to pin down. Here is her conclusion to the highly inconclusive recording session of The Doors, who had waited a long while for singer Jim Morrison to make an appearance, although that would prove anticlimactic:

> Morrison sat down again on the leather couch and leaned back. He lit a match. He studied the flame awhile and then very slowly, very deliberately lowered it to the fly of his black vinyl pants. [Keyboardist Ray] Manzarek watched him. The girl who was rubbing Manzarek's shoulders did not look at anyone. There was a sense that no one was going to leave the room, ever. It would be some weeks before The Doors finished recording this album. I did not see it through.

We can notice a couple of things here. Besides, that is, these being some strange cats. One is the reliance on short, declarative sentences with few modifiers. Very Hemingway. The second is that there is almost no rise in emotional temperature. While in this instance we may conclude that drugs are involved, that flatness is evident in nearly every vignette in the essay. Even when the characters are animated, the narration levels them out, as with that "ever" in "no one was going to leave the room, ever." It carries a kind of deadening finality, adding to the affectless quality of the experience. And third, her closing sentence, "I did not see it through," brings things back to her. We never know what her purpose had been in being present, who had sent her or who had admitted her or what the endgame might have been, had she seen it through. The only thing that matters, finally, is less the image of this band than her perception of that image.

This passage is less about its ostensible subject than it is about the experience of the witness-scribe, Joan Didion. In that regard, if not necessarily others, "The White Album" resembles other New Journalistic efforts. Is she one of *them*? Maybe, but . . . But maybe it doesn't matter. She is what she is. Her method is her own, although it may overlap with others. Her concern with perfect sentences (something she has spoken of repeatedly), for the clean line, is a signature element. Don't look for that in Hunter Thompson.

Come to think of it, maybe Didion is emblematic of the New Journalism precisely because she does not fit comfortably into the category (I'm not sure it coheres sufficiently to qualify as a "genre"): it may well be that there is no such beast as New Journalism, only a collection of individuals who arrived on the scene at more or less the same time and threw various wrenches—each after his or her own fashion—into the works of conventional journalism. The ironized attitude toward all subjects of Tom

Wolfe, the madcap adventurism of Thompson, the cool distance of Didion—what have they to do with one another, really? And why should they? These writers are not club-joiners, much less law-givers. Nothing about them suggests a "movement," let alone a coherent one. The one thing that connects them is that each was looking for new ways to tell true stories. It turned out to be plenty new.

Immersive Journalism

THERE IS A PEACOCK quality to much of the New Journalism. "Hey, look at me," the text fairly screams, "I can be really clever." Quite often, the claim is true, but one wonders how many imitations, pale or overwrought as the case may be, died on editorial slush piles. These are writers who want to be noticed, who want to be seen as part of the story, in the case of Thompson, to *be* the story. Peacocks are showy, striking, but maybe not for everyone. Besides, do we want every piece of nonfiction we read to make a spectacle of itself? Sometimes, we just want the writer to burrow into the story. At the same time, we may not want the writing to be devoid of personality or to read like a generic *New York Times* story from 1957. Turns out, there's a solution for that, a method whereby the journalist can immerse herself in the story without distracting our attention. And a handful of journalists have gotten very good at it.

In the early 1980s, I started hearing an odd buzz among my literary friends. Literary buzz is hardly odd in itself; it is the stuff of life in English and related departments, "Have you read," "Did you see," "Have you talked to anyone about . . . ?" Conversations about new books are the background hum, something to take the mind off the latest batch of mildly competent student essays or hottest campus gossip. But these opening salvos to a discussion weren't about the usual stuff—the latest novel, a volume of poetry by an old friend, the current French critical atrocity—but about something folks in English departments almost never talk about. Rocks. Landscape. Plate tectonics. In short, geology.

Having spent my sophomore year of college rooming with a rocks jock, I had a bit of experience with how wrapped up some people can become with matters geological. Just not, you know, *my* people. So, I thought, what gives? Why are otherwise sober and serious scholars of literature suddenly giddy over a book about what lies between us and the molten center of the earth? The answer, it turns out, was not "geology" but "literature." I should have known. My colleagues, you see, didn't care merely about a category but about any writing that rises above the ordinary, and this book was as far from ordinary as you can get. *Basin and Range* (1981), as matters turned out, was the first of four standalone volumes that would come out over the next decade or so and, together with a previously unpublished essay, constitute *Annals of the Former World* (1998), the *magnum opus* that would win a Pulitzer Prize for John McPhee.

But here's the thing: it's not a book about geology. Or perhaps it's only partly about geology. It's really about two other, not-unrelated, things: understanding the world the author inhabits, and the people who make that understanding possible. There is almost nothing in John McPhee's world that is beneath his notice or that he can't work his magic on. He has, after all, written a book entirely about oranges and another on the historical and cultural importance of shad, a fish that almost no one living more than two hundred miles from the Atlantic Ocean knows or cares about. Robert Frost objected to being called a "nature poet," since he claimed that fewer than a half dozen of his poems had no human presence. So it is with McPhee. Like oranges, like shad, the story of geology—which after all is the story not of rocks but of the study thereof—is the story of humans interacting with their world. In this case, it is the story of humans decoding the puzzle of earth's formation.

How does one write about something entirely beyond our capacity for comprehension, about what the earth looked like a long time ago? No, not last year or the sixties or the time of Jesus. Way back. Two hundred million years ago, add or subtract a few, when the space that would become the Atlantic Ocean was occupied instead by land masses that would move off to the far sides of the globe, to become India, Africa, Australia, Antarctica. There is no chance we mere mortals, with our threescore and ten allotted years, can grasp such numbers. In terms of geologic time, we're like the tribe whose concept of numbers only goes to two: one, two, many. Is there any way to help us to see that far back? McPhee strikes upon the expedient of an imaginary road trip across the country on Interstate 80. By using this device, he can let us relate this bizarre world to the one we actually know, and he can place us at points along the way by name-dropping familiar places: New York, Ohio, Council Bluffs, Iowa, Nebraska, Wyoming, Sacramento, San Francisco.

"If you were to make that trip in the Triassic—New York to San Francisco, Interstate 80, say roughly at the end of Triassic time—you would move west from the nonexistent Hudson River with the Palisades Sill ten thousand feet down." Wait! No

Hudson? No cliffs rising dramatically above its west bank? And so it goes as we cross the space that will become our country, all the way to the West Coast, which is also not where, to our minds, it belongs: "Then, at roughly the point where the Sierran foothills will end and the Central Valley will begin—at Auburn, California—you move beyond the shelf and over deep ocean. There are probably some islands out there somewhere, but fundamentally you are crossing above ocean crustal floor that reaches to the China Sea. Below you there is no hint of North America, no hint of the valley or the hills where Sacramento and San Francisco will be." Toto, I've a feeling we're not in Kansas anymore. But that's I-70, so never mind.

We're still lost, but now we're lost in ways we can pin on a map of the familiar world. I can't imagine a world in which Sacramento is at the bottom of the ocean, but at least I know where that will be in a hundred million years or so when it rises from the brine. McPhee has shown his plan for his tetralogy in this early passage from book one: connect the unfamiliar, the bizarre, the incomprehensible to something accessible, whether it is a map or the person studying whatever phenomenon is at hand. He knows better than to batter us about the head and shoulders with hard data, and he wants us to know that he will ease us through the hard bits, which will be everything except for the articles and conjunctions. The concepts and the facts of the earth sciences are just plain difficult, and so is talking about them. One of the notions McPhee mastered early on in his career is that the harder the subject matter, the more gentle and supportive the discussion must be in order to lead bewildered readers to safer shores.

And then there's the terminology: Triassic, Pennsylvanian, Devonian, craton, sedimentary, igneous, orogeny. What a mess

of labels! There may be no field of human endeavor more bedev-
iled by nomenclature than geology, and that includes the military.
In fact, McPhee does a riff far better than I could manage in
the section, early in *Basin and Range*, on the maddening—and
proliferating—array of terms employed by geologists. After say-
ing that the nomenclature would have attracted the attention of
Gilbert and Sullivan, he provides a sort of patter song jammed
with terms reminiscent of their operettas, or perhaps of Tom
Lehrer's song "The Elements," which consists of the entire peri-
odic table at the time of its composition. These terms range from
the comparatively simple (pigeonite, samsonite) to the insanely
convoluted (Metakirchheimerite, Clinoptilolite). Indeed, there
seem to have been some sort of unholy linguistic liaisons between
ancient Greek, German, and various other languages, not inevi-
tably excluding Klingon. Readers may find their eyes swimming
even as they realize that the passage is intensely funny. Opposing
the traditional "granite" with the newer "granodiorite" for a rock
that is a variety of the former, he opines that "the enthusiasm
geologists show for adding new words to their conversation is, if
anything, exceeded by their affection for the old. They are not
about to drop granite. They say granodiorite when they are in
church and granite the rest of the week."

What we learn from this passage, which is something we really
need to know, is that he understands how difficult this material
is and will be on our side as we struggle to keep up. The section,
untitled on the page, is noted in the table of contents as "Why
Would an English Major Write about Rocks?" It begins with his
own mystification in his undergraduate geology course as terms
"came floating down the room like paper airplanes," which may,
as intended, allay our fears a bit. It's nice to have someone repre-

senting our own distance from the subject: if this guy can get up to speed on all the technical material, maybe there's hope for us.

Now, his question comes with some obligations attached, not least the need to establish some authority. There is no way that an English major who took a course or so in geology can write this book, much less the whole tetralogy. Clearly, such a person must latch onto others who actually know and study the field. Which suits John McPhee right down to the ground he's writing about. He may be the ride-along king of American journalism. In his career he has hitched lifts on tugboats, coal trains, merchant ships, long-haul tractor-trailers, pickup trucks, and canoes. Given half the chance, he might have gone on the space shuttle for a story. Each book in the group revolves around his observing and interrogating an earth scientist or two whose expertise covers a part of his journey about which he wishes to know more. In *Basin and Range*, he latches onto geologists Karen Kleinspehn and Kenneth Deffeyes as his guides and mentors. From there he finds others in the field who can explain the trickier aspects of a notoriously tricky area of study. This arrangement is as it must be. A working journalist is an expert in one area of human endeavor: writing about stuff. But that's a good area, since it involves finding information the writer does not already possess, then processing, synthesizing, and disseminating it. McPhee is not different from the rest of his field, just much, much better at it. He rarely ventures an opinion on anything technical, although he passes along many opinions belonging to the researchers. Instead, he limits his own thoughts to those he has about said researchers, who amaze, delight, and not infrequently confound him.

Okay, so how is this like or unlike New Journalism? Or the traditional kind, for that matter?

Humility, chiefly. McPhee doesn't lack for confidence or ambition. No one undertakes writing on the scale he does while doubting he has the ability to complete the work. Nor is he shy about insinuating himself into places—the cab of a train engine, the wheelhouse of a tug—that most of us would feel we have no right to step. But believing in your talents is not the same as putting yourself on display. It's just that, when it comes to the writing, the story comes first. Try saying that of Hunter Thompson. Yet McPhee is more immersed in his subject matter than many other journalists, in part because he has so much time to pursue his research and in part because he is writing about living, breathing stories. Yes, even when the subject is rocks. It's the people who matter. The other thing that sets him off from many other writers is his artfulness. By that, I do not mean something cutesy, like employing a lot of rhetorical flourishes. What I intend, rather, is the way that he brings the implements of fiction writing—point of view, careful use of the telling detail, chapter organization, effective presentation of dialogue, a knowledge of what to omit and why, the poetic use of language (in its best, non-flowery sense).

McPhee is sometimes lumped with the New Journalists, sometimes with Creative Nonfiction (which makes him a sort of pioneer in that field), and sometimes in a little club whose membership numbers one.

Creative Nonfiction

OF THESE THREE GENRES, creative nonfiction is the newcomer. It seems to have arrived a decade or so later than participatory journalism, so mid-to-late-1970s, although instances of it can be found much earlier. Numerous sources cite James Agee's *Let Us Now Praise Famous Men*, detailing the lives of poor tenant farmers during the Depression, as an early instance. Of course, Agee had the advantage of wonderfully evocative photos by Walker Evans, something few such works can boast. Others would go back still further, to Henry David Thoreau's *Walden* (1854) and *A Week on the Concord and Merrimack Rivers* (1849), to find models. The first is well known, but the second, ostensibly an account of a float trip he took with his late brother some years earlier, morphs into an elegy for that brother, becoming a fitting archetype of the creative nonfiction enterprise.

The modernists did a lot of work that we would call "creative" or "literary" nonfiction. Virginia Woolf's *A Room of One's Own* or "Modern Fiction," or D. H. Lawrence's "Reflections on the Death of a Porcupine" or "Fantasia of the Unconscious," or Ernest Hemingway's *Death in the Afternoon* or *A Moveable Feast* all stand as examples of nonfiction as a literary pursuit, as do efforts by many of their contemporaries.

One of the later examples, although an early one in the development of this contemporary movement, would be Annie Dillard's *Pilgrim at Tinker Creek* (1974). That work, covering an entire year and divided into four sections mirroring the seasons, explores the natural world by her home near Roanoke, Virginia, in the Blue Ridge Mountains. In the course of her examinations, although the narrator is never named, she ruminates on nature, consciousness, religion, solitude, the inevitable cruelty of nature, and the problem of evil. The narrative goes where it goes, when it decides to go there. In this regard as in so many others, the book follows the example of Thoreau's *Walden*, on which she wrote her master's thesis. The creek, for instance, functions as she claimed in that thesis that Thoreau's pond did, as a center around which the book is organized. True, she set herself the task of observing her home water for just one year, not the two that consumed Thoreau, but the principle is much the same.

Don't panic: you can perfectly understand what Dillard writes even if you've never read Thoreau, even if you've never heard of him, although you may wonder why this guy gets mentioned without first or middle names twice in the first chapter. Otherwise, it's clear sailing.

Here's what you may notice. Dillard writes this memoir of noticing the world as if she is writing a novel. The opening, in fact, could easily be from a novel, with its memory of a tomcat who used to jump, bloody from fighting others of his kind or catching small creatures, through the open bedroom window and land on the narrator's chest. That memory opens out into other observations and memories, of comparing herself to medieval religious hermits, of living along Tinker Creek in a valley of the Blue Ridge, of watching a green frog being consumed by a giant water bug, of the beef cattle across the creek, of the Koran and Blaise Pascal, of the arrow-making of "certain Indians," and of her central project, which is to learn to see and know her immediate surroundings. As in a novel, her solitude is noted but not explained, as if something we will learn later, and her background before Tinker Creek is left unsaid. That she comes as an outsider is clear enough from the newness of her way of perceiving this space.

That first chapter, then, becomes a model for how the book will proceed, veering between careful noticing and sudden shifts of subject in which we move from frogs to Eskimos, from pinochle to arctic exploration. The kaleidoscopic nature of these shifts—each crystalline in itself but with only a tenuous connection to the one before or after—led Eudora Welty, in an otherwise glowing review in the *New York Times*, to admit that in some of Dillard's more fanciful flights, the reviewer does not know what the author is talking about.

That becomes the main question we must ask of this book, or any work of creative nonfiction: what is the author talking about, and why does she express it as she does? Welty's uncertainties are momentary and localized, while we want an answer on a more global level. In this case, it becomes clear very early that Dillard's main concern is with *seeing* the world as it is. Her second chapter is called, in fact, "Seeing," and concerns itself with the difference between what experts notice that ordinary folk do not, as when a herpetologist comes down off a hillside with a sack full of snakes, a hillside that a local told him had no snakes, or with the difficulty in seeing for early recipients, blind from birth with cataracts, after surgery removed the clouds from their sight. Seeing, it turns out, is a lifelong habit. Beyond mere seeing, though, Dillard is concerned with what we these days might call, with our embrace of Buddhist terminology if not practice, "mindfulness," the habit of turning sensation into something deeper, more meaningful. For what Dillard really wants to consider is creation, and the possibility of a creator, in a manic sort of teleology: discerning the nature of the Watchmaker by intensive study of the watch.

McPhee and Dillard represent, as it were, two poles of creative nonfiction, the reportorial and the autobiographical. It is certainly possible, as McPhee demonstrates again and again, to write from the *inside* of something other than the self; it appears to be a matter of immersion in that object of consideration, coal trains or otherwise. Dillard, by contrast, shows that consideration of the Other can be a doorway into exploration of the self. *Pilgrim at Tinker Creek*, as set out by the first word of the title, is ultimately concerned with the growth of the writer/narrator/character. Neither of these approaches is right or wrong; they are simply approaches, merely means to different ends. While there has been an explosion of creative nonfiction over the last quarter century or so, it remains a genre in progress, something like the early novel of the eighteenth century. This condition is extremely fertile, since there is nothing ruled out or required on the basis of long-standing practice, there being no practice that has stood long. Nor is there a substantial body of criticism, much less of theorizing, about creative nonfiction, although that work is coming. Soon. We do not know, in short, what the genre can become, so instead we watch it in the act of becoming.

Writing about and from the self has always been with us, and it is always evolving. What these newer personal forms, New Journalism and creative nonfiction, have taught us is that the building blocks of narrative or discursive nonfiction are largely identical to those of traditional realistic fiction: point-of-view selection, narrative voice, tone and mood, scene construction and sequencing, dialogue, control of diction, tension, flashbacks, foreshadowing, and all the rest. As we have noted with Wolfe, they can even touch on such arcana as stream-of-consciousness or indirect free speech techniques. Not every work will employ all of these, of course, but they may and will use any number in any combination their writers desire. What this broad technical palette reminds us is that, after all, nonfiction writing is first and foremost *writing*, a branch on the tree of literature.

10

From the Inside Out

Essay and Opinion

Personal Essay

THE *ESSAY* HAS GOTTEN a bad rap for a while now. Let's say the last century or so. Or whenever its first name became "student," as in, the *student essay*, that soggy, apologetic attempt to please a secondary school teacher with the fewest possible words on an unwished-for subject stretched over the most inflexible framework available. It is sometimes called a "theme" in these matters, but if you look up "theme" in this context, dictionaries will tell you that it is a "student essay on an assigned topic." The problem, to a large extent, is that the form is taught in terms of how to build it—rigidly, often—rather than of what it can achieve. Some of you will have learned that it should have five paragraphs (kind of limiting in itself, but we'll pass over that), that its first paragraph should contain its main statement of purpose, called the *thesis sentence*, followed by its younger cousins, the *topic sentences* of each body paragraph, which paragraphs will feature, in exact order, the relevant sentences as their first statements, bringing us to a point of exhaustion where the sentences in question are repeated, in reverse order, in something quaintly called the *conclusion*, although point of exhaustion might be a better term. This soul-deadening exercise is designed not to teach good writing but to impose structure on the fourteen-year-old mind. Not every method of instruction is so brutalizing, but many come close.

Is it any wonder, then, that upon hearing the word "essay," people run in horror? Who would want to read such a monstrosity?

The real essay, on the other hand, is one of the most sinuous, adaptable forms in all of literature. Only the novel can begin to compete with it for sheer variety. Essays can be formal or informal, objective or personal, philosophical or scientific or humorous. They have been around for centuries, and we can even date their first appearance, 1580, when Michel de Montaigne published two volumes he called *Essais*. He took the word from a Middle French verb, *essayer*, to try or attempt, and he took seriously the notion that these were trial pieces. So seriously, in fact, that he went back again and again to some of them, revising until his death. Since that time, most essayists have dropped the notion of endless change and improvement and regarded their published essays as finished products, so the form need not hold the threat of being an endless work loop for the creator. The idea caught on. Francis Bacon published the first English book to be called *Essays* in 1597, and by 1609, playwright Ben Jonson had given us the term *essayist* for one who essays in print. Such persons have stayed busy ever since.

And why not? You can do just about anything with an essay. Montaigne wrote his on topics as elevated as "Of Sadness and Sorrow" and "That to Study Philosophy Is to Learn to Die" and as lowly as "Of Smells" and "Of Posting" (letters in the mail). The idea that one can write essays about anything really caught on. Aldous Huxley, no slouch in this department himself, says in the preface to his *Collected Essays* (1958) that the beauty of the form is that it provides a platform "for saying almost everything about almost anything." Who could object to that?

Some eras have embraced the form more than others. The English nineteenth century saw huge enthusiasm for the form in both the earlier, Romantic period (Charles Lamb, Thomas De Quincey) and the later, Victorian era (Thomas Carlyle, John Henry Newman, Thomas Babington Macaulay, Walter Pater). The modernist period of the early-to-mid twentieth century was not a great age—everyone in the literary set was too busy writing manifestos or blowing up the traditional expectations for what their chosen genre could accomplish—but writers such as D. H. Lawrence, Virginia Woolf, and George Orwell produced remarkable work. Lawrence's "Reflections on the Death of a Porcupine" and Orwell's "Shooting an Elephant" are brilliant explorations of death and the hand we sometimes take in meting it out; it is well worth any reader's time to make their acquaintance. Woolf's fame as an essayist rests chiefly, but by no means exclusively, on her championing a woman's right to write, *A Room of One's Own*, but her essays on the state of literature, especially the modern novel, are provocative and ornery in their own ways. The later twentieth century and early years of the twenty-first have produced a remarkable array of essayists covering every conceivable topic. African American writers from James Baldwin to Martin Luther

King Jr. to Alice Walker to bell hooks to Ta-Nehisi Coates have written brilliantly on race, as have Native Americans N. Scott Momaday, Leslie Marmon Silko, Janet Campbell Hale, and Sherman Alexie, among many others. But that is not the only subject. In fact, it is hard to find a subject that has not been touched by really interesting essayists, from poetry (Seamus Heaney, Geoffrey Hill, Adrienne Rich) to art (Julian Barnes, Simon Schama) to computers (Tracy Kidder) to personal experience (David Sedaris) to feminism (Kate Millett, Betty Friedan, Gloria Steinem) to antifeminism (Norman Mailer) to belief and disbelief (Marilynne Robinson, Christopher Hitchens) to, well, you name it.

These writers range from the deadly serious to the maniacally comic and from the formal to the familiar. What all share is a deeply personal connection between the essayist and his or her work: the form and tone of the essay must fit the writer like a suit, even if that suit, as in Sedaris's case, is that of a Christmas elf. We can all spot a King speech or essay within the first paragraph; some of us can hear Julian Barnes in an essay even with a wall between it and us—and will walk through that wall to read it. The combination of self-deprecation and sly derision would let us pick Sedaris out of a literary-police lineup. Writers tend to find what works for them and, having found it, return to the scene of their success. D. H. Lawrence's hectoring tone and hammering repetition marks him out as being no one but himself. Woolf's mannerisms, less confrontational, identify her just as surely.

By its very nature, the essay demands a special sort of attention. In the first place, we need to know how the author is placed vis-à-vis the material. Some writers take a sort of Joycean seat above and, as it were, behind the work, metaphorically paring their fingernails, as Stephen Dedalus describes it in *A Portrait of the Artist as a Young Man.* Their detachment may be genuine or, as seems more common to me, theatrical; since the words are clearly coming from a writer, having the writer appear disinterested rings slightly untrue. Still, some can pull it off.

Others will be right in the thick of things, painting, as Seamus Heaney said of Francisco Goya, with their fists and elbows. They slug it out in full view of readers, the essayist not as impartial juror but as pugilist.

What should interest us, however, is not the degree of attachment but the reason behind it. We will get to John Henry Newman again when we discuss autobiography, but he also wrote some of the great essays of his or any other era. That his autobiography, *Apologia Pro Vita Sua* (1864), is intensely personal is beyond dispute, but the same can be said of *The Idea of a University* (1852, 1858), which makes no such overt nod toward his life yet rests entirely on his experiences and views of university life. A collection of essays called "Confessions"—and there have been quite a few since Augustine—is easy to see as personal, as is Thoreau's "Civil Disobedience." But that is no less true for the vast majority of essays on all topics; *this is me*, they declare, *this is what I think.* Perhaps this quality no longer seems radical in an age when any semi-sentient creature with opposable thumbs can tweet out personal thoughts however ill informed or badly written at all times of day, but in its origins, the essay was radical precisely because it was personal.

Scholarship in the late Renaissance was inevitably written with careful attention to the past, to philosophical and religious antecedents. Thought bowed down before authority. Suddenly, along came this new thing, obedient to no institutional practice because it belonged to no institution, no tradition. The early essayists were inventing not only a mode of thought but a form in which that thought could be displayed. In doing so, their chief concern seems to have been establishing the self as the source of insight, a very modern stance. Pre-Enlightenment knowledge, like wisdom and power, was hierarchical: it came ultimately from God and not directly but via his messengers, from the Pope successively down until the local priest informed his parishioners. In such an environment the essay, in the sense that we understand it, makes no sense. Things began to change, though, with the Reformation, Protestantism finding it had less and less use for hierarchies sacred or profane. Nor did it take social philosophy long to catch up. The ultimate political expression of this Enlightenment insistence on the individual, the Declaration of Independence, is essentially an argumentative essay whose true audience is not the British crown but his American subjects. The essay, in fact, is the form by which the Enlightenment moved forward, and not merely because of John Locke's *Essay Concerning Human Understanding* (1690). Baruch Spinoza, David Hume, Adam Smith, Voltaire, René Descartes, and Immanuel Kant were all accomplished, persuasive essayists. It is not unreasonable to assert that our world looks the way it does chiefly because of the essay. And no two of them, I promise, sound like each other.

That's sort of the point, isn't it? To think like oneself, write like oneself, to sound like oneself and no other. Is that ego? You bet it is. E. B. White got it about right when he said, "Only a person who is congenitally self-centered has the effrontery and the stamina to write essays." White was being cheeky here, and more than a little self-deprecating, since *Stuart Little* and *Charlotte's Web* notwithstanding, the bulk of his career was taken up with writing essays. That element of ego, however, does not make the essayist an egomaniac. It just doesn't exclude one. Look, the point of the essay is to express the self. Someone, I can't remember who, said that an essay should fit its writer as perfectly as a bespoke suit of clothes. In other words, it drapes itself around its writer, revealing his thoughts and being. Sometimes it shapes them. The British novelist E. M. Forster stated it best in a question, "How do I know what I think until I see what I say?" In its truest form, the essay is an exploration of the self and some aspect of the world. That aspect can be art or war or death or youth or model railroading. What the essay uncovers is how the self relates to that topic.

Contemporary British novelist Julian Barnes is one of the foremost practitioners of the essay-as-exploration. His topics are as varied as death (*Nothing to Be Frightened Of*, 2008), grief at his wife's passing (*Levels of Life*, 2013), art (*Keeping an Eye Open*, 2015), his love affair with France (*Something to Declare*, 2002), writers who have influenced him (*Through the Window: Seventeen Essays and a Short Story*, 2012). Indeed, he is so comfortable in this mode that several of his novels are assembled from pieces, some of which are essays in the characters' voices. I read the final chapter of his defining novel, *Flaubert's Parrot* (1984), in the *New York Times Book Review* not knowing it was a novel chapter, and it worked just fine as a standalone essay. Later, when I had made the acquaintance of the book's protagonist-narrator, it did work better. Part of Barnes's charm is that he is, well, charming. His essayistic persona is friendly, engaging, humorous without being cutting, knowing. One critic describes his essays as "exquisitely humorous."

We can contrast that approach with his friend Christopher Hitchens, whose work is brilliant, strident, at times painfully witty, and often derisive of those who disagree with him. Hitchens was a professional contrarian, seeming to require something to argue against—which was an asset when he was attacking the hypocrisies of organized religion in staking out his position as an atheist in *God Is Not Great* (2007)—and he found much in his world that demanded argument against it. He also came equipped with a lacerating wit and a will to use it. Among his admirers and, later, his opponents, the casual term "Hitch-slapped" came into vogue for the victims of his debate barbs that were designed to demean and humiliate. One cannot imagine someone being "Julian-slapped," both because the term is so unwieldy and because that rhetorical mischief is so unlike Barnes. The rhetorical suit that fits Hitchens so well bags and pinches in unfortunate places on Barnes. And vice versa, of course.

The garment tailored for Marilynne Robinson would suit neither of them. Robinson, the award-winning American novelist, is also a prolific essayist whose calling card is earnestness, high seriousness of both moral and intellectual purpose. Her touch is not light, as with Barnes, nor cruel, as sometimes with Hitchens. Writing on the state of public higher education in "Save Our Public Universities" in the March 2016 edition of *Harper's*, she begins by invoking both Emerson's "The American Scholar" and Alexis de Tocqueville's *Democracy in America* (2 vols.,1835,1840). Hard to get much more high-minded than that. Her plan, however, involves more than merely seeking famous antecedents. She employs them as evidence that America was once an aspirational place, seeking to better itself by bettering its people; one of her chief data points is the Land Grant Act (officially the Morrill Act of 1862) that created the land-grant university system, one per state, for educating persons who in previous ages would have had no hope of higher education. Against this aspirational, which is for her to say spiritual, nature, she contrasts the countervailing materialist impulse in American culture. The resulting essay is wide-ranging as it touches on wage disparities, Henry Ford's enlightened economic treatment of workers, the current disparagement of higher education that does anything but train workers for specific jobs, the decline of cultural institutions and traditional values, utilitarianism, and of course the plea to continue supporting public universities, among many topics. She makes a persuasive case. At the same time, hardly anyone will finish the essay and declare, "That was fun," as might be the case with Barnes, or "That was shocking," as with Hitchens. Uplifting, maybe, thought-provoking, certainly, even improving. And all of that would be fine with Robinson. Her aims are different from either of the other writers just named, and her means are very much her own. Yet each of them writes essays that other humans actually read with profit. How boring the world would be if all essays followed the same paint-by-numbers template that we have forced upon student "essayists," whom we expect to do anything in the world except "essay" their subject or themselves.

One thing that great essayists never do is leave you in doubt as to what they think. The "thesis" may not reside where your English classes taught you to put one, but it will be in there somewhere that makes sense, early or late, and it will have several components:

- It will be firm and clear.
- It will be original—profound, unique, or, if revisiting older truths, imparting a new spin to them.

✏ It will drive the rest of the essay. If arising early, it will inform what follows; if coming toward the end, everything will have been building toward it. Yes, even the digressions.

There's a lot aspiring writers can learn from where—and why—professional essayists position their theses. The world contains more possibilities than dreamt of in your five-paragraph theme.

What, then, should we make of this form that is so elastic, so widespread, yet so profoundly personal? We might begin by trying to see it not as something concrete but as an ideal, a goal toward which each writer strives according to his or her own lights. If we are to understand essays, we might need recourse to Ezra Pound's triple criteria of criticism:

1. What was the author trying to do?
2. Did he or she succeed in doing it?
3. Was it worth doing?

Come to think of it, we could do far worse than apply those in every artistic thing we seek to judge. I would expand the first question somewhat to something like, "What was the author trying to do, and how did she try to do it?" That larger question allows for not just aims but means. How does she structure her essay? What sort of voice does she adopt? What is her tone? What does the logic of the essay look like? And so on. From there, the expansion of the second question follows naturally from the sorts of questions we ask in pursuing the first. The third remains short and relatively sweet.

Our examination of individual essays and essayists will, over time, allow us to apprehend more fully the possibilities of the form which, as we already know, can say almost everything about almost anything.

Opinion

A man must be both stupid and uncharitable who
believes there is no virtue or truth but on his own side.
—Joseph Addison

There is a kind of writing that occurs only in nonfiction works. Fiction has no need of it, and in fact fiction writers are generally counseled to avoid it. Poetry can live without it, although it flirted with it for a spell in the eighteenth century. Newspapers have a lot of it, most magazines somewhat less. This kind of writing appears in the one place in a paper where objectivity holds no value, fairness is rather shaky. And in whatever form, by whatever writer, roughly half of the reading audience will disagree with the content.

We are of course speaking here of opinion writing, which term covers a multitude of sins and one or two virtues. Opinions come in various forms: editorials, columns, political cartoons, op-eds (trust me, they're different), and expert commentary (sometimes called "punditry," although that term has fallen into disrepute along with some pundits). Opinion writing tends to be the province of the news department, although a certain amount has always landed on the sports pages. Taken together, this category of writing is more loosely tethered to fact, more open to loose interpretation of events, more forgiving (even encouraging, some would say) of open bias, less governed by the strict rules of journalistic structure, yet still obliged to follow the general contours of nonfiction. That is, it can't be (well, shouldn't be) wholly invented, and for best outcomes, it should be approximately believable.

Back in the mists of journalistic time, the eighteenth century to be precise, the essay was opinion. Were we to ask Joseph Addison and Richard Steele if their writing in *The Spectator* was essay or opinion, they would have looked at us very strangely; for them, to *essay* was to express opinions—in their case, somewhat less political than those of the writers of *The Federalist*, James Madison, John Jay, and Alexander Hamilton, whose aim was Constitutional ratification. Men of the Enlightenment wore their opinions as they wore waistcoats: automatically, reflexively, comfortably. That we now regard opinion as a separate category is in some ways an accident of publishing history. *The Spectator* was a daily *paper*, but without "news" prefixing the noun. It brought daily observations on culture and morality—indeed sought to "marry wit to morality"—without any attempt to chronicle the doings of Parliament or the latest carriage crash. When daily journalism developed into reportage of events of note and then into something resembling objective coverage, there needed to be a place for essays carrying opinions, and eventually a firewall between the two, lest opinions and editorials appear to corrupt the fairness of the reporting. As we discussed earlier, this led to the Op-Ed page(s), the designated space for writing with a slant.

In America, the roster of departed opinion and crusading newspaper columnists is long and varied: Will Rogers, Drew Pearson, Andy Rooney, Molly Ivins, Jack Anderson, Herb Caen,

Jimmy Breslin, Erma Bombeck, William Safire, and Mike Royko. Their subjects ranged from the distinctly political to the whimsical, from the international to the local. More than a few had reputations as cranks, which was part of their appeal. One of Mike Royko's great themes was the iniquity of introducing the use of gloves into Chicago softball (played with a larger and slower-moving ball than that employed in the rest of the republic). You have to admire a man who takes a strong stand on so momentous a topic. Among current practitioners, the miscellany is nearly as great: Mitch Albom, Mona Charen, E. J. Dionne, David Brooks, Jonah Goldberg, Connie Schultz, Clarence Page, Kathleen Parker, Eugene Robinson, Paul Krugman, Cal Thomas, Michelle Malkin, and Leonard Pitts. Outside of advice and humor columnists, who find themselves on the other side of a different wall, the slant has been more decidedly political and the slants left or right sharper, although both have always been a component of opinion writing. There is almost nothing that can be said about all these personages except this: they have not been afraid to express their thoughts. Otherwise, they're all over the place.

One area that should interest us especially is their approach to argumentative fairness. Only a fool would expect a political columnist to present the opposing side as fully and accurately as her own, and one thing I know about you is that you're no fool (the jury is still out on me). But there are degrees of fairness. Some columnists—Charen, Thomas, Krugman—happily set up straw men, putting improbable words into the mouths of hypothetical liberals or conservatives, depending on the slant. For others it is a struggle; Goldberg falls into the pit of caricature, endeavors to climb out and aim for some sort of equanimity, but nearly always backslides.

Dionne suffers from something like the liberal version of this malady, although his slips are slightly more occasional, slightly less egregious. A few—Schultz, Parker, Brooks (mostly, with head-scratching exceptions), Page—generally play it down the middle, favoring their own viewpoint, naturally, but not being preposterous about the opposing side. It ain't easy, folks. If you doubt that, try writing a few pieces in the style of your favorite columnist. Or the one you most despise. Either will work.

In attempts at equal treatment, many papers marshal opinion columns as binary pairs. One paper I sometimes read, the *Dayton Daily News*, has two opinion columns each day, one "From the Left" and one "From the Right." Why two? Why not seven? Do differences of opinion exist only as dichotomies, polar opposites holding themselves in repulsive balance? I'm sure it has to do with the American two-party system, although that has the effect of reinforcing an idea that is far from inevitable. *USA Today* has one editorial that emerges from its editorial board each day, then one from an outside voice. Most commonly, that voice is in opposition to whatever the paper's editorial stance proves to be. On May 22, 2018, the main editorial was on President Trump's immigration policy and how, rather than pushing the more extreme and largely unworkable aspects of his aspirations, he should pursue a more centrist position and "focus on the doable." The corresponding opinion was written by Mark Krikorian, executive director of the Center for Immigration Studies, a hard-right, immigration-skeptic group (and favored source by Trump for "fun facts" about immigration) that has argued, among other things, that "birth tourism"—the practice of coming temporarily to the United States in order to have a baby on American soil and gain birthright citizenship—has been a growing phenomenon, a falsehood that has been debunked by multiple sources, including the fact-checking operation PolitiFact, that have shown that such births have actually been on the decline. Care to guess how much Krikorian agreed with the main editorial? Are those the only possibilities on immigration? Of course not. But they are as many as fit in the constrained space of the modern, mass-circulation newspaper. And so we get point-counterpoint.

If we are to read opinions and editorials with profit—that is, if we are to glean useful something from them beyond confirmation of our biases—we need to ask a few questions.

- ✏ FIRST, DO THE "FACTS" SQUARE WITH WHAT WE ACTUALLY KNOW ABOUT THE WORLD? I often find myself balking at some claim that brings me up short with a response that feels more than says, that doesn't sound right to me. From that little nagging voice, I know that sooner or later I'll have to do some fact-checking. Might as well be sooner, so that dubious factoids don't stick. Happily, this is easier than ever. When I read a newspaper, I nearly always have two devices at hand with which I can do a quick browser search (often, I'm reading it on one), and the results surface in about as long as it takes me to type the question. How do we develop that little nagging voice? Practice. Reading reliable, objective sources about what the world actually looks like. For all the abuse that mainstream media take from those on the loonier fringes, our major news sources are actually pretty trustworthy. Perfect? No. But more accurate than most of the alternatives.
- ✏ SECOND, IS THE SOURCE OF THAT ASSERTION RELIABLE? If the issue is tobacco use and the source is the tobacco

industry, I'm not buying. Hell, if the issue is anything and the source is the tobacco industry, I'm not buying. Those folks have not proved to be paragons of honesty down the decades. For me, and I hope for you, facts are more likely to be trustworthy if they come from independent sources whose money is not derived from products involved in the story. Facebook is no more likely to tell the truth about internet security than Koch Industries is about energy extraction. Each has too much at stake.

☞ ARE THE FACTS BEING USED FAIRLY OR MISAPPLIED? Cherry-picked factoids are worse than none at all. If the columnist pulls out a tiny sliver of a statistic, my skin itches. What we want to know is if the columnist, before sending in his copy, could honestly add a disclaimer, "No facts were harmed in the making of this opinion."

☞ ARE FRIENDS AND ENEMIES (THE LATTER ESPECIALLY) BEING QUOTED ACCURATELY? We've all seen quotes taken out of context and made to say the opposite of what was originally intended. Yes, so-and-so did say those six words in sequence, but if you omit the "not" that preceded them, you've just committed intellectual fraud.

☞ DO THE ARGUMENTS ACTUALLY SUPPORT THE CLAIMS THAT ARE MADE, OR DO THEY REQUIRE A PREEXISTING BIAS IN LINE WITH THE WRITER'S? If all you are doing is preaching to the choir, what's the point? You don't have to convert your opponents (a nearly impossible job in any case), but the argument should at least have a chance with an impartial, intelligent observer who has not yet decided what she thinks.

Practicing this sort of questioning of opinion-writing, of anything, really, won't guarantee that we won't get bamboozled, but it will make the likelihood somewhat less.

Whether they deal with the writer's life, the essay and the opinion are two of the most revealing personal forms of writing. They reveal innermost thoughts, long-held beliefs, habits of mind, loves and hates. They reveal who the writer is. And they bring us into contact with the minds of others. We need more of that.

11

Life from the Inside

Reading Autobiography and Memoir

YOU MIGHT THINK, ASSUMING you thought about it at all, that writing about the self would be the truest form of nonfiction possible. After all, who could be more of an expert on a subject than the person writing about the life he or she actually lived? Surely we can count on getting the real story there. Which leads to a simple question about autobiography and memoir:

Have you ever read one?

I have long counseled students of fiction to start doubting the narrator's veracity if they see the word "I" on the first page. That warning excludes dialogue, of course, and concentrates on the narration itself. The same is true of nonfiction. In a story or novel, authors generally employ a first-person narrator (the "I" in question) when they want to hide something. That narrator may be too naive to understand what she's experiencing, as when children—or adults recalling their childhood—are employed.

A narrator of great old age may have lapses of memory. Others simply have something to hide and want to put the best face on what is a hideous picture. The narrators of *A Clockwork Orange* and *Lolita* are both the protagonists of their novels. And horrible people. They seek (or, more accurately, their writers cause them to seek) to win over their readers with charm and wordplay—see? he's clever, so he can't be that bad—so that we will give them a pass on unforgivable behavior. Most first-person narrators aren't so awful, but nearly all of them give us some reason to doubt their truthfulness.

So what about autobiography and memoir? Their narrators have the same issue, but with this difference: the narrator-protagonists are the authors' presentation of themselves.

Before we go further, a bit of definition. We often, in casual conversation, use *memoir* and *autobiography* interchangeably. That won't quite work for literary discussion (we actually do have one or two standards here, however mild). So here's a way to think of it. An autobiography is a special kind of biography. What is special is that it is written from the inside; what is biographical is that it is the story of a life. The chief difference in terms of subject matter is that biography covers the death of its subject, something that is difficult in a form that requires the subject to still be breathing. And the memoir? The word is derived from the French for memory or reminiscence. Those reminiscences can be as wide as a full life, but they are more often part of a smaller slice. We speak of presidential memoirs, which typically limit themselves more or less to the period when the person was actually president, or memoirs of a general's time leading his troops, or even memoirs of someone who suffered through a particular trauma.

Such a work is under no obligation to cover the memoirist's birth or wedding or appendectomy. Such topics come into the memoir only if they somehow bear upon it. While memoir is a species of autobiographical writing, it would be a mistake to speak of it as the same as autobiography. We can separate works by scope and intent. Henry David Thoreau's *Walden* (1854) limits itself to a specific period of the author's life, those two years, two months, and two days (talk about artistically arranged experience!) that he spent living alone in a hand-built cabin in the woods by Concord's most famous pond. His prior experiences count not at all in this tale except if some earlier lesson impinges on the immediate experience. Pioneering flier Beryl Markham's *West with the Night* (1942) focuses on her famous flight to become the first person to make a solo Atlantic crossing from east to west. She brings in her early Kenyan upbringing and experiences as a racehorse trainer and bush pilot as necessary preliminaries, but always with an eye on the main purpose, using them to explain how she became the person capable of this remarkable feat. Were this memoir a standard autobiography, the transatlantic flight would simply be one of any number of episodes retold and given no more weight than any of the others.

But back to the dubious veracity of first-person nonfiction. This begins, in America at least, with your Father. Of the Founding sort. *The Autobiography of Benjamin Franklin* (1791) begins as a letter from a father to a son, just the sort of thing that any ordinary inventor-entrepreneur-patriot-citizen-social-improver-statesman-visionary writes to his son late in his life to let the lad have the benefit of whatever accumulated wisdom the old boy has acquired. But as with so many things, it wouldn't stay in its intended genre. What began as a simple letter (as if there were such a thing with old Ben) became an exercise in creating an American Myth. Or rather, the Myth of the American.

Have autobiographies always had such a sketchy relation to truth? The real truth is that we cannot know. If we go back to something like the beginning, to, say, Augustine's *Confessions* (ca. 400 C.E.), we find ourselves hampered by a serious lack of external sources. The only "facts" we can ascertain reside in the *Confessions* themselves. Was Augustine of Hippo as much of a rascal as he purports to have been prior to his conversion? Stealing pears when he had better pears at home? How terrible! As for veracity, we have only his version. What we do know is that no story of redemption can be compelling without some sinful nature from which the protagonist needs to be redeemed. And also that almost every spiritual autobiography since Augustine's has dutifully followed the sin-to-grace path he laid out. Even Franklin's *Autobiography*, with its impulse toward improving its readers, owes at least its transfiguring zeal to the long line of spiritual autobiographies stretching back to the Bishop of Hippo Regius. The ostensible purpose of the *Confessions* is to detail a life leading to conversion to Christianity. In reality, though, the work serves as an exhortation and guide to conversion for its readers.

One of Augustine's great inheritors is John Henry, Cardinal Newman (1801–90), who wrote one of the key spiritual autobiographies, *Apologia Pro Vita Sua* (Justification or Defense of His Life). If I had my way, that would be the title of every autobiography; librarians and bookstore workers might hold a different view. Newman was already an important religious figure in England, the vicar of St. Mary's College, Oxford, and a leading thinker and writer in the "Oxford Movement," a group that sought to return the Church of England to practices closer to the Catholic Church. Ultimately, his dissatisfaction with Anglicanism would lead to his switching to Catholicism in 1847 and eventually becoming first the rector of the new Catholic University of Ireland (now University College, Dublin) and later the cardinal deacon of San Giorgio in Velabro in Rome. His split with the Church of England occasioned a series of attacks impugning his honesty and character by fellow clergyman Charles Kingsley. His response was the *Apologia*. Contrary to the way its title sounds, the book is no part of an apology but instead, hewing to the word's Latin meaning, a very spirited defense of his life choices, particularly his decision to leave Canterbury for Rome. And his real weapon is style:

> He was the first who taught me to weigh my words, and to be cautious in my statements. He led me to that mode of limiting and clearing my sense in discussion and in controversy, and of distinguishing between cognate ideas, and of obviating mistakes by anticipation, which to my surprise has been since considered, even in quarters friendly to me, to savour of the polemics of Rome. He is a man of most exact mind himself, and he used to snub me severely, on reading, as he was kind enough to do, the first sermons that I wrote, and other compositions which I was engaged upon.

Newman employs parallel sentence openings that start out deceptively simple and declarative: "He was the first," "He led me," "He is a man." Of course, being a Victorian writer, he can allow no statement to remain simple and declarative for long. The second sentence, for instance, develops its own parallel structure with the prepositional phrases "that mode of limiting and clearing my sense . . . of distinguishing between cognate ideas . . . of obviating mistakes." The result is an elegance even when he is a bit fussy, as was his era, with the hanging of ornaments and baubles on his tree of rhetoric. The "he" of this passage is Dr. Hawkins, the first curate with whom Newman had sustained close working contact, who made a profound impression on the young future cardinal. Clearly, Hawkins did not grade sermons on the curve, and his pupil took the lessons to heart. The occasion for the book is an attack by Charles Kingsley of the Church of England on the resignation of Newman as vicar of St. Mary's Oxford preparatory to his conversion to Catholicism. Much of Newman's counterattack involves the shoddy language used by Kingsley, and Dr. Hawkins's editorial comments could not possibly be more severe than Newman's against Kingsley. Much of the *Apologia* concerns itself with Kingsley's argument, but a good deal rests on the critique by a brilliant essayist of a much shoddier one. Writing well is the best revenge.

Who are the inheritors of the Newman autobiography? In one sense, everyone who came after, since the good cardinal explained for one and all that the self-life is an excellent vessel for self-justification. More particularly, though, there are two groups for whom self-justification holds a mighty appeal. The first would be politicians. These days every candidate for president must present an autobiography detailing his formative experiences and political-spiritual growth; the universal subtitle could be "Who I Am and How I Got This Way." This trend has been around for a while but became more pronounced after Barack Obama's one-two punch of *Dreams from My Father* (2004) and *The Au-*

dacity of Hope (2006) in the run-up to his national prominence and election to the presidency. In the subsequent elections, virtually every serious candidate, and, given the sheer number of hopefuls, some less serious models, has published some booklike object. The main exception would be the eventual 2016 winner, Donald Trump, but he had published *The Art of the Deal* (1987) years earlier. A majority of these works, including Trump's, have been ghostwritten, given that sufficient time and a gift with the language (not to mention the ability to sit still) are not prerequisites for the Oval Office. The ultraconservative right attacked Obama's books as being ghostwritten by declared radical and former Weather Underground member Bill Ayers. The goal was to taint Obama with guilt by association with an extremist boogeyman and contained not a little racism in its insinuation that a former editor of the *Harvard Law Review* was incapable of writing his own book. When Ayers made a jokey "confession," the ultra-right, predictably, lost its mind. One thing we can ascertain about the ones that we know to be ghosted is that the spirits have been influenced by the nineteenth century's most famous religious convert, or at least by others who have followed his model. They incline toward a growing awareness of a larger purpose than the self, a road-to-Damascus moment when the scales fell away and revealed their true belief, and a path forward to their present situation. And why do they sound so much alike? Because the structure works, the narrative works. You have to have a pretty darned good reason to bother us with your presidential ambitions, and the pre-candidacy autobiography helps to justify what in other terms might look like (and often is) rank opportunism.

As a side note, the exit-interview version of the campaign autobiography is the presidential memoir, the most famous of which is probably that of Ulysses S. Grant. The old soldier, next door to penniless and dying of throat cancer (all those cigars and whiskey having caught up with him), wrote his *Personal Memoirs* in a headlong rush during his final months. The book was sold by personal subscription, and no less than Mark Twain offered him a 75 percent royalty for the finished product. Grant completed his task mere days before he died, but the stratagem worked: Julia Grant became a very wealthy woman. In this case, "presidential memoir" is a misnomer, since it is by a former president but covers only his military career. There were only three autobiographies or memoirs by nineteenth-century presidents, the other two being by Martin Van Buren and James Buchanan, but beginning with Teddy Roosevelt, most modern ex-presidents have penned at least one book. Even the silent Calvin Coolidge got in on the game. Some are memoirs specific to their time in office; some, like Dwight Eisenhower's *At Ease: Stories I Tell to Friends* (1967), focus on events from various life points; and some, like Bill Clinton's *My Life* (2004), are comprehensive autobiographies. The benefits run in both directions. Of course, readers, both contemporary and future, want to know what went on in the minds of the most powerful men on earth, and those men, besides meeting financial needs (there were no presidential pensions before 1958), wish to, with apologies to John Milton, justify their ways to men—and women. So the post-presidency memoir, like the qualifying autobiography, follows Newman's pattern of autobiography as *apologia*.

And that second great inheritor? Music autobiographies. I have several sitting around on real and virtual shelves, and they show a strong trend toward validation. Pete Townshend's *Who I Am* (2012) concerns itself chiefly with explaining his guitar-smashing as an act of deliberate artistic destruction rather than the actions of an impulsive narcissist. Neil Young's *Waging Heavy Peace* (2012) tries to establish that its author is as contrarian and visionary as befits rock's Jeremiah, the man who wrote the anthemic "Ohio." And Steven Tyler's *Does the Noise in My Head Bother You?* (2011) reminds readers that he really is as scattered and wacky (he frequently gets facts and titles wrong) as they suppose and makes a case to adore him anyway. Structurally, the three are very different. Townshend's is tightly structured along chronological lines. Young's is notably nonlinear, moving thematically and subjectively as the spirit moves the author, who refused the help of a ghostwriter, thereby preserving the idiosyncratic nature of his thought process. And Tyler's is, well, let's just say flighty. But all three are united in their request: respect me, understand me, love me. I won't deny that this category can be expanded to take in nearly everyone in entertainment, but it seems particularly compelling in musical genres designed for the young and written by folks who no longer are.

Before we forget entirely about Franklin's first-person life story, let us say that it actually is an autobiography in the sense that it undertakes to tell the entire story of his life to date. By definition, no one can write the story of his or her entire life, since part of that story is forever out of reach of the living author. There's an old, almost universal joke about the canny but taciturn rustic—from Ireland or Vermont or Virginia or New Brunswick or wherever men of few words reside—and the loquacious visitor determined to draw him (it's always a him in the versions I've heard) out. "So," asks the outsider, "have you lived here all your life?" The answer is two words long: "Not yet." Autobiography is like that, missing the natural ending.

Like Augustine, Franklin sometimes tars himself more than circumstances warrant, as when he makes the point that as a young person he had not yet learned the value of thrift. Newly arrived in Philadelphia as a runaway apprentice, he spent too much of his money "buying three great rolls" from the baker only to find that this purchase was as unwieldy as it was wasteful, and he leaves us with the comic image of him walking down the street munching on one of the rolls while having the others tucked one under each arm. He calls such a mistake an *erratum*, a term he borrows from his career as a printer, *errata* being errors in printing that at one time were corrected on slips of paper tucked into the pages where the mistakes occur. These particular errata serve much the same purpose as Augustine's sins: hard to show improvement in a life if the need for such is not demonstrated. Franklin's blunders are hardly the darkest of crimes, but he is intent on making better citizens, not saving souls.

It is worth noting that Franklin's *Autobiography* was written over the course of years and that larger events, not least among them the American Revolution, took place. And a breach occurred between father and son when the younger remained loyal to Britain. The device, then, of the letter became not merely a fiction but a bridge too far after Book One (of four). It had served its purpose, though, and most of us recall the entire thing as an extended letter.

A special class of autobiographical writing that has gained prominence in recent years is the death memoir. Works like Paul Kalanithi's *When Breath Becomes Air* (2016) and Randy Pausch's *The Last Lecture* (2008) are cancer memoirs written by young men surprised by terminal illness. Both were men of science, Kalanithi a brilliant surgeon, Pausch a professor of computer science, so they bring analytical minds to bear on their circumstances. Kalanithi, an English major at Stanford, is also a man of letters who brings a literary sensibility to his enterprise; Pausch, less literary, enlists Jeffrey Zaslow as coauthor. Neither survived to see his book in print. There have been numerous others taking all manner of approaches to the ways writing transpires, including not only the matter of coauthors but also structure, voice, pace—in short, everything authors in a genre usually differ over. The one constant among death memoirs is that the author is facing a certain and quite proximate end.

Then there are the memoirs not by sufferers of fatal maladies or misadventures but by their survivors. Two of those left behind, it turns out, have been among our most celebrated writers. Journalist and memoirist Joan Didion wrote *The Year of Magical Thinking* (2005), which won the National Book Award, after the heart-attack death of her husband, John Gregory Dunne, and *Blue Nights* (2011), about the experience of grief at the loss of her daughter, Quintana. And lauded, prolific novelist Joyce Carol Oates's *A Widow's Story* (2011) dealt with the loss of her husband, Raymond Smith.

Perhaps the most inventive approach to the death memoir is written by a professional in the field. Thomas Lynch, a noted poet as well as an undertaker, published one of the least likely bestsellers of recent decades, *The Undertaking* (1997). The book explains the curious relationships undertakers have with the dead and the living and is filled with anecdotes that bring his occupation to life, as it were, including he and his brother handling the embalming and funeral of their own father. It was, he says, the last gift they could give the man who shaped their lives.

In a sense, it is impossible for an American to escape the long shadow of Franklin when writing an autobiography. The best course of action might be to embrace it, acknowledge the debt, and ring the changes of one's own contribution to the genre. Few have done so to greater effect than Ta-Nehisi Coates in his 2015 *Between the World and Me*. As Franklin had done more than two centuries earlier, Coates begins by addressing his son, but with an urgency unknown in the original. That earlier work aims at self-improvement and, with it, societal improvement, the later survival in a country where survival is far from assured for young black men. From the first pages, Coates attacks the concept of race, the construction of "democracy," and the notion of America. He is writing in the wake of the killing of young black men and women by authorities in tragic or foolish or accidental circumstances— for selling cigarettes, for asking for help, for playing with a toy gun at age twelve—with an all-too-real knowledge that neither he nor his son are ever completely safe. Franklin never addressed such matters, could not have conceived of them nor seen that they existed.

From there, Coates's book moves away from the merely autobiographical—not that there's anything "mere" about auto-biography. It is, by turns, essay, social analysis, historical critique, and searing warning to a vulnerable young man. And autobiography. It becomes Franklin meets James Baldwin/Malcolm X/ Martin Luther King Jr./Old Testament Prophet. That may seem a great deal to put on a slim volume (around one hundred fifty pages), but dire necessity drives this text. If we wanted to put a simplistic label (and aren't they all?) on it, we might call the book a memoir-essay, although that would fall well short of the mark.

As with Franklin's autobiography or the most famous African American autobiography, *Narrative of the Life of Frederick Douglass* (1845), the life is used as illustration of some core values or successes or failings in the larger society. Douglass's *Narrative* is much more than a perils-of-Pauline series of travails and struggles; its ultimate aim is to convince a target audience, chiefly white Northerners who had not made up their minds on the slavery question, that it was high time for decisions and that there was only one available moral choice. Such an argument might seem almost quaint, were it not for the fact that Ta-Nehisi Coates must make much the same one, substituting a contemporary outrage against black Americans in place of "slavery," some one hundred sixty years after the original.

The chief argument of this essay is that the fate of the black male body is never entirely at the disposition of the black male in question; too many forces from gangs to the police to society at large have the power to take that life away, not just from Coates or his son but from any American boy or man descended from Africans, to "destroy" or "take" or "steal" my body away from me, as he puts it. He further argues that there can be no real freedom so long as one does not possess the power of determination over one's own fate. When a life can be snuffed out for trivial mistakes—walking down the wrong street, making an inadvertent gesture that is misconstrued, reaching for a wallet in front of a jumpy lawman, waiting to pick up a child at school or a friend from the mall—and sometimes for no mistake at all, then the owner of that life lacks a basic autonomy that white people, or to quote him, "those Americans who believe that they are white," can take as a given.

Here's the question we might want to ask of *Between the World and Me*: what does that formal decision of copying Franklin's opening gambit tell us about Coates's argument? That device situates him in a specific tradition of American autobiography, but not one that invited him in. Franklin's tale of success applies, Coates knows, to Americans of European descent and only a limited portion of those, as Old Ben's caustic remarks about German immigrants to Philadelphia indicate, just as he knows that many of Franklin's achievements were accomplished by working closely with men who owned other human beings and by bowing to those men's demands regarding that chattel property, all of it of African descent. By framing his argument as a letter to his son, Coates hammers on the door of an institution once closed to him. His ostensible autobiography reaches out in multiple directions at once, out into societal events, back into history, into relations between races and even within his own race, into personal identity when aspects of identity are stripped from the person, into the contest of ideas between Malcolm and Martin. His is a very busy text, never willing to settle for a single, simple answer. This should not surprise us, however. There's a whole lot more going on beyond a life story in either *The Autobiography of Benjamin Franklin* or *Narrative of the Life of Frederick Douglass*.

12

That Is So Last Year

Reading History and Biography

THE WORLD OF NONFICTION divides human experience into two
time frames: *Now* and *Everything Before Now*. How much be-
fore? How far back would you like to go? The Trojan War (circa
1300 BCE) exists in *EBN* but so also do the Clinton and Bush ad-
ministrations, with Obama's following quickly. Events discussed
in historical works do not need to be back in the mists of time,
only earlier enough that we are now looking back at them from
a suitable distance (by which we mean, not last week). *Now* is
always moving forward, leaving more and more *Everything Before*
in its wake.

The difference between, say, Katherine Boo's *Behind the
Beautiful Forevers* (2012) and David Grann's *Killers of the Flower
Moon* (2017) is time. Boo reveals the hidden world of a Mumbai
slum that exists, however much we might wish it weren't true,
in the twenty-first century, while Grann exposes the murderous

conspiracy against wealthy Osage tribal members during the 1920s. And that difference matters in a number of ways, among them the nature of the available information. Boo has the advantage of being able to interview her subjects. Grann's subjects are unavailable, since almost a century had passed between the events and the writing. On the other hand, he has a deeper written record on which to draw, which includes interviews, court records, journals, and letters as *primary* documents and articles, novels, nonfiction books, court reviews among the *secondary* documents. By "primary," we mean any firsthand source, or source by someone who was actually present. A "secondary" source is one that relies on received information. So a journal entry by a crime victim is primary; if a writer draws upon that journal to analyze the events, the resulting article or book would be a secondary source for some future researcher. For Boo, the secondary record is fairly thin, although she can draw on many sources that discuss the world's poorest neighborhoods generally.

What books and articles on contemporaneous events offer is immediacy: we are looking at events or situations that are happening right now. What the passage of time affords, by contrast, and what historical works provide is perspective. Both types of writing are valuable. *Behind the Beautiful Forevers* is news in the broadest sense, information readers need to understand their world as it currently exists. How is it possible that such poverty exists in the world? How is it that most of us have no idea how desperate lives are in places we never see because we don't look? Katherine Boo is reporting from the front, looking on our behalf and sending us this detailed, unsettling dispatch from a war that poverty is clearly winning. *Killers of the Flower Moon*, on the other hand, is taking the long view, allowing us to see one of the ugliest chapters in a long and ugly history of treatment of Native peoples. David Grann is not so much a reporter as a compiler, amassing and then sifting through a mountain of information on a story from ninety years earlier to fill in a major gap in our understanding of race relations. Our need for this knowledge is no less acute for the passage of decades.

Histories come in various denominations. We are accustomed to the great-man-great-event sort of history, whether of George Washington and the beginnings of the American presidency or George Custer and the Battle of the Little Bighorn. These can lean more toward the biography of the protagonist or the events he or she brings about. But histories can also be about ordinary men and women caught up in something far larger than themselves. Stephen Ambrose's *Undaunted Courage* or Doris Kearns Goodwin's *Team of Rivals* stand as examples of the former, David McCullough's *1776* or Tom Brokaw's *The Greatest Generation* of the latter.

Ambrose's book follows the exploits of Lewis and Clark's expedition to open up the West, but it does so, as we have said before, through Lewis's perspective. The strategy here is that Lewis is the more compelling figure, in part because of his short, tragic life, but also because of his meteoric rise. That he was also the ranking officer (he had been a captain to Clark's second lieutenant, although both are treated as "Captain" on the expedition) may also have played a role in Ambrose's decision. Clark is also covered extensively, but Lewis receives the star treatment, along with his president, Thomas Jefferson, who completed the Louisiana Purchase and commissioned the grueling quest to "discover" the new real estate he had bought. Ambrose is exhaustive in his treatment of the journey, drawing heavily on the journals the two

leaders kept as well as correspondence with Jefferson and con-
temporaneous sources of many types. And while he is generally
favorable to the project and the people involved, he doesn't fail to
mention their shortcomings, as when Lewis neglects to inform
his president that their survival over the winter was made possi-
ble by the generosity of the Mandans in sharing their corn; the
resulting report suggests that the land itself supplied adequately
for their nutritional needs, which was not the case. He reports
the challenges and sometimes surprising assistance the Corps of
Discovery encountered from Native American tribes, at times
displaying a wry humor. He is also sympathetic toward the native
peoples encountered, the friendly tribes and individuals certainly,
but also the Sioux, who were frequently obstreperous. Rather
than merely seeing them as blocking characters in a narrative, he
examines the reasons they might have had for being hostile to
strangers, since the Corps was not the first incursion by outsiders
in the history of the Plains.

This work is in a sense the easiest sort of history to follow,
tracing a large event—in this case a massive series of events—
through the experience of a single person. When in doubt, the
author always doubles back to Meriwether Lewis. Are there
downsides to this approach? Of course. Every writing decision
is a choice based on what is gained and what is lost. In exchange
for greater coherence, Ambrose sacrifices the variety of views.
This is likely a necessary element since the two captains are very
nearly the only literate persons on the journey, so their views are
captured in a way that Sacagawea's or the enlisted men's are not.
Nevertheless, an argument can be made that the story is as much
Clark's as Lewis's, and that in fact each person on this journey

had his or her own epic adventure. *The Odyssey*, however, admits of no hero but Odysseus.

An alternative to the single-focus history is what we might think of as the mosaic approach, a narrative without a central figure but with a thematic or temporal lodestar. Both McCullough and Brokaw follow this pattern. We can best understand McCullough's book as a biography of the single most consequential year in American history. His approach is a discontinuous narrative, moving from place to place as the date and events dictate. In order to do the story justice, he must present not only tales from up and down the colonies—the newly declared States by midyear—but also from the chambers of power in England. Travel and communication being what they were in the late eighteenth century, there is an inevitable lag between, say, the signing of the Declaration on July 4 and the British response some weeks later. King George and Parliament may have anticipated that the action would come, but expectation and certain knowledge are two different things. The other notable aspect of the narrative is that McCullough focuses on persons great and small, not forgetting that this incipient war was more than a contest between two men named George. He recounts the experience of an ordinary soldier in the army when his unit was called forward during the disastrous rout of the Battle of Brooklyn:

> Private Joseph Martin, one of those in the units ordered
> to march to the Brooklyn ferry, remembered the cheers of
> the soldiers as they embarked, and the answering cheers
> of the spectators who thronged the wharfs to watch the
> excitement. "They all wished us good luck apparently."

For his own part, Private Martin could only think of the horrors of war "in all their hideousness."

When they arrived at the battle, his worst fears were confirmed. Discovering an officer who made a spectacle of his fear and alarm, thereby making the scene even worse for his men, "A fine soldier you are, I thought, a fine officer, an exemplary man for young soldiers! I would have suffered anything short of death than have made such an exhibition of myself." In passages such as this, McCullough shows us the character of the common enlisted men and the not-always-sunny relationship with their leaders.

There are numerous nonfiction works with a four-digit (usually) numerical title. You can find multiple titles for 1066, the year of the Norman Conquest of England. Books about major disruptions or, at least as common, the year just prior to calamity are popular. Thus we have *1913* in various guises. Would you like that by Florian Illies (2013), Charles Emmerson (also 2013, centenaries being what they are), Oliver DeMille (2012, jumping the gun a little), or Paul Ham (back to 2013)? You have only to ask. Want to know about Columbus's impact on the new world? Charles C. Mann gives us *1491: New Revelations of the Americas before Columbus* (2005) and *1493: Uncovering the New World Columbus Created* (2011). Wait, you cry, what about the year he landed? No sweat. Felipe Fernández-Armesto covers that in *1492: The Year the World Began* (2009). The thing is, these titles and many, *many* more like them arise from the same impulse as McCullough's book: the desire to carve out a space small enough that a deep dive into it avoids resembling a ship's anchor.

Brokaw's book, in contrast, which stands as a tribute to a generation that was shaped by the privations of the Great Depression and that made its mark in the cataclysm that was World War II, is much more fragmentary and pointillist. In a series of chapters drawn from oral or written testimony, Brokaw presents forty-seven profiles—thirty of "Normal People" and another seventeen of those who went on to achievements in the public realm—of men and women whose contributions helped win the war. The chapters average under ten book pages in hardcover; none runs more than a dozen. The book makes no pretensions at being an exhaustive treatment of the war, no claims as to strategy or policy. Rather, this is a book of lives, reminding us of all the lives that were risked to turn back tyranny and oppression, of young people called away from quiet or noisy private lives by an enterprise vastly larger than anything they could have imagined. To that end, he allows his subjects as much voice as space can accommodate, moving between narrative overview and direct quotation from either the participants or their family members in each profile. Take, for instance, his handling of the story of Lloyd Kilmer, the son of a Minnesota farmer who went bankrupt during the Depression. Kilmer, despite having never been in an airplane, was determined to become an airman, which he did, piloting a bomber during the early months of the US involvement until, on June 29, 1944, just three weeks after D-Day, his plane was shot down, crash-landing near Beemster, Holland. It was his sixteenth mission. He and his crew were taken prisoner, and he remained a prisoner of war for the duration, until his camp's liberation on April 26, 1945. After the war, he would earn a degree from Creighton University and have a successful career in business and local government in Omaha while raising a family with Marie, the girlfriend whose memory kept him going during the ten months in Stalag 7A. When he retired to Sun City West near Phoenix, he began a campaign to affix American flags (something he noticed lacking on his first Fourth of July there) "to each of the hundred power poles along the [main] boulevard," which goal he achieved in short order. Here is Lloyd's account of his plane being hit: "One shell went through the wing, rupturing the gas tanks, and starting a fire. Another burst knocked the propeller off an engine. Other planes were exploding all around us. We could see parachutes coming out of some—and others with no parachutes. We were in big trouble." Count on the man who was there to give you the story straight, with no extra drama. The facts supply plenty.

Brokaw's goal is not to present a comprehensive overview, which would be massive and unwieldy in the extreme, but a broad canvas filled with miniatures. In so doing, he can move from people who became businessmen or farmers or presidents (George H. W. Bush, who flew for the navy) or famous television chefs (Julia Child, who worked in the Office of Strategic Services, the forerunner to the CIA). The point of the book is that the heroes of the Second Great War came from every place and every background to fight and then dispersed equally widely to help build postwar America. The structure—a large accumulation of brief biographical vignettes—served to underscore that purpose. As we learned from the example of John McPhee earlier, every successful nonfiction work must find the structure adequate to its task; the best ones find the perfect structure to accomplish their ends.

This will surprise almost none of you, but publishing is a fashion industry. Turn one Harry Potter–style success loose in the world and suddenly all of publishing is madly chasing the next boy wizard, the next school of magic series. Let one *Gone Girl* take flight, and within a couple of months we will be swamped with books bearing the word *girl* on their spines. This is no less true of histories and biographies. At one time, both concerned themselves chiefly with the star attractions of our past. That means big wars and the generals who (mostly) won them. Famous statesmen, with the emphasis on the second syllable. Famous writers and artists and composers, chiefly male. See any pattern? Oh, there were occasional books about famous help-meets, if those wives or lovers kicked up enough of a ruckus or drowned in difficulty. Occasionally, a book on Abigail Adams, Dolley Madison, or Mary Todd Lincoln might appear either because of the atmosphere of mythmaking (Madison, especially) or incredible suffering (Lincoln) that surrounded the First Ladies. Mostly, however, history and biography were the province of Great-Men-and-the-Acts-that-Made-Them-Great. A biography of Mrs. Charles Dickens? Get serious. His mistress, maybe, since Ellen Ternan was an actress, famous in her own right, but not poor, long-suffering, misused Catherine Hogarth Dickens. Even her beautiful younger sister Mary, known to be the model for every "young, beautiful, and good" doomed heroine in his novels, had a better chance of being profiled.

Then in the late twentieth century, something changed. In large measure because of second-wave feminism, great men's wives also seemed like material for serious study. There had always been interest in those who, like Zelda Fitzgerald, were intimately tied to their husbands' public personae, especially if, also like Zelda, their stories carried elements of scandal or madness in their own right. The biography that really set this trend rolling was *Nora*, Brenda Maddox's life of James Joyce's wife (1988). Much of the early writing on Joyce characterized Nora as a hapless figure, at best an uneducated, non-literary, incompetent housekeeper from the West of Ireland, at worst a sharp-tongued harridan who made her celebrated husband's life hell. These accounts were written by or based on the view of Joyce's male friends and fellow literary stars, who could see nothing to account for Joyce's utter devotion to his other half. Their prejudice was abetted by leaning heavily on her family surname, Barnacle. Worse fortune in the matter of naming has rarely occurred. True, in his brilliant *James Joyce* (1959), a work that forever changed literary biography, and not inevitably for the better (bigger is truly not always better), Richard Ellmann does much better by Nora, even ending with the story of her funeral, at which the presiding priest referred to her as "a great sinner" (*eine grosse Sünderin*), leading to the book's most touching line. "No epithet," Ellmann writes, "could have been less apt." Still, even for him Nora remains a peripheral figure. Maddox, happily, became the first to bring this supposedly peripheral life to center stage, depicting a much more complex woman than any previous writer on the Joyce ménage. Sometimes in publishing, virtue is rewarded; *Nora* appeared to critical acclaim and excellent sales.

From there, the race was on. The last thirty years have seen biographies of Georgie Hyde-Lees Yeats (wife of W. B.), Frieda Lawrence (wife of D. H.), Véra Nabokov (wife of Vladimir), pretty much every Hemingway wife, some repeatedly, Zelda again, Sophia Tolstoy (wife of Leo), Constance Lloyd Wilde (wife of Oscar), Lee Krasner (wife of Jackson Pollock), and so many more. There is a special case in the trend in women's biographies about not a wife but a work colleague: *Rosalind Franklin: The Dark Lady of DNA* (2002). There is even a new-ish class of novel, the artist's wife/partner/lover book, of which the most successful is probably Paula McLain's *The Paris Wife* (2011). The day I wrote this list I heard of *The Age of Light*, a new bio-novel by Whitney Scharer of Lee Miller, the assistant to as well as fellow photographer and lover of experimental visual artist Man Ray. And why should this not be so? The wives, lovers, and friends of famous male artists constituted a largely untouched field of information. To continue ignoring them would simply be extending the insult. Maddox was clearly on to something.

It is always tempting when discussing history to drag out George Santayana's bromide about ignorance dooming us to repeat it, but I don't think that gets at the real need for historical understanding. First of all, evidence from every quarter suggests that we humans inevitably repeat every sort of folly, however knowledgeable we are about past performance. The greater argument for knowing history is that we cannot possibly comprehend our present without understanding our past. To think, for instance, that a single event, whether the Emancipation Proclamation or Rosa Parks refusing to move to the back of the bus or Martin Luther King's "I Have a Dream" speech, somehow rectified relations between black and white citizens of the republic is sheer lunacy. Those moments and movements are justly celebrated, but they are not the entire story. A book like Margot Lee Shetterly's *Hidden Figures*, which shows us the NASA triumphs that were made possible by black female mathematicians and physicists, while at the same time pointing out the difficulties they faced because of their race and gender, adds depth and complexity to the saga of the struggle for racial equality. Similarly, David McCullough's *1776* fleshes out our understanding of that founding year by including not merely famous leaders but also ordinary men and women who helped to shape events. Ron Chernow's biography helps restore to prominence Alexander Hamilton, who for many of us was little more than a footnote, dying in a duel over obscure reasons in our high school history textbooks.

Perhaps the most troubling book from a Santayanian perspective is Grann's *Killers of the Flower Moon*. The Osage murders of the 1920s were, as he details, not incidental misfortunes but a horrific campaign of murder driven by greed, racism, innate viciousness, and official indifference. A particularly disturbing element is the patient violence required for white men to become the lovers or husbands of Osage women in order to murder them with poisoned whiskey (although they were not opposed to guns and nitroglycerin when dealing with women or men). Grann's book is like a terrible wreck from which we can't avert our gaze. At least, readers will feel, this is ninety years and more in the past, the last major outrage in a long, bloody history of murderous impulses carried out against the original inhabitants of the land.

Or so we thought. Something closer to the truth became general knowledge in 2018–2019 with reports of a series of disappearances of women across Indian Country dating back more than a decade. A great many of the cases have not been solved. It turns out that Native women are, depending on location, up to ten times more likely than the overall population to be victims of murder. As with the Osage murders, the current situation is a stain on the character of America; that this should happen in such numbers is appalling. Yet happen it does. Was David Grann prescient when he chose his subject? Did he understand the extent to which the problem of violence against Native people, women especially, has never really left? Probably not, but his work shines a light on one of the darkest aspects of life in America, one that has been with us since colonialization and shows too few signs of abating. What he did discover was that the killings went on long after the supposed perpetrators had been identified. Many Osage died while under government-ordered guardianship; some "guardians" had client deaths of 100 percent. The resulting windfalls made some of those men quite wealthy, and most went unpunished.

For those of us who would embrace the ideal of social progress, such stories are repulsive. This is not why we read nonfiction, to find out that things have not improved, that crises continue or reemerge periodically, that the two founding crimes of America—slavery and genocide—continue to stain the national soul. But it may be why we need to.

Ultimately, biography and history are merely tools available to writers and the reading public, and like most tools, they have no innate morality. Writers have to supply that, if it is to exist, just as readers must approve or disapprove of the result. A great many lives of great leaders and major historical events, especially those works closest in time to their subjects, have been written in something like bad faith, glorifying and lionizing war criminals as heroes, painting unjust incursions as acts directed by Divine Providence. Nowhere has this been more true than in dealing with our twin Original Sins, slavery and the treatment of Native Americans. We may wish to believe, with Martin Luther King Jr. (and before him, the abolitionist minister Theodore Parker) that "the arc of the moral universe is long, but it bends toward justice," but it will not bend thusly without some work from those who seek justice. Among that number are invariably writers. I said earlier in the chapter that the key element in these works is time. In this case, time allows later writers to look at the falsehoods often present in first-generation biographies and histories and to offer correctives, as with Dee Brown's *Bury My Heart at Wounded Knee: An Indian History of the American West* (1970), a history of westward expansionism from a Native American viewpoint, and Vine Deloria Jr.'s *Custer Died for Your Sins: An Indian Manifesto* (1969). Yet what can be gained can also be lost, and recent times have proved that a society is capable of backsliding along that moral arc. There will always be writers and readers eager to return to some earlier, personally advantageous status quo. Readers interested in a more perfect union, then, must recognize those retrograde efforts for what they are, a drag against the movement of history. As former Attorney General Eric Holder said of Dr. King's maxim, that arc only bends toward justice with a little pulling from us.

13

On the Stump

Reading Political Writing

POLITICAL WRITING HAS A long and not inevitably glorious history. Oh, there are high points. Niccolo Macchiavelli's *The Prince* (1532) is a treatise on the exercise of power in societies where that power resides in a single set of hands. That's back there a ways in the history of political philosophy, which stretches in the west from Plato (*The Republic*) and Aristotle (*On Politics*) to Thomas Hobbes (*Leviathan*) and John Locke (*Two Treatises of Government*) to Alexander Hamilton, James Madison, and John Jay (*The Federalist Papers*), Karl Marx and Friedrich Engels (*The Communist Manifesto*), but we can only take so much of that. A great deal of political writing is soggy analysis of this or that aspect of the current state of governance in whatever locale, and that proves even less bearable. Even a cursory summary of the history of political writing would take up volumes and in any case be quite beyond my poor powers. Neither of us wants that.

Instead, let's look at a fairly recent phenomenon in political writing, the examination of a current president. Such writing has gone on for a long, long time, of course, but there was an explosion of it after the 2016 election victory of Donald Trump. Nearly everything about that election and the subsequent administration has been unusual—extreme reactions by adherents and opponents, transgressive behavior by the chief executive, cabinet appointments from beyond the pale, rejection of longtime allies and embrace of totalitarian thugs, simply everything—and the avalanche of political tomes is no exception. Whether this presidency proves to be transformational or a curious blind alley, it will be abundantly documented. The commentariat made a huge number of pronouncements about the likelihood of a Trump victory; the commentariat was largely mistaken. I heard David Brooks declare on multiple occasions that Trump was simply "not a serious person" and that voters would see through him in either the Republican primaries or the general election. Whatever one may think of Mr. Brooks's premise, his conclusions were clearly in error, even allowing a bit of latitude for Trump's loss in the popular vote totals. Since then, a number of books have come out that examine some aspect of that election season or his administration. Among the latter, there are kiss-and-tells, minus the kissing, from campaign or White House insiders, the most explosive of which was Omarosa Manigault Newman's *Unhinged: An Insider's Account of the Trump White House* (2018), which, among other charges, claimed that Trump repeatedly used racist language on the set of his reality show *The Apprentice* and that a presidential daughter-in-law had tried to buy Omarosa's (she uses her first name mononymously) silence with a promise of a senior position in the 2020 campaign. Given the record rate of turnover in the administration, there is little likelihood of any slackening in the pace of tell-all books from former officials.

There is another sort of book, however, that at least promises a bit more objectivity: the outsider exposé. Those books typically fall into three types: celebrity reporting, direct observation, and investigative journalism. In Trump's case, 2018 brought all three. The year began with a bang when Michael Wolff's *Fire and Fury: Inside the Trump White House* started bookstore stampedes on just the fifth day of the year. It was followed a few months later by former FBI director James Comey's *A Higher Loyalty: Truth, Lies, and Leadership*, followed late in the year by Bob Woodward's *Fear: Trump in the White House*. Wolff had heretofore been known chiefly as a celebrity portraitist. Comey was an unwilling first-time author forced by circumstance to defend his reputation. And Woodward, of course, possibly the most respected investigative journalist in the country, had helped bring down a corrupt president when he was the first name of "and Bernstein." Only one man, it seemed, could bring these authors together on a common subject.

Fire and Fury and Outrage

QUICK: WHAT WAS THE most incendiary book of 2018? Its title answers that question: *Fire and Fury* by Michael Wolff. It generated plenty of both on the Right and the Left as well as straight down the middle. Only the most politically disengaged reader could have no opinion. My description of that personage is probably a contradiction in terms, since someone that disengaged would be unlikely to read the book. Wolff, a career celebrity journalist, saw an opportunity to cover the first several months of a White House under a celebrity president. Granted a surprising level of access by someone in the West Wing (the likeliest party seems to have been then White House chief strategist Steve Bannon), Wolff camped out in the West Wing and enticed its denizens to talk to him. And boy, did they talk. His subtitle is *Inside the Trump White House*, but it could just as well have been called *Loose Lips Sink Ships of State*. The result—full of self-justifications, backbiting, gossip, envy, and dubious grasps on reality—is like *Peyton Place*, only a lot less sexy. The question from day one was whether it also resembles Grace Metalious's novel in another respect: how much of it is fiction.

The book launched with its own version of firestorm and fury in tow as commentators weighed in on all sides. President Trump himself characterized the book as fiction and its author as a fraud. Annalisa Quinn of National Public Radio, in reviewing the book, concluded, "Much of the narrative is not substantively different from information found in other reporting on the president. But many other reporters have been restrained and careful where Wolff is shameless." Indeed, numerous commentators acknowledged that a preponderance of information in the book—on personalities, motivations, in-fighting, actions—had already been confirmed by other, more sober sources. Michael D'Antonio, himself author of the 2015 exposé *Never Enough: Donald Trump and the Pursuit of Success*, lists the many things that Wolff claims that people familiar with Trump and his White House already knew to be true, those that ring true but that Wolff fails to cite his sources sufficiently to be entirely credible, and those like late-night goings-on when the author was not present as instances of free-floating claims whose veracity is impossible to know. Since D'Antonio's book was credited for being accurate and well sourced by the *Financial Times*, among others, his judgments on unsourced material must be afforded some weight.

In their regular Friday afternoon roundtable on NPR, David Brooks and E. J. Dionne agreed—somewhat—that the book contains a good bit of truth. Dionne, the liberal side of this mild-mannered point-counterpoint discussion, focused on the big picture, that the portrait of dysfunctional life in the West Wing as painted by Wolff follows the contours of many other reports on the same scene. Brooks, the traditional conservative foil, cited the direct quotes and the widening rift between Trump and Steve Bannon as things he thought most likely true. He then went on to cite the book's shady methods as a major problem not only for readers but for mainstream journalists, whose public relations situation was already precarious: "I worry about us becoming even more delegitimized by simply baying to this guy." That *Fire and Fury* will become an instance of Gresham's Law, that bad journalistic money will drive out the good by tainting all of it, has been addressed elsewhere but rarely with the vehemence and clarity that Brooks has brought to the idea here and in his columns.

Fox News was rather less restrained. On *The Five* on January 5, 2018, Dana Perino, Geraldo Rivera, and Jesse Watters fell all over themselves to discredit claims from the book while using fact-free opinions and debatable assertions of their own. At one point, they agreed that First Daughter Ivanka could not have said that her father was not smart because daughters simply wouldn't say that of fathers. But of course daughters—and sons—would and do say a great many things about parents. Rivera led the charge on another front, that Wolff interviewed the president for only three hours total over nine months. His fellow roundtablers quickly followed suit, insisting that if he talked so little to the subject of the book, then it must be fiction. But Trump himself is not the subject of his book, his snarling visage on the cover notwithstanding. Rather, *Fire and Fury* is about the Trump White House, in particular, the way that a host of people with strong views saw their boss and one another in ways entirely suited to their needs rather than those more nearly corresponding to objective reality. In this regard, the administration is not unlike others, where competing interests and personal loyalties and antipathies always play a role in how the place functions. Or doesn't. The chief difference here is that we had not a No-Drama Obama who sought to smooth ruffled feathers but a chief executive famous for setting cats among the pigeons whether in his private business operations or his reality television shows.

Sean Hannity found plenty to dislike on his eponymous nighttime show, but nothing galled him like the claim (a single line late in the book) that he had supplied questions ahead of his Harrisburg, Pennsylvania, interview with Trump, loosely citing something like journalistic ethics. He would seem in a position to know whether he supplied those disputed questions. On the other hand, Hannity's oft-strained relations with truth serve him poorly in refuting a charge merely on the basis of his word. Moreover, his long-standing claim that he is an entertainer, a talker, and not a journalist makes falling back on journalistic ethics less than convincing. The fact of the matter is that, absent a recording of some verifiable statement from an administration insider or Hannity himself, we cannot know with any certainty whether the questions found their way into the president's hands or not. What seems most likely is that Wolff *heard* that from some unnamed source with an ax to grind against either Hannity or Trump, then reported that claim, without any second sourcing or fact-checking, in his typical, omniscient, I-just-know narration as one last juicy tidbit on the way to The End.

So here's the question on that matter: does it matter? In the grand scheme of things in general or the grandiose scheme of the book, does a single line, almost a throwaway line, carry that much weight? On one level, not very much. Whatever Mr. Hannity may think of the accusation, his legion of followers won't care, and his equally large coalition of detractors could hardly think less of him. Such is the life of a communications lightning rod. Nor does the statement invalidate the book as a whole. Whatever validity the book possesses or lacks for readers is long since established by page 309. But the claim matters very much as exemplar: just as readers wonder whether the statement is true and based on a reliable source or a bogus invention of an audience-hungry writer, so, too, will they wonder about the book as a whole. For there is no attribution to a source here, no attested documentation, not even any hint that there might be a source or a sliver of evidence, only an assertion that it is true because it is written. Huge patches of the book follow that same pattern. That cannot be enough for discerning readers. Such behavior is why David Brooks says that the quotes and events recorded by other, more reputable, outlets are the only thing he feels good about trusting as real.

What Brooks is getting at is that there are legitimate reasons to doubt Wolff's information. Yes, much of the harshest criticisms came from Trump partisans, some of whom like Hannity have attacked every negative story about Trump, even those with witnesses in the millions, since he began his campaign for office. Those criticisms, moreover, often strain credulity in their own right. But there are sober, serious people (Brooks's favorite kind—and mine, truth be told) who find much to dislike about Wolff's breathless, often under-sourced scandalmongering, even as they recognize that much of what he relates has been corroborated by other, better reporting. In which case, we are far better off consulting those other sources.

So what about ordinary people? What do we think about this book? Here's what *Fire and Fury* comes down to: a Rorschach test whose appearance is determined not by the subject but by the eyes that each observer brings to it. All one has to do is read the comment stream on any website, blog, Facebook, or Twitter post with the slightest political tinge to see that, not only are we in disagreement with one another, we seem to be living in separate realities governed not by fact but by tribe. And that is especially true where the content has anything to do with this president or the candidate he defeated. It seems that no one can be convinced of anything except what they already believe they know. Or know they believe.

And that is simply wrong. We can do better. We can be better. We need to be better.

How did we reach this sorry state of affairs? There are several lines of inquiry that we can develop a bit later. For now, I would suggest two items for your delectation. The first is the Great Leveling of Information brought on by the internet. You may remember the tagline for *Alien*, "In space, no one can hear you scream." The modern-day equivalent, also describing a horror film, is, "In cyberspace, no one can hear you lie."

What sorts of problems does Wolff's book present readers? The big one is the absence of attribution; in other words, how on earth did the author acquire the knowledge he claims to possess?

This example is but one of many. Speaking of Jared Kushner's attempt to make his first administrative success by bringing his father-in-law and Enrique Peña Nieto together for a meeting despite all of Trump's bashing of the Mexican president during and after the campaign, Wolff asserts, "Kushner called up the ninety-three-year-old [Henry] Kissinger for advice. This was both to flatter the old man and to be able to name drop, but it was actually also for real advice. [. . .] It was what Kushner believed he should be doing: quietly following behind the president and with added nuance and subtlety clarifying the president's intentions, if not recasting them entirely." Really? "Kushner *believed*"? "To be able to name drop"? By my count, there is precisely one person in the world equipped to tell us what Jared Kushner believes as anything other than speculation. And that person is unlikely to share that information. If he had confided anything to that effect, moreover, why would the author not trumpet that fact? Because he does not claim that Kushner or any other person described the motivations behind the action, a reasonable person can only conclude that (a) he invented an explanation for Kushner's reaching out to Dr. Kissinger beyond wishing to consult a famous diplomat with massive experience in foreign affairs or (b) he accepted without analysis a tale told to him by some second party who may or may not know anything about Kushner's state of mind and, given what Wolff claims about White House personalities throughout the book, who as likely as not has something other than the presidential son-in-law's best interests at heart.

Does it mean that the anecdote is false? Not inevitably. It could be true, unlikely as that seems. But we absolutely can't accept it as factual or true. Instead, we must treat it the way we would gossip—warily.

And here's the problem with this omniscient approach: it reads like fiction and might just be. When those magnificent all-seeing and all-knowing narrators of Charles Dickens or Gabriel García Marquez swoop in on an unsuspecting character to reveal his most secret thoughts, the ones he keeps buried deep in his heart, they can do that because they stand in relation to the story as God to his creation; no moat around the heart, no citadel around the mind is proof against their predations. We accept their revelations as truths because they are acting at the behest of their authors, whose stories they tell. Fictional truth is entirely an internal matter. But a writer of nonfiction is not a novelist. Truth is not his to decide. Rather than merely assert, he must adduce evidence to convince us of the veracity of his claims. That evidence can be physical—anything from an email to a literal smoking gun—or reliable testimony. What is reliable in this case? A witness in a position to know. First-person witnesses are simultaneously the most reliable and the least. Most reliable because they were present. If they performed an action, they not only know where and when and how but also, assuming they care to say, what they were thinking at the time. And least? For the reason that we have laws against lying to police and perjury. But also because in the heat of the moment a direct participant may not have the clearest experience of that moment.

Wolff puts us on alert in his author's note, which reminds us why we must always pay attention to openings. He says that the book is based on conversations with not only the president but also his aides and *the people they spoke with*. In other words, before we know anything else, we know (or have the opportunity to know) that much of what comes thereafter will be based on secondhand—at best—reports of incidents and conversations. This, I believe, is one reason for the lack of attribution in many cases. To say that he learned something from Bannon or Kushner is one thing; to say that the information came not from either of those gentlemen nor from someone they told but from someone to whom they in turn related the tale is quite another. A story, in other words, of a story of a story. That's pretty far out toward the rim of the administrative solar system. Who would want to parade sources in such a case? At the end of the author's note, he attempts to ameliorate the damage of non-attribution by intimating that *everyone, simply everyone* talked to him at length:

> For whatever reason, almost everyone I contacted—senior members of the White House staff as well as dedicated observers of it—shared large amounts of time with me and went to great effort to help shed light on the unique nature of life in the Trump White House. In the end, what I witnessed, and what this book is about, is a group of people who have struggled, each in their own way, to come to terms with the meaning of working for Donald Trump.

Clearly, what he wishes us to understand about his effort is that it is neither a biography nor an exposé of the man himself but a sort of group portrait, a dysfunctional family photo. His sources would seem, if we take him at his word, to include other journalists, although it is hard to fathom any journalist worth his or her salt giving away any tidbit of the sort that so much of this book rests on. The one exception that makes sense is if that tidbit were so scurrilous as to risk not merely a suit for but a judgment of libel. And such items abound in the book.

Later, Trump and his apologists would attack Wolff for basing his book on a mere three hours of talk with the president himself. But a discussion of what Donald Trump thinks is the last thing the work presumes to be; rather, it is, overtly, about Trump as prism, the way that the light he deflects shines differently on different people, often because of the biases and needs they bring to their viewing.

It seems to be the fate of everyone who touches this book that they must pronounce judgment upon it and its several subjects. If that is true, here is mine: *a plague on all their houses*. Also condos, penthouses, golf resorts, and garden sheds. It is hard to envisage how one could bring together a more odious group of sycophants, leakers, back-biters and front-stabbers, gossips, incompetents, would-be messiahs, self-aggrandizers, and graspers after personal gain. And that includes the president of the United States.

And his ersatz Boswell. Under no circumstances is Wolff in the clear. He comes across as sleazy, disingenuous, smug, and more than a little cavalier with the truth. His greatest crime is not some mischaracterization of the chief executive or the functioning or malfunctioning of his administration but the disrepute into which he drags legitimate journalists. Because the truth is that he is not a journalist but a celebrity gossip. And the book is not journalism, political analysis, or current events reporting. To qualify as any of those latter things, there would have to be some evidence that the author had consulted any written work on the subject of the presidency, or on public policy, that he had talked with any reputable journalist who could independently confirm some of his dodgier claims, that he ever entertained a doubt about what his cadre of West Wing infighters tattled to him about their associates. Those things he breezily declines to do. It is much more fun to retail character assassinations than to track down their accuracy. He is a one-man instance of Gresham's Law, that bad money drives out good money, or in this case, bad-faith journalism (or journalism-like object) drives out faith in good journalism. There are entire organizations dedicated not to being believed but to casting doubt on the very enterprise—news gathering and dissemination—that they seem to be engaged in, the goal being, evidently, to discredit all writing, all broadcast journalism, all opinion writing, to drag everyone and everything involved in the profession down into the same muck. To his credit, Wolff manages to accomplish this feat without half trying.

But his ignoring of convention and standards of diligence doesn't mean that his information is wrong. Or right. Only un-trustworthy. The author's stock-in-trade is the seamless narrative, part of what makes the celebrity profile so appealing to readers. In this case, however, the urge toward seamlessness, toward a glib, smooth surface, drives him away from verifiability. How dull it is to break the illusion of knowing all with trivialities like who actually said what, and in what context! Readers are accustomed to narrative unreliability, the notion that the story's foundation can't be trusted. In fiction. Nearly the only reason to employ a first-person narrator in a novel or short story is so that he or she can hide, distort, skip over, or misconstrue essential facts. This can be accomplished through deliberate action (think *Lolita* or *A Clockwork Orange*, where the narrators have plenty of reason to be less than forthright) or misunderstanding (as with nearly every child narrator). We not only give authors a pass for such diddling of the truth; we celebrate them for it. We should not countenance the same tomfoolery, the same unreliability, in nonfiction, where the facts just might matter.

But here's something else to consider: if Wolff were making this up, why wouldn't he come up with something we haven't already heard? As a great many commentators with better knowledge than I have declared, there is almost nothing in the book that we did not already know, had not already heard, could not already intuit about this White House. Yes, there is some colorful slagging off, mostly by Steve Bannon, of colleagues and bosses, but hardly a new revelation about anything of substance in the bunch. Readers who are paying attention must wonder whether this proves that his stories are therefore approximately true or that the existing cultural narrative of a White House in disarray provided good cover for salacious gossip of dubious provenance. Whatever the conclusion, the Trump administration is neither exonerated nor further damned by his tepid tattling. Whatever one's views on Wolff or his work, the book offers itself as an object lesson on what journalism should avoid if it is to be trustworthy:

- excessive or exclusive use of hearsay as evidence (secondary and secondhand sources are not the same)
- omniscient narration (the journalist has not been born who can see into the minds of others)
- lack of appropriate attribution of sources (someone, somewhere, sometime must appear as an actual source)

Wolff is a triple threat in the bad journalist game.

Loyalties High and Low

NOT INFREQUENTLY, POLITICAL WRITING takes the form of memoir. It has become *de rigueur* by this point, for instance, for potential presidential candidates to author some very personal book whose real purpose is to serve as a campaign advertisement that lays out claims of serious intent and equally serious merit. The great hazard for devoted readers of these tomes (chiefly limited to reporters condemned to follow the campaign trail) is that the overdose of earnestness sparks a violent lurch in the direction of cynicism. Equal and opposite reactions occur in politics as much as physics. And as failed candidacies litter the campaign landscape, so do presidential-hopeful memoirs burden remainder tables from one end of this great land to the other.

Occasionally, however, a different sort of memoir grows out of the soil of electioneering: the bystander chronicle. I don't mean the sort of participatory journalism that descends from Hunter S. Thompson's *Fear and Loathing on the Campaign Trail* but rather the work of those who, willingly or otherwise, find themselves in the candidates' comet tails. In the "otherwise" category, we could include former FBI director James Comey, who found himself at the center of the maelstrom while dealing with the issue of Hillary Clinton's private email servers in summer and fall 2016 and again, related to President Donald Trump's response to the investigation into alleged Russian interference in the election, during the following winter. Even as director of the FBI, he could hardly have foreseen, as the Times Square ball dropped the curtain on 2015, the scope of the controversies coming his way (and partly precipitated by him) in the following fifteen months.

His turbulent extended year concluded with his firing by Trump on May 9, 2017, for reasons he has variously offered as Comey's "unfair" handling of the Clinton email affair (which explanation strains credulity given Trump's own lock-her-up, "Crooked Hillary" rhetoric on the campaign trail and even long after the inauguration), a lack of personal loyalty, and a desire to eliminate the pressure of the Russia investigation. The *Washington Post* reported the day after the firing that Trump was angry that Comey refused to support his claim that the Obama administration had wiretapped the phones of the Trump campaign, a claim that has been debunked by FBI documents but that Trump continued to peddle more than a year later. Comey then testified before the Senate Intelligence Committee on June 8, during which he described the strangely personal nature of his meetings with the new president, who asked for loyalty and said that he hoped that Comey could "let the [former general Michael] Flynn investigation go." In testimony, he asserted that neither of the other two presidents he served had ever made requests of that sort. The Senate hearing appeared to conclude the Comey saga, until news of a book deal reached the public.

That book, *A Higher Loyalty: Truth, Lies, and Leadership*, became the second blockbuster on the new administration, after Wolff's *Fire and Fury* earlier in the year. Unlike that previous book, however, Comey's was a memoir as well as a reflection on recent events; it was his *Apologia Pro Vita Sua*, his justification for his life, the life that led up to and carried him through his own year of living dangerously.

Reaction to the book was swift—indeed so swift in some cases as to predate the first day of sales or even the release of review copies. The Republican National Committee started a website with the sole aim to discredit Comey, and for good measure created two attack ads assailing his credibility and honor, calling him a "leaker" and—*quelle horreur!*—a "Washington insider." RNC chair Ronna Romney McDaniel said that "when you read it, Comey discredits himself," which pronouncement she managed without having undertaken the decisive act of reading it. Democrats were hardly more satisfied, having inveighed against the author for months over his handling of the Clinton email affair, particularly his erroneous announcement less than two weeks before the election that another large cache had been found on disgraced congressman Anthony Weiner's laptop. In time, the truth would be revealed that the emails were virtually all copies that Weiner's then wife and top Clinton aide, Huma Abedin, had downloaded from her work computer. The key phrase here, however, is "in time," for by the time the truth came out, the damage was complete. While Clinton won the popular vote for president, she lost the electoral college by less than the margin of three swing states, Michigan, Pennsylvania, and Wisconsin, that a fortnight before the election had polled as solidly, if narrowly, in her column. The margin in each of those states was in turn minuscule, as tiny as 0.3 percent (13,080 votes) in Michigan. Was Comey's "revelation" of newly discovered emails the deciding factor? One can never know, but the turn in polling was virtually instantaneous from that fateful afternoon. Given the election outcome, Dems were unlikely to forgive and forget, however much they liked what he had to tell America about its new president.

What a dispassionate observer, should such a mythical beast exist, would have witnessed was a universal rush to judgment of the book based on *a priori* opinions about the man and his conduct as FBI director. Those negative opinions proved no impediment to sales, which topped 600,000 in all formats for the first week after the drop date (April 17, 2018), eclipsing both Clinton's *What Happened* (300,000) and Wolff's *Fire and Fury* (200,000). All three books continued to appear on the bestseller lists for months after release.

Nothing in this, not sales or attacks *ad hominem* or praise or partisans choosing sides, tells us anything about the book. For that, there is only one remedy. In the case of a book upon which everyone has a definite point of view and where so many people have axes to grind that one wonders if we might run out of grindstones, we cannot really trust to any single review or analysis. We have to read the book ourselves.

So, how is it?

Patience. See prior paragraph. Since my thinking may be as colored as anyone else's, I won't tell you what to believe about the book, nor what to believe in it. I can make a couple of general statements, after which there are a few recommendations I would suggest for *how* to read it, details to watch for in order to establish its trustworthiness. First of all, the style is . . . stolid. Workmanlike. As a prose stylist, Comey is no Cardinal Newman. There is nothing one could describe as "soaring" or "regal" or even "elegant" here, words which have often been attached to Newman's writing. On the other hand, the language is clean and suited to its purpose. Most of all, the prose reminds us that its author is an attorney, accustomed to direct, accessible modes of address. One does not wish, after all, to leave a jury to tease out a tricky metaphor. There are lawyers, of course, who give themselves over to wild flights of rhetoric, as the late Johnny Cochran, he of the O. J. Simpson defense team, was wont to do, but such persons are rarely career prosecutors. Mystification favors the defense, whichever side introduces it into the proceedings. That lawyerly manner leads us to a second point: Comey builds his case meticulously, brick by argumentative brick, until he has a wall to be proud of. He is workmanlike also in the matter of construction at the larger scale than individual words and sentences. He crafts his story at any given point so that there are not holes an opponent can pick apart, nor crevices into which the unwary may fall. His writing may be unflashy, but it gives no cause for complaint. Indeed, as Michiko Kakutani noted in her *New York Times* review, his pacing of the stories is commendable.

Comey takes great care in attribution of sources. Wherever he can name the speaker in a situation, he does so. He is scrupulous in all the ways that Wolff is slipshod. This is the major reason that Wolff's book is breezy where Comey's may at times plod. Facts carry weight.

Curiously in a book so consumed with logical process, Comey's logic falls into disarray in discussing the two decisions he and his colleagues made during the fall of 2016. Those two major decisions involved revealing the early stages of the Russian interference investigation, including involvement of at least one staffer for Donald Trump, which would have proved damaging to the Trump campaign, and revealing the Weiner/Abedin/Clinton laptop-email discovery. For the first, Comey ultimately decided that revealing the Russia investigation in full would afford Trump, almost certain to lose anyway, with a basis for complaint that the forces of the State were arrayed against him. Since Trump had for months been complaining the system was "rigged," whatever he meant by that, he certainly would have seized on any rationale that salved his ego. For the second, Comey ultimately decided to go forward with revelation, reasoning that concealment (his word) would taint the newly inaugurated President Clinton with a whiff—and maybe more than a whiff—of scandal, something with which her history was not unacquainted. True, others had input on these issues, including his own investigative teams at the FBI and the Obama White House, including the president himself. Even so, Comey presents himself as oddly passive in the first case, more dynamically involved with the second. What careful observers will note is that in each case the decisions redounded to the benefit of the Trump campaign. This combination had Democrats howling with outrage first when he made the Clinton email statement eleven days before the election and again when, during his Senate hearing, he revealed the decision-making process regarding the Russia investigation. Did those decisions swing the presidential election? We can never know, since there is no way to play out the election without those decisions. Democrats have their conclusions, Republicans their own.

But our conclusion needs to be about the book and not the original actions. As readers, we owe it to writers to observe their standards for the narrative or argument they pursue. It is unreasonable and unproductive to take Ernest Hemingway to task, for instance, for not being William Faulkner. As Ezra Pound suggested, the first two (of three) criteria for the critic are what was the author trying to do, and did she succeed in doing it? In Comey's case, what he is attempting to do is pretty obvious. On that second point, however, things are less straightforward. Readers must decide whether his *narrative* procedure violates his customary practice in the book. And this decision is no small point. His portrayal of these events is the heart of the book. Indeed, it is the reason the book exists. The argument runs something like this: everything in my life, all the choices I made, the lessons I learned, the past cases I participated in—all of what I have been telling you about—led to this moment, this choice, or these choices, in a crisis. Beyond that, it led to the way I am portraying those choices. Pretty big stakes here.

And he funks it.

I don't mean the decision itself. Like almost everyone, I have my opinions of all those events; like many, mine have shifted a bit with additional information, although the baseline has remained the same. You will have yours, too, if you know anything about said events. No, what I mean is that he funks it rhetorically. In a narrative that has thus far been fairly muscular about his role in decision making, he suddenly turns quite passive. On his announcement that no further action was called for and no charges were being recommended about the original Clinton email investigation, he says he took the highly unusual step of making a formal announcement by declaring that "the American people needed and deserved transparency." That is probably true, as far as it goes. It does not, however, explain his word choice in calling her use of a private, unsecured server "extremely reckless," which as he goes on to note prompted the right-wing commentariat to take it as a euphemism for "grossly negligent," something that in the world of national security law actually is a crime, although only one person has ever been prosecuted under the statute and that person was not convicted. "Reckless" would have worked, *sans* adverb, if he felt he must address that aspect of the case. In looking back, he says that he regrets the phrase but does so in language suggesting that he couldn't foresee its effect, which would make him the only sentient being in North America who failed to do so. Virtually everyone who heard his statement gasped, half of them with delight at the political hay to be made, the other half in horror at the hay that was going to be made by the first half. The rhetorical strategy to give himself a pass for not seeing what should have been plain to see simply doesn't wash. Comey has been smarter than that throughout the book, making this look like special pleading for a really bad decision.

When he moves on to the Russian interference story, he employs a different strategy: shift the blame. The FBI knew in the summer of 2016 that the Russians were involved on several fronts in a scheme to shift public opinion from Hillary Clinton to Donald Trump. It also knew, moreover, that at least one Trump campaign staffer, George Papadopoulos, had been in contact with Russian operatives. And indeed, the FBI did what it should and alerted the American people, albeit in a vague, general way, to that attempted interference. In February 2017. Why the delay? Because, Comey says, the Bureau was concerned that revealing it during the campaign would undermine its credibility as an honest broker if one side or the other felt its fortunes harmed. Moreover, when he discussed this with the Obama White House, the president and his staff worried that it would look as if they were trying to affect the outcome of the election. This sentiment was expressed in a conversation about how alerting the public might "inoculate" them against the Russian perfidy. He does not say who suggested such a political vaccination of the body politic, only that "we discussed" it, which tells us it wasn't him. He does mention that he introduced the thought that such an inoculation might backfire, quickly adding that Obama himself seized upon it as a problem. Ultimately, more than a month passed before the administration decided to write a document telling the American people about the matter, by which time it was widely bruited

about in the press. Comey, along with his team, decided that add-
ing their signatures was unnecessary.

Finally, in late October, he dropped the bombshell about the
Weiner/Abedin laptop containing a trove of emails. Then, a mere
two days before the election, he issued an exculpatory statement
that, again, no criminal activity had taken place. So why had the
Bureau Clinton team (code-named, for no clear reason, "Mid-
year") not read the emails to establish that they were not mere
copies of things already seen (as the vast majority turned out to
be)? Because, Comey says, there were too many of them to read
before the election. So why not read, say, a hundred, and if noth-
ing seemed amiss, another hundred and another? If all seemed
well, the Midyear team could proceed at leisure and a statement
could be issued in the fullness of time. Why rush to reveal? For
two reasons, it would seem. First, he was concerned that if word
got out later that the FBI knew something and didn't say so, there
would be hell to pay from Republicans. And second, because he
made a rhetorical blunder in real life. The two choices—two
doors, as in Frank Stockton's "The Lady, or the Tiger?"—he la-
beled as "Speak" and "Conceal," a classic false dichotomy. Those
two words are not antonyms. Concealment is not the only alter-
native to speaking; it contains a value judgment that is lacking
in the first term. It colors the decision to keep silent for a little
while with dishonesty where that is not an inevitable conclusion.
Suppose we replaced his terms with "Act Hastily" or "Jump to
Conclusions" and "Hold Fast and Work in Silence." The conclu-
sion he reached then seems less inescapable. His choice of "Con-
ceal" as the second term appears to have been dictated by the
assumed complaint that would come his way.

So then, here's the problem with this tangle of decisions, or rather, with his presentation of them: in placing the impetus else-where for decisions, he avoids the bulk of the responsibility and immunizes himself, to coin a phrase, against charges of "hav-ing his thumb on the scale" of the election, as he at one point describes the perception he wants to avoid. Consider his choice to issue a statement about the Clinton emails even though there was a finding of no criminality. The reason: anger from the po-litical Right. And the decision not to announce a problem with Russian interference, and a likely finding of criminality by Pap-adopoulos (who ultimately pleaded guilty): anger by the Right. The announcement about the Weiner laptop? Republican anger. Nor does he ever address what seems the most telling instance of a failure of leadership: tasking the Obama administration with deciding a course of action on the Russia investigation. He had no difficulty bypassing the president in the two Hillary matters, but in seeking Obama's views on the Russia matter, he had to have known, at some level, the untenable situation he inflicted on the president: once Obama knew of the investigation, there was no way for him to go public without infuriating the Right. In a book that is so often self-reflective and even self-critical, these two chapters (ten: Roadkill, and eleven: Speak or Conceal) demonstrate a serious lapse of the level of introspection he has taught us to expect. I find a great deal to admire about the book, and about its author, but this failure at the most critical juncture of the book is a disappointment.

Comey has turned out to be a trailblazer in the lawman-removed-from-office-memoir subgenre. Both former US attorney for the Southern District of New York Preet Bharara (*Doing Jus-tice: A Prosecutor's Thoughts on Crime, Punishment, and the Rule of Law*) and former acting director of the Federal Bureau of Investigation Andrew McCabe (*The Threat: How the FBI Protects America in the Age of Terror and Trump*) published books in early 2019 following firings that seemed designed to demean (in the case of McCabe, twenty-six hours before he became eligible for retirement). Given the rate of dismissals in the Department of Justice and the virulence of Trump's rhetoric about it, they are unlikely to be the last of their breed.

Oh, yeah—remember Pound's third criterion? Was it worth doing? Your results may vary.

Real Power Is *Fear*

WHATEVER ELSE THE TRUMP administration may prove to be in time, it has been a godsend for the publishing industry. From the first moments after the inauguration—indeed, from the day after the election—oceans of ink have spilled across mountains of paper. Part of this is the nature of Donald Trump's interaction with the world: he is so omnipresent in the media he supposedly despises that he alone provides an inexhaustible supply of quotes, misstatements, policy proposals and reversals, personal attacks, and outright falsehoods. From long before his Twitter über-celebrity status, even from long before he starred on *The Apprentice*, he carved out a role for himself as an outspoken, outsized personality always ready with a statement for the press. Even when not requested. The trove of information on the president-elect was a sort of preexisting condition.

And then there was the team he assembled and constantly reassembled throughout his campaign and transition and first years in the White House. A group of greater self-aggrandizers would be difficult to amass if one tried. His key man during the latter campaign season and through the transition was Steve Bannon, whose sense of his value to the republic was out of all proportion to anything he had ever actually accomplished. When your highest station is executive chairman of Breitbart News, the far-right news-aggregator website that traffics in wild conspiracy theories and deliberate misinformation, you can scarcely claim to be at the center of American cultural life. Once in the White House, he was notorious for picking battles with very nearly everyone, including Ivanka Trump and Jared Kushner, which may have sealed his ultimate exile. Bannon, however, was only the most notable instance of the backbiting one-upmanship running throughout the West Wing. According to many commentators, another thing about this crowd was that they really, really liked to talk about themselves and air their grievances against one another. As a result, this administration became known as the leakiest in living memory. Every administration has a few people who like the idea of being insiders and who prove their *bona fides* by talking out of school. This one seemed to be a full-time race to find a reporter to talk to, often in an effort to make their rivals look bad. And when fired or forced to resign, as so many were, wagging tongues went into overdrive. A number of White House functionaries, like former *Apprentice* contestant Omarosa Manigault Newman, were barely over the threshold before books appeared under their names. (She was dismissed from her duties on January 20, 2018 after exactly one year, and her book came out on August 14.) When Michael Wolff's *Fire and Fury* first came out, one of the criticisms was that no one could have found so many persons so willing to speak with him. By the time 2018 had ended, though, the only real question was if there had been anyone who didn't seek him out.

Another beneficiary of the loose-lips brigade was Bob Woodward, whose *Fear: Trump in the White House* provided the year-end closing bracket to Wolff's opener. Woodward is legendary for getting unwilling witnesses to history to speak with him, a trait that has marked him since his early pairing with Carl Bernstein during the Nixon downfall. This time out, he must have been astonished at how easy his job had become over the years. Like Wolff, he declines to mention the names of his sources, but his record-keeping is as fabled as his interviewing skills, and he has, in case sources accuse him of inventing their contributions, notes and recordings of virtually all his interviews. Besides, decades of rock-solid reporting have earned him some leeway unavailable to the more celebrity-driven, gossipy Wolff. In a prefatory Note to Readers, he is clearer about his sources than Wolff. Interviews were conducted on deep background, meaning that he could quote but not identify whom he was quoting. He does say that the speakers were either "first-hand participants" or "witnesses" to the events and conversations described, and since Trump declined to be interviewed, that narrows the field a good deal. Often, there were only two people in the room. He also states that he had access to "meeting notes, personal diaries, files and government or personal documents" as sources for "exact quotations." As ever, he understands that working in such a fraught environment, the reporter needs to be extremely scrupulous about sources and materials.

Sometimes, the story may have come from any of several persons present at a meeting. Other times, we need not wonder. Trump dismissed his chief of staff Reince Priebus on July 28,

2017, in truly Trumpian fashion. On a plane ride back from Long Island, Priebus and the president talked in the private cabin on Air Force One. Priebus had already submitted his resignation, but he was hoping to leave with a bit of dignity intact. Trump had agreed that they would find the right time to make the announcement, possibly later in the weekend, as his chief of staff had suggested, and gave him a big hug, telling him, "You're the man." Before Priebus could drive away from the tarmac after landing, he received a notification of the tweet announcing that General John Kelly, heretofore the secretary of the Department of Homeland Security, was the new chief of staff. Trump neglected to mention that he had not yet offered Kelly the job. Now, there are only two people in the world who could relate that story; one of them is most unlikely to portray himself as that callous. A few pages later, Woodward offers this rumination from the now-former chief of staff:

> Months after his departure from the White House, Priebus made a final assessment: He believed he had been surrounded in the West Wing by high-ranking natural killers with no requirement to produce regular work products—a plan, a speech, the outline of a strategy, a budget, a daily or weekly schedule. They were roving interlopers, a band of chaos creators.

He specifically identifies Kellyanne Conway, Bannon, Ivanka, and Jared Kushner as the chaos agents, whose goal is not to merely win a debate but to crush the opposition. Again, this can have come from no source but Priebus, who by that point had nothing left to fear from Team Trump. A year and a half later, Kelly would find himself in a position to compare notes with Priebus on falling from presidential grace.

The book is a steady stream of tales told out of school by an almost endless supply of indifferent scholars, most of whom had earned either detention or expulsion in this school with only one rule: don't piss off the boss.

What is remarkable about *Fear* is how unremarkable it is. That is to say, a great deal of what Woodward reports had already formally appeared or been bruited about for months before his book appeared. At the very least, the broad contours of the saga he weaves were widely known: the rivalries, the explosive personalities of numerous parties, Bannon and the president not least among them, the subterfuges and low-level spying of this internecine warfare. Some specifics are genuinely new, such as Gary Cohn allegedly hiding a potentially ruinous draft decree from his boss until Trump lost interest. At such revelations the reader must sit up and say, "Wow!" The truly new or surprising material is in a sense indemnified against doubt by the way so much of the book merely ratifies general knowledge about the workings of this dysfunctional operation.

It turns out that 2018 was, indeed, a huge year for political writing. All three of these books had lengthy stays atop the bestseller list, generated massive discussion, and proved that anything that touches this president or is touched by him ignites strong passions. And yet none of them was the bestselling book by a figure connected to the White House. For that, one has to turn to a book that hardly dealt with current White House shenanigans, that took no stance on most debates of the last two years, in which a president appears as a secondary figure, and that is written by the only party able to give orders to the most powerful man in the world whose given name is Barack. Michelle Obama's *Becoming* was second to Woodward's *Fear* in first day sales with a mere 750,000 but not only overtook its predecessor but managed to outsell every other hardcover *book* of any genre. In fifteen days. By the end of March 2019, it had surpassed ten million in sales and was well on its way, if it wasn't already (international sales figures can be notoriously hard to pin down), to becoming the bestselling memoir of all time. Not bad for an uplifting, largely optimistic story of personal development and public service. That may, of course be part of its appeal. In a year of relentless negativity and stories of scandal and dysfunction, readers may have been yearning for something with a positive outlook.

14

The Universe of Ideas/Ideas of the Universe

Reading Science and Tech Writing

HERE ARE TWO STATEMENTS that are logically incompatible but nevertheless true: (1) We are living in a great age of science writing, and (2) We are living in a wildly antiscientific age. Ain't logic grand?

First things first. Science writing since, say, 1970 has an incredible starting lineup and a deep, powerhouse bench. Whether in astronomy with Carl Sagan (*Cosmos*, *Pale Blue Dot*), Brian Greene (*The Elegant Universe*), Neil deGrasse Tyson (*Astrophysics for People in a Hurry*), and Stephen Hawking (*A Brief History of Time*); biology with E. O. Wilson (*On Human Nature*, *The Ants*), Jane Goodall (*My Friends the Wild Chimpanzees*, *The Chimpanzees of Gombe*), Stephen Jay Gould (*The Panda's Thumb*, *The Structure of Evolutionary Theory*), and Lewis Thomas (*The Lives of a Cell*); cognitive sciences with Oliver Sacks (*The Man Who Mistook His Wife for a Hat*, *The Mind's Eye*, *Awakenings*), Steven

Pinker (*How the Mind Works*, *The Language Instinct*), and Noam Chomsky (*Language and Mind*, *What Kind of Creatures Are We?*), scientist-writers, many of them leading scholars in their fields, have offered us up-to-the-minute reports from the front lines of scientific research. You can hardly expect to keep up with all the really excellent books and articles on science for the general reader, so rapidly do they appear. So, there's the good news.

The bad? Large swaths of the public refuse delivery of all this scientific news. For some, it is specific: no evolution noise, please. They may even embrace other forms of science, so Darwinism is out but findings (or some findings) regarding embryonic develop-ment hold appeal. For others, it is more comprehensive: they dis-trust all scientific findings, including those that are demonstrably true. You have to work really hard to deny your senses *and* the photographic record to be a member of the Flat Earth Society. But the comprehensive science and technology rejecters are likely few. It's difficult to foreswear all modern knowledge in favor of a Pre–Industrial Age ethos. The Amish do so, but they don't post their objections on Twitter. More prevalent are those who zero in on one or two areas of objectionable knowledge. Evolution, earth sciences, and astrophysics tend to be the *bêtes noires* for those who reject those fields because the findings upend strongly held reli-gious beliefs. For those with a literalist interpretation of the Bible, for instance, it is impossible to square the age of the universe at something just under fourteen billion years with a scriptural age of around six thousand years. Archbishop James Ussher, in the seventeenth century, for instance, calculated the moment of creation to be in the year 4,004 B.C. by the Julian calendar. On October 22. At 6:00 P.M. I do not know what day of the week that would be. Ussher remains a favorite date-calculator among creationists, although many doubt his methodology as being too scientific and not sufficiently religious. Nor is this belief confined to the age of Oliver Cromwell. A man named Ken Ham has founded a Creation Museum in Kentucky, complete with a replica of Noah's Ark and animatronic dinosaurs coexisting with humans. Even mainstream Christian leaders have criticized Ham and his museum not only for bad science but for bringing religion into disrepute. Clearly, someone is wrong by a factor of roughly two million. For those whose belief runs toward extractive energy, the Bad Science award goes to climate science. Not for nothing did former vice president Al Gore call his film about global warming *An Inconvenient Truth* (2006); the reality of climate change will be inconvenient for someone, whether coastal lowland dwellers or coal mining and petroleum drilling companies or those of us who want our energy at the lowest price.

Neither of these two areas of rejection, it should be noted, exists in large numbers outside the United States. Europeans tend to be bemused by the American tendency toward refusal of scientific consensus for whatever reason, particularly when that consensus among specialists is as high as 97 percent, as in the case of climate change. And no one who sees their religious creation myths as just that, stories that helped explain the world to an earlier people who lacked our scientific understanding, has cause to resist the findings of science regarding the universe or one insignificant planet and its development of living organisms. Nor, I hasten to add, is this opposition shared by anything remotely like a majority of Americans. But the presence of a vocal minority can make for a skewed discussion of facts and theories. The state superintendent of Arizona has recently placed on its panel regarding the state science curriculum Joseph Kezele, a creationist who is adamant that the earth is younger than six thousand years old, that dinosaurs (but only the young ones because of size issues) were present on Noah's Ark, and that enough scientific evidence exists to back up the story of creation in Genesis. That evidence may require a bit of squinting to bring into focus—and to lock out the mountains of evidence against it. But this is where the United States, unique among advanced countries, finds itself these days. We've reached a point where science journalist Michael Specter felt the need to publish *Denialism: How Irrational Thinking Hinders Scientific Progress, Harms the Planet, and Threatens Our Lives* (2009).

That resistance, then, is what scientist-writers are up against when they write for a public audience. If scientists like Brian Greene and Neil deGrasse Tyson, who actually study the origins of the universe, sometimes sound a little strident or peevish in their writings, it's because deniers have rejected that evidential mountain range through willful ignorance or rigid religious belief or a hatred of institutions, including the institution of scientific inquiry.

There are basically three types of writing in the sciences, or perhaps three positions from which writing about science happens. The first is the *expert testimony*. This is the sort of writing I refer to at the beginning of this chapter: the professional scientist, often a star in his or her field, offers a report on the latest findings in that field with analysis or speculation as to what those discoveries entail. If Stephen Hawking offers us *A Brief History of Time*, we know we should sit up and pay attention, even if we likely won't understand everything (or much of anything) he has to say. He is the intrepid explorer of an undiscovered country, the first to peer in from the border of the known world, telling us what he has seen and what he thinks may lie beyond his current range of vision.

The second type is the *amateur profile*; like any profile, it takes as its subject not (or not only) the science but the scientist as well. The types of writing that fall under the profile category lie along a continuum. At one end would be the pure profile, works such as Margot Lee Shetterly's *Hidden Figures*, the story of the remarkable African American women loaded with mathematical talent and achievement but limited by race and gender as to what occupations they could follow, who became the "computers" who performed the calculations that kept the early NASA missions safe from launch to splashdown. By focusing on four of the women—Dorothy Vaughan, Mary Jackson, Katherine Johnson, and Christine Darden—Shetterly reveals the barriers these numbers wizards had to surmount simply to do the jobs the space program needed done. One could very well argue whether the book is about science at all, or whether it is really a social history or a study of race relations at a particularly fraught moment, but it is undeniable that science lies at the center of the story, whatever the true import of the work. At the other end would be something on the order of John McPhee's *Annals of the Former World* in which he employs his profiles of key earth scientists as a way into the mysteries of a field of inquiry he could not possibly understand without their explanations and guidance. McPhee, a layperson, is our representative and translator, our Dr. Watson to so many Sherlocks, in a bewildering world in which neither the timescale nor the phenomena (nor, for that matter, the language used to describe either) are comprehensible to anyone but experts. In this case, the scientists are not the subjects, as they are in Shetterly's book, but conduits to a subject as mystifying as it is fascinating.

The third type of science writing is what we can think of as *journalistic compilation*. In such works, a writer surveys a field, usually an emerging subfield (we scarcely need a survey of, say, Newtonian physics), and reports on the direction of this new line of inquiry. I have called it journalistic compilation chiefly because it is largely undertaken by journalists, but perhaps *scholarly* compilation would be equally apt: a fair number of such works are written by professors and researchers in disciplines other than the one that forms the subject of the article or book. An example would be Cathy N. Davidson's *Now You See It: How the Brain Science of Attention Will Transform the Way We Live, Work, and Learn* (2011). Davidson is an Americanist by training and taught for decades in English departments, venues not noted for a high density of brain scientists, at Duke and Michigan State universities. Yet she also has long found brain science intriguing and cofounded HASTAC, "a virtual organization" (written thus in 2010; today no one would bother) of scholars and educators interested in learning in the new digital age. The acronym stands for Humanities, Arts, Science, and Technology Alliance and Collaboratory, a mouthful that explains why everyone involved simply calls it "Haystack." So she is not precisely a stranger to the phenomenon of brains interacting with digital environments.

What these three strands demonstrate is that science writing relies on expertise. The first variety originates in professional expertise by men and women who have spent their entire lives in intense study of their chosen fields. The second type taps directly into that body of expert knowledge by closely examining the work of science professionals; we can think of it as expertise at a remove. The third type, then, is at one more remove, one more degree of separation. In this subgenre, the expertise is largely gleaned from writing by true experts as the scholar/journalist immerses herself or himself in the literature of the field, compiling, explaining, and analyzing all of that learning.

Many science writers, either because of professional specialization or amateur interest, stick to a single field of study. Brian Greene knows the loftier reaches of physics the way I know— actually, I don't know anything the way he knows that. Michio Kaku is much the same, with a special love for string theory. On the other side of the intellectual fence, some writers are catholic in their tastes, writing about anything as long as it is interesting. And what could possibly be more interesting than the earth and how it got this way?

A handful of writers become a brand unto themselves. That's clear enough in fiction, where Stephen King becomes synonymous with a type of horror novel unlike anyone else or Robert B. Parker combines tough-guy action with self-aware insouciance to stake out his own hard-boiled detective territory in his Spenser novels. But it's no less true in nonfiction. In 2000 a staffer at *The New Yorker* published a book about the working of the collective mind that wasn't quite like anything readers had encountered before. It wasn't just the subject matter but the light touch with technical information, the homely analogies, the vivid examples, and the soothing voice that made *The Tipping Point: How Little Things Can Make a Big Difference* a bestseller and Malcolm Gladwell a household name. In subsequent books such as *Blink: The Power of Thinking without Thinking* (2005) and *Outliers: The Story of Success* (2008), he cemented his reputation for demonstrating how factors we overlook or never consider might play large roles in the way our lives turn out. In *Blink*, he explains the processes, called *thin-slicing*, by which we make what we typically think of as "intuitive" decisions. In *Outliers*, he examines how sociological and biological factors ranging from educational opportunity to the date of birth can affect whether a person succeeds or not. In all these books, he employs a massive amount of social science research, often of the kind that upends conventional thinking, ranging from psychology to sociology to behavioral economics.

He established his process in *The Tipping Point*, in which he uses examples as various as a sudden, unforeseeable surge in popularity of Hush Puppies shoes in the 1990s, the drop in the murder rate in New York City, and a sociological experiment in which hundreds of subjects tried to reach a specific person hundreds of miles away, the results of which showed a statistical near-impossibility that a very large number of these efforts filtered through just three persons (unknown to the subjects) in the target person's city. These examples afford Gladwell the opportunity to talk about "tipping points," those moments when scattered actions coalesce into a movement or wave. His method employs recent findings in the social sciences, especially the intersection of psychology and sociology, as a means of explaining how certain social phenomena take place. How is it, for instance, that an expert in a field can arrive at a solid conclusion in that area of knowledge while the rest of us are trying to figure out what the question is? How is it that a small movement suddenly takes off? Why is it that some people with talent and even genius fail to prosper while others with fewer innate advantages succeed? In each case, the answers are not always as obvious as it seems they would be.

Gladwell's detractors, psychologist and linguist Steven Pinker among them, have found his work simplistic or based on false dichotomies, even on cherry-picked data, but he has found a large and welcoming audience as well as much critical praise. Still, the negative challenges remind us that we should be hesitant about taking scientific or social research at face value without substantive evidence. If Gladwell has a failing, it is that he too glibly tosses around the research he cites without drilling down into it; in effect, he doesn't always show his work when using the numbers. Nevertheless, Gladwell's work has proved to be very popular and influential. What's his real strategy? Getting readers to think in new ways or to listen to others who are looking at human behavior with new eyes. A pretty considerable achievement, don't you think?

Let's face it, not all scientists are great communicators. That's fine, their main jobs being to conduct research and share their findings with colleagues in their fields. But the rest of us need periodic reports from the frontier, just to see what the smart kids have been up to. Happily, some research and theoretical scientists are very good at carrying that news, their talent encompassing not only being really smart but also the ability to explain things so that people like me can understand. Most of the writers we discuss in this chapter are journalists who have made science their home for a book or two or maybe a whole career. It's nice, though, to hear sometimes from the men and women who are intimately connected to the work going on out there on the boundary of the known.

Neil deGrasse Tyson is one of those people. He is director of the Hayden Planetarium in New York City, with degrees from

Harvard, University of Texas, and Columbia. Definitely one
of the smart kids. His *Astrophysics for People in a Hurry*, on the
other hand, is for the rest of us. He invites us into his world,
anticipating our anxieties and doubts about a field that is not
only beyond our contribution but also frequently counterintu-
itive. He employs familiar comparisons and lucid explanations
for the incomprehensible—which is most of it. The scale of al-
most everything is too vast for our imaginations to really grasp.
In his first chapter, dealing with the birth of the universe, he
describes the tremendous difficulties we face: "In the beginning,
nearly fourteen billion years ago, all the space and all the matter
and all the energy of the known universe was contained in a vol-
ume less than one-trillionth the size of the period at the end of
this sentence." And right there, we think, okay, I'm lost. We're
not, though, because he stands us up and makes sure we feel
grounded. Which is good, because things are about to get worse.
He describes a dizzying series of microevents in that first instant,
when the universe, still consisting only of subatomic particles for
mass and photons for energy, expanded vastly, to "one hundred
billion trillion-trillionths of a meter," while the various compo-
nents split as if choosing up sides for a game of Red Rover. And
then a single sentence set off between single asterisks above and
below, "A trillionth of a second has passed since the beginning."
To most of us, that will sound like it is still pretty beginning-ish.
He will continue with this construction, walking us through a
millionth of a second, then one second to two minutes. And in
that two minutes, the universe has grown to "a few light-years
across."

Wait a minute! The operation expanded to a distance that
would take light, at the speed we know (186,000 miles per sec-

ond), a few *years* to cross in one hundred twenty *seconds?* Is that even possible? Evidently, yes. The propulsion of the Big Bang, as we have come to call it, was such that the laws of physics were unenforceable. Anything is possible, he tells us, when the temperature of the nascent universe is a billion degrees.

Through all this frenetic action, all manner of things came into being, quarks and antiquarks (because what's a quark without its anti?), hadrons, bosons, protons, neutrons, electrons, leptons (of which electrons are one type), and positrons among them. One or two of those we have even heard of. The hadrons, in particular, will turn out to be important. A hadron is two or more quarks (don't ask) yoked together by something called the *strong force.* From them, the building blocks of matter, protons and neutrons chiefly, emerge. This whole discussion is mind-blowing, but Tyson brings it into the realm of the imaginable: "Those loners [the one in a billion hadrons that survived this mad dash away from the blast point] would ultimately get to have all the fun: serving as the ultimate source of matter to create galaxies, stars, planets, and petunias." The petunias, I believe, save us. Galaxies are still beyond us, but we get flowers. Even if we don't know their names. They, at least, are on our scale.

And therein lies the challenge for the physicist seeking to explain his or her field for the rest of us. Everything is either way too huge or way too tiny for mere mortals to visualize. We have the focal length of a 55 millimeter camera lens, not of the Hubble Space Telescope or an electron microscope, and we can only really comprehend things we can "see." The scientist-writer (or the science journalist, for that matter) has to enable our ability to see things outside our range. Nor is that true only in physics. Biology, chemistry, medicine, brain science, geology, and most certainly mathematics have all gotten well beyond us. We can't puzzle our way through scientific papers, even if we had access, which the majority of us do not. Small wonder, aside from the general rejection of expertise, that some people have doubts, if not outright hostility, toward the scientific consensus on such matters as evolution or climate change.

How should we approach writing on science where we don't even understand the questions, much less the answers? As with all nonfiction, with care. Not suspicion, which suggests a starting point grounded in paranoia, but with intelligent questions. First, who or what is the source of this knowledge? We do well to rely on people with research knowledge in a field. E. O. Wilson is a truly great biologist, and the main man if you want to know about ants, but I don't think he's the guy I turn to if I want to learn the latest in microcircuitry. Which is okay; he mostly sticks to ants. So many of the smoke-blowers in fields where the science is settled turn out to be folks who may have a science or engineering background but not a speck of experience in the matter at hand. The problem with the objections to, say, climate change is that they often rest on "some scientists." Until we know who those scientists are and what credentials they can present, that's so much smoke. They may have scientifically valid points, but their position needs proving.

Does this mean the writer must be a scientist? Not at all. She may be a professional writer, but her sources should be strong figures in their field. When John McPhee writes about rocks, he does so while standing on a foundation of knowledge acquired from geologists who have spent their entire lives pursuing this special terrain.

Another issue with belief: evidence. A real expert can cite facts and figures until you are begging for relief. A fake expert, or his followers, will likely focus on a single data point in hopes that it undermines faith in the massive data advantage of the other side. Or else hammer on "what about" questions that often turn out to be counterfactual. For a number of years, climate deniers recited a figure about a single area in the North Atlantic where the temperature did not rise. The idea was that this one factoid somehow outweighed the overwhelming number of data points all showing rises in every other measurable location. Or they bring out something like, "But what about the Greenland (or Antarctic) ice sheet that's actually expanding?" Neither of which happens to be true, by the way, but it slows down proponents and seems as if facts are being presented. But they're not, because truth is what makes a fact a fact. Creationists, aside from changing what they call themselves, are fond of pointing out some hole in the fossil record as evidence that seems to disprove evolution. But a hole in the fossil record is just that, a hole. Not proof that the thing never existed but merely that it hasn't been found. Paleontologists recently unveiled the largest Tyrannosaurus rex ever discovered. Until it was discovered, no recorded T. Rex had ever been that big. Didn't mean none had ever been thus, only that none found *yet* had been. We can see evolution at work all the time, often prompted by our efforts. Indiscriminate use of antibiotics has resulted in multiple-resistant or even universally resistant bacterial "superbugs," on which antibiotics have no effect. Similarly profligate dispersal of Roundup (glyphosate) has raised resistance in weeds, producing stronger agricultural nuisances. That's evolution before our eyes, no fossils required.

The point here is that we need to examine the kinds of arguments being made, especially when those arguments appear to fly in the face of the findings of a majority of scientists. Way back when I took driver's education, we were taught something called *defensive driving*, which meant not only taking in what was happening immediately before our eyes (important in its own right) but to "drive ahead" and spot potential problems so we could avoid them. We need to practice what I think of as *defensive reading*, to be on the lookout for a coming logical wreck. Because like drivers, not all writers have our best interests at heart.

Defensive reading is as much an attitude as a technique. More than anything, it means that we do not accept anything we read at face value. That we ask writers to earn their keep, earn our trust. It may sound like cynicism but is more nearly its opposite. Cynicism is a pose—oh, you can't trust any of them—a dismissal of everything we read because some of what we read is misleading or false. Rather, it is more like a social contract: if a piece of writing demonstrates its legitimacy, we will give ourselves fully to it. Having found it to be accurate, honest, earnest, interesting, we can settle in wholeheartedly. Before that, however, proof must be offered that it is these things. Which means that we are going to ask some questions. We're going to *interrogate the text*. Sounds ominous, doesn't it? But it's not. We already do it, consciously or unconsciously. The early paragraphs of an article or early pages of a book are always a negotiation between doubt and belief. Is this going to be worth my while? How do I feel about the writer? Is this someone I want to spend time with? Someone I can trust? Does this page make me want to read the next one?

All we're doing in this interrogation is taking an instinctual and implicit process and making it rational and explicit via a series of questions. We'll go into more detail later, but here is the bare-bones outline:

- Is the writing engaging?
- Is the argument valid?
- Is the evidence solid? Does it back up the claims made?
- Are the sources reliable? Are they being used fairly?
- Do the conclusions follow from the material presented?

Doesn't this sound pretty much like what you do when you read? Life is too short to read books and articles that waste our time with nonsense and misinformation. When we read about science, we are trying to learn about the reality we inhabit. Same with history or biography or current events or any subject of non-fiction. And we can only discover that reality if our reading gives us the straight scoop. Good science writing fascinates us and enriches our lives; science writing that seeks to mislead us simply steals time we never get back. Which one do you want to read?

{ **Interrogating the Text** }

Three Questions

In *Draft No. 4*, his excellent book on the art and craft of non-fiction writing, John McPhee recounts his relationship with the long, long, longtime editor of *The New Yorker*, William Shawn. As editorially ferocious as he was personally diffident, Mr. Shawn (as he was inevitably called around the magazine's offices) would invariably ask one or more of the following questions about any piece McPhee submitted: "How do you know?" "How could you know?" and "How can you possibly know that?" Since the writer covered topics as diverse as oranges, a cultural history of shad, and geological deep history of North America, and since these are topics about which English majors are not inevitably knowledgeable, Mr. Shawn was justified to question his state of knowledge.

Beyond the writer-editor dynamic, however, lies a truth we can use as readers of nonfiction: we need to ask questions of the article or book and its author. This process is called *interrogating the text,* and taken to its limit, it can be pretty exhaustive, not to mention exhausting. But let's focus for the moment on just those questions. We've touched on most of these in earlier chapters, but sometimes it's helpful to bring concepts into a single site. There's actually a question that hides in plain sight before Mr. Shawn's three, so let's start back one step with just this: *Do you really know this?* Then we can move forward with the others.

- How do you know, assuming you do?
- How can you?
- Is it even possible for you to know, and if so, how?

Asking these questions does not mean that the writer is a liar or that we do not believe her. Rather, it is a means of holding her to account. There are a couple of very good reasons for this. First, although the vast majority of fact-based writers are honest and honorable people, there are, as we shall see later on, spectacular examples of the other sort, writers-as-scumbags. And second, we just might want to check her work and do some further investigations of our own.

In addition to these defensive-reading purposes, these questions also move us toward greater understanding of the process a writer has employed. Stephen Ambrose was in his later years when he wrote *Undaunted Courage*, but not sufficiently old to have been able to interview either Lewis or Clark. Same with Ron Chernow and *Alexander Hamilton*. Laura Hillenbrand faced an additional impediment in *Seabiscuit*: her key witness, had he still been alive, could only whinny. In all of these cases, writers can only "know" what they know through primary and secondary sources. The first group includes journals, letters, diaries, and published works by the person in question. Secondary works would be everything about that person or event by folks who were someone else. The good news is that most writers are at pains to tell us just how they know what they know. Usually, they tell us in the text what sources they're using for any particular piece of information that they can't readily know on their own. Some employ notes of either the foot- (bottom of page) or end- (end of book) variety. Others go further and provide a bibliography, sometimes called Works Cited, of all sources consulted that turned out to have a bearing on the work at hand. Chernow's *Hamilton* has eight tightly packed, double column pages of bibliography; his endnotes run to forty pages. By contrast, Malcolm Gladwell uses endnotes but typically not bibliographies. In my own books, I eschew notes, attempting to avoid a heavy, academic feel, although I am at pains to state in the text where I acquired any piece of specialized knowledge. This policy also offers one of the rare occasions for me to use "eschew," so that's a bonus. The goal is the same, to shine a light on the sources to which we are indebted. Some writers are less forthcoming, mostly for good and sound reasons. Exposé writers, as we have seen, need to protect their sources with anonymity, or else no one would talk to them. Even then, the good ones tell us as much as they can whenever they can so that we have faith in their process.

Obviously, you are not interested in tracking down every source in an activity that is already a lengthy undertaking, the reading of a book-length piece of nonfiction. So, when should you check things out? You can mostly gloss over external facts, that so-and-so wrote to you-know-who on such-and-such a date. If there is a note there, you can move ahead. Where I would (and do) grow curious is when it comes to internal matters. If I see the words "thought" or "imagined," for instance, in a work where the person thinking or imagining something was physically unavailable to the author, I want to know just how the author knows this to be the case. There really should be a citation of some sort there. It can be a mention in the text or a numbered note, but I expect to see a letter or a journal entry where the principal actually admitted that thought or imagination transpired.

Interrogate the Writer

Our checklist begins, of course, with the person responsible for this piece of writing. Our curiosity on this matter points toward the authority of the author. Seems almost rational, doesn't it?

- Who is the writer? What credentials does she bring to the project?
- Why is she to be believed or not? What claims does she have to our trust? How does she earn it?
- Does she exhibit the professionalism demanded for this task?

Interrogate the Sources

What does the writer know and how does she know it? Inquiring minds—that's us, by the way—are going to want to know.

- Quality: How good are the sources? Are they authoritative? Are the authors consulted experts? Hint: when they are, the writer is eager to tell you so. You won't need the bibliography. If the sources are periodicals, are they respected? The difference between a major daily paper and a supermarket tabloid is meaningful.

- ✏ Honesty: Is material from sources being presented accurately and fairly? This is tough to evaluate. One helpful hint is to notice how often source material is presented with editorial comments appended. If this happens too much (you'll know), you may not be getting a complete picture.
- ✏ Aptness: Is the source material being applied to the argument in a way that makes sense? This is often another feel test: "gee, that 'evidence' seems a little squirrelly." Accept no rodents!

Interrogate the Data

MOST OF US AREN'T scientists. We may not even have understood our high school science classes, which in any case didn't prepare us for jobs at NASA or Fermi Labs.

Here are some things to watch for when people use data. Some are misuses, others merely elements of that use it behooves us to notice:

- ✏ Incomplete or inaccurate evidence
- ✏ Reliance on a single data point
- ✏ Misapplying data to show something untrue
- ✏ Attacking *anything* other than the data of the other side
- ✏ Attacking the scientists, not the science

- False analogy
- Appeal to extremes (a bogus attempt at *reductio ad absurdum*)
- Context: numbers tell us very little unless we know what they measure. How are they being interpreted?
- Sources: where are these numbers coming from? Is the source rock-solid or Jell-O-shaky? Does it have something to gain by fudging them? Can we discern the methodology behind them?

Interrogate the Argument

What we're doing here is checking to see if the argument holds together.

- Basis: Does the argument appeal to reason or only (or chiefly) to emotion?
- Preaching to the choir: Does the logic actually hold up under scrutiny, or does it require preexisting bias in its favor? This is a cherished technique among politicians, most of whom aren't seeking to win arguments but to stir their desired audience (their base, in current parlance) to action.
- Logical construction: For each point, does the evidence support the premise? Go back to the Toulmin Method we spoke of earlier and look at the *claims, grounds,* and *warrants* on offer. Does the supporting evidence, the ground, actually support the claim? Does the expository linkage, the warrant, actually connect the two? Or do the

parts simply lie next to one another, hoping we will make connections that the writer or speaker failed to make?

- Cherry-picking: does the argument suppress annoying details in an attempt to gloss over its own weak spots?
- Glibness: does the argument rely on logic and thought or only on lofty rhetoric? Elegant expression is nothing to be ashamed of, but it shouldn't be the entirety of an argument's appeal.
- Ad hominem(ity): does the argument resort to name-calling? That rarely indicates a writer or speaker believes he occupies the intellectual high ground.

Interrogating Bias

WHEN WE INVESTIGATE THE matter of bias, the type of writing will matter greatly. A piece purporting to be objective reportage is held to a different standard of objectivity from an opinion piece. Even with the latter, though, there is such a thing as going too far.

- Does the writer exhibit (or admit) bias on the subject?
- Is that bias open or hidden? If hidden, is that because it is suppressed or attempting to deceive?
- Does it affect her judgment?
- Does she fairly represent the opposing view and take it on based on the merits, or does she misrepresent that view with an eye toward gaining an unfair advantage?
- Is the writer's bias managed appropriately for the type of writing?

Emerging
Media

15

Reading Internet Sources

Or, Beyond Here There Be Monsters

THUS FAR WE HAVE dealt with traditional sources of information, chiefly print but also some broadcast. And we have seen that there are pitfalls and bad actors aplenty, although the vast majority of writers are diligent, responsible, and probably kind to their pets. Best of all, if they weren't honest, readers had a pretty good idea of whom to blame. Friends, we've been living in a fools' paradise. Welcome to the nightmare.

How We Got Here

THE INTERNET AND, WITH it, the World Wide Web, came along more or less coincident with the Clinton administration in the early 1990s, although it would be unfair to saddle anyone there with that culpability. In any case, it seemed like a good idea at the time. Its predecessor, ARPANET, a network of linked networks among government and research agencies, was built in the 1960s, all the more remarkable when one considers how few and how primitive computers were in that time. That was decommissioned in 1990, the newer internet having developed during the 1980s and the first commercial use of the new internet beginning in 1989. It was right about then that Tim Berners-Lee invented the World Wide Web, a network—or web, hence the name—that would connect sources of information via the use of *hypertext*, a marking system (all of two months old at that point) readable by computers so that we could all watch cat videos and receive offers of immense riches from Nigerian princes. In 1990, he invented the first web browser, the means by which we could search for those videos and monetary offers, and then in 1993 the first commercial browser, MOSAIC, was invented and from there it took about five minutes to be overrun by *email spam* and online pornography. According to Wikipedia (another entity we'll get to shortly), the internet at that point became fully commercialized. Some might say weaponized, but we'll withhold judgment for now.

Here's the problem with the internet. It holds a universe of useful information available at any moment that the inquisitive mind may want to know, say, Roy Orbison's birthday. It is also blazingly faster than anything in prior human experience, hence the nickname, the Information Superhighway. But it also has a universe of bad information. You know how our actual universe was once thought to be made up of matter and energy, but now we find that there is also *dark matter* and *dark energy*, the mere existence of which makes my head swim? It's like that, except that the cosmos has no malicious intent. It took physicists and cosmologists hundreds of years to get from matter to dark matter conceptually, and then only because the equations that everyone knew were right didn't work out, so they went in search of something not yet seen that made the numbers fall into place. In the case of *dark information*, it took about a nanosecond for some bad actor to realize that this new wonderland was ripe for all sorts of malice and confusion.

This state of things is not the *fault* of the internet but something more like its inevitable condition. In space, as the movie blurb went, no one can hear you scream. In cyberspace, no one can hear you lie. Or rather, everyone can, but there's no one to say that you did. The internet is impartial; in that respect, it's like the universe. It isn't even exactly a thing. It is a network of networks, a vast web connecting all manner of data collecting other webs. We can paraphrase Julian Barnes here and say that this net is a collection of holes tied together with digital string, and each of those holes is another collection of holes and string. And every one of those nets—and everything it contains—is just as valid as any other net or its contents. As with everything to do with computers, it is nothing more than a series of ones and zeros, and neither one nor zero has an opinion. Or a conscience.

Let's take a moment to clarify matters. Most of us use the words *internet* and *World Wide Web* interchangeably, because in our minds they are where we go to do stuff in cyberspace. We're wrong. The internet is a *network* of *interconnected* computer systems—servers and mainframes and supercomputers and all of the wiring and connecting devices—that exists as a global-scale hardware host for whatever users might want to put on it. You are computer-savvy enough to know that the thing that runs on hardware is software, and one of the biggest collections of software on the internet is the World Wide Web. The web is a vast network of content. And it lives on the internet. Now, we can muck this up with a bunch of acronyms (HTTP, HTML, TPP/IP, and so on), but do you want that, really? Thought not. Besides, what we want is a clear picture of what these two terms mean. So one more time: internet—hardware, World Wide Web—software.

To summarize, then, the military begat ARPANET, and ARPANET begat the internet (with, seriously, some help from congressman-then-senator Al Gore, making him a sort of midwife), and the internet became the cradle for the World Wide Web, which was begat by Tim Berners-Lee, and the web begat mayhem. It turns out, there are twin oceans, called *information* and *dark information*, except that the oceans are not side by side but mingled together and virtually impossible to sort out. And swimmers in that mixed superocean can't even agree on which is which. This sorry state is partly by design and partly by design failure, and it rests on one terrible fact. The design part? The creators of this new information stream foresaw the value of the democratization of information. Power to the people, right on! In theory, much more of the world's population could have access to and even the chance to contribute to the universe of knowledge that human beings have spent millennia creating. No longer would the prohibitive price of, say, the *Encyclopedia Britannica* stand between the thirst for learning and its satiation. That is very noble, and to a large degree it has proved true, although the cost of devices is fairly prohibitive in its own right. Alas, that plan contained one fatal flaw: quality control. There was no guarantee that the newly enfranchised contributors would act in good faith but rather a virtual certainty that large numbers, motivated by self-interest or greed or mischief, would not. Because here's the terrible fact (cue the ominous horror-film trailer music) again: **In cyberspace, no one can hear you lie.**

On the web, truth and lie look exactly alike, and the lie can look better with the right packaging. Despite the highest level of educational attainment in history, the world today is as subject to hoax and fraud as it has ever been. Perhaps even more so. Why? Lack of critical thinking. An inability to ask the right questions of assertions and claims and even supposed evidence brought to bear on a subject. This isn't all of the problem, but too many of us receive information emotionally or viscerally rather than rationally. If, for instance, someone tells us something that plays to our prejudices, or if we like the person offering that something, we're all too inclined to believe. And I mean that both ways, that we are overly likely to believe and that *all of us* get caught in that trap. Which, like all others, is a trap best avoided.

You have a plan, no doubt? A five-year plan? Twelve-step program?

Nothing so formal as that. Just two words: *think better.* That's a solution to a lot of our problems, and we are, based on available evidence, really pretty terrible at it. How do we think better? I get an image here of shutting my eyes tight and squeezing to pull my temples toward each other and thereby press my brain into activity. Pretty sure that won't work. We're not adept at thinking better thoughts on cue. Our poor minds are generally doing their best, which is a scary thought. But if we can't come up with better ideas, maybe we can start with asking better questions. And here is where numbers help. Not every question we come up with will be a gem, but if we ask enough of them, perhaps one or two good ones will slink in with all the junk. Then, if we pay attention to which questions were good, and just maybe with why they were good, we can bring up our good-to-bad ratio over time. How can we go about that task of asking questions, of trying to think better?

I have one suggestion, and it's not easy: **Act like an editor**.

After all, someone should. But no one does. Here's what I mean. Internet falsehoods are so prolific and so hard to stop precisely because of the nature of the internet. No gatekeepers. Whatever those are, they have a bad reputation these days. "Gatekeepers" sound like folks who set up unreasonable barriers to keep good people from doing what they want to do. Such thinking is predicated on two errors: that barriers are perforce unreasonable, and that people are always good. If we stop and think for just a moment, we know that neither of those assumptions is invariably true. For most of the history of printed and broadcast material, those gatekeepers have been called *editors*. Often an adjective will be appended to, usually before, the noun, as in managing editor, acquisition editor, copy editor, and even editor in chief, which breaks the word-order pattern. And they all have basically one job: keep the talent—writers, reporters, anchors—from screwing up. Which we are wont to do. Editors are gatekeepers, no question. And if you are one of the very large number who have had your brilliant book or article or story or poem rejected, you will probably dispute my previous statement about "unreasonable" barriers. I am and I have. But reason is a big part of the job. An editor asks questions all the time: is this idea promising? Does this person pull it off? Will anyone want to read the resulting piece? Is that the right wording? Is this assertion accurate? Is it adequately explained? Supported by evidence?

So here's the problem: by and large, web-based sources lack editors. That means that there has been no effort to filter out nonsense, confusion, or even outright fraud. Which means that, in turn, *we* have to become the filters. The best way of filtering is, as we discussed a bit ago, by interrogating the text, by asking a series of questions that just might illuminate the accuracy, sincerity, and reliability of the claims being made.

Up till now, I have been suggesting that we can treat web-based texts like print-based texts because they in some way resemble them. But you and I know that's not really true. A great many "texts" online are single sentences or scattered phrases, not necessarily well written or thought through. Internet *memes* are not exactly Emersonian essays. And comments by readers bear little resemblance to judicial decisions, being more often knee-jerk reactions based on emotion or prejudice. So, then, we have a situation that poses a screwy question: how does one act like an editor with materials that may be impervious to editing? After all, what good is a copy editor where there is no copy to edit? The first thing for us to do is dispense with the notion that an editor moves words around and fixes spelling. Many do those things, but that is the primary activity for a very small subset of editors. Instead, we should think of them as specialists in the art of thinking: they bring reason and judgment to bear on texts. And they can do that whatever the text may look like. After all, a children's book that is all pictures, no words, still had an editor who judged how well it told its story or presented its idea without any words, accepted it, worked with the creator to improve it, saw that all the details were handled consistently (that the pink hippo on page two was still both pink and a hippo on page fourteen), and on and on. In other words, they interrogate the text, asking that series of questions about appropriateness and accuracy and logic that must be asked.

That's what we need to do, become *de facto* editors asking

those questions about accuracy and fairness and bias that we discussed earlier as means by which we interrogate texts. We have to do the heavy lifting here. No one else will carry that weight if we don't. Most of all, we have to insist on integrity on the part of writers: no shirking obligations, no lying to us, no fudging facts. Yes, it takes a little time and effort; on the other hand, how much of our time and effort are wasted when we're hoodwinked?

Listicles, Blogs, and Memes, Oh My!

I don't think a complete taxonomy of the internet ecosystem is possible at this early stage of its history. Maybe not even desirable. Among other things, how do we deal with the dark web, which most users of the World Wide version have never seen? But even beyond that, everything on the web is in constant flux. Old forms are sloughed off like so many snakeskins, while new forms arise constantly and others shape-change at the drop of an electronic hat. We never know what humans may like or respond to until we discover that someone has started a totally new form of communication. Who on earth, prior to 2006, could have imagined that people would actually *like* using an app that severely limited the scale of their communication? Severely, as in 140 characters? Suddenly, though, there was this thing called Twitter and it fairly rapidly took flight. For that matter, who would think that a LISTSERV (essentially a self-selecting email list) designed to rate the attractiveness of female Harvard students could become the biggest social media phenomenon in the world? But that's how we got Facebook.

Web-Specific Forms

SO WHAT SORTS OF communication do we find on the web? And what can be done about them?

- Reviews—of books and babies, movies and movers, plays and plumbers, persons and pizzas, as well as furnace repair services, builders, restaurants, and, well, everything.
- Lists—often known as *listicles* (a portmanteau word of "list" and "article") and inclining toward the snarky.
- News—and "news"—items, whether borrowed from established sources, self-generated, or, frankly, invented out of whole cloth. Conventional news sources often also generate a stream of daily updates to keep up with rapidly changing events.
- Videos—not necessarily of cats, but those are the ones for which YouTube became notorious.
- Photos—cats here, too, but also dogs and food and small children and sweaty softball teams and food and political leaders and perp walks and food. Did I mention food?
- Websites—an informational site for companies, services, products, persons. Websites can have many pages (and sometimes much searching, as anyone who has tried to find information on a university website can attest). Most pages on websites tend to be static, as opposed to . . .
- Blogs—like websites, these can serve an almost limitless range of purposes from conveying timely information to massaging pure vanity. Unlike websites (of which they

can be a page), blogs are dynamic and frequently updated with new entries (hence the name, an amalgam of *web* and *log*).

☞ Social media—posts here are by user-members and run the gamut from "here's a question I just had" to shared items from anywhere in the webiverse.

☞ Personal opinion—because isn't that the meaning of life, to discover what everyone else thinks on every conceivable topic? Informed opinions and uninformed ones count for about the same (remember that bit about the neutrality of zeros and ones?).

☞ Help and how-to—whatever task you seek to master, someone out there has text instructions or a video explaining how to do it. On the downside, it proves difficult to operate a saber saw and film the action at the same time, so the quality of videos is often sketchy. And no, dear hearts, not everyone is a natural performer, including a lot of folks who believe they are. On the positive, I have successfully installed devices from toilet flush mechanisms to an anchor trolley for my kayak with how-to videos.

☞ Discussion boards—these question-and-answer hangouts for like-minded individuals were a staple of the early WWW, where they had moderators (how quaint!) and where I was once in one on *Finnegans Wake* that included students, Joyce scholars, and superfans. No kidding. And while other forms have taken over a lot of cyberspace, communities of people wanting to share knowledge on a common interest still exist. In the case of a site like Reddit, the form has changed so much that it hardly seems like the old-style discussion boards, but that's essentially what a *subreddit* is: a subsidiary gathering that self-selects for discussion of a specific topic.

- E-commerce—selling stuff, whether merchandise or ideologies, is big business online. Sometimes the selling looks just like what it is; at others, sellers are hiding their real intent, which is more true of commerce in ideas rather than things.

- Memes—images, textual items, videos, often of humorous intent, that are intended to spread virally online. In pre-internet times, a meme (first coined by British evolutionary biologist Richard Dawkins in 1976) was defined as a cultural equivalent to a gene, a unit of cultural information that might pass from person to person and thereby propagate over time. It can be an idea, behavior, mode of dress, worldview, or item of style. The 1980s mullet haircut could thus be viewed as a meme, although, happily, it lacked the staying power of a gene.

How Wikipedia Murdered Truth

THERE IS ONE OTHER outcome of all this democratizing that we should take into account. Because everyone can contribute information, the web is equally welcoming to amateur and expert alike. In consequence, there is sometimes a reaction against experts as somehow throwing their weight around, as bullies, as (worst of all) elitists. That's unfortunate, since research does not equate with falsification any more than earnestness with truth. One of the places we see the war between levels of expertise is on

Wikipedia. Wikipedia is a remarkable cultural experiment, based on a belief in the wisdom of crowds. Anyone can contribute information to any article, assuming they meet one or two basic requirements (citing a secondary source being one, although clearly that one is not always enforced). This openness means that all information on the site is suspect. The vast majority of entries are accurate, and some are lovingly curated by interested experts and responsible amateurs. So crowd-wisdom mostly works. But there are always outliers, individuals who have a bee in their scholarly bonnets about a famous person or incident. If they are sufficiently determined, they can not only bring dubious information to a page but keep changing any corrections back until the other side wears out. Worse, the gatekeepers at Wikipedia are as likely to side with them as with the party with greater knowledge.

A few years ago, a friend of mine, a scholar of the eighteenth century, noticed that the entry on the boy poet and hoaxer Thomas Chatterton was using outdated information about his death, declaring it a suicide. The current state of knowledge, after a 2004 article by a professor at the University of Bristol (Chatterton's hometown) caused scholars to rethink that Romantic era myth, was that while it could have been suicide, it was more likely an accidental overdose, since the instrument of death, arsenic, was also the accepted cure for gonorrhea, and that Chatterton was also taking opium, the combination of which could have proved fatal. The poet was also making money from his writing, contrary to the stories told by Robert Southey and other nineteenth-century writers of an impoverished and hopeless youth driven to madness. Okay, my friend thought, this story needs balance. So she edited the page to reflect the change in the field of Chatterton scholarship (with citations). The next day, her edits were gone.

She put them back in. Next day, gone again. She put them back in. After several rounds of this contest of wills, she contacted Wikipedia. Look, she said, I have a doctorate in this area, Chatterton is one of my specialties, I'm up on this latest discovery, and whoever keeps changing this back is making the page worse. Care to guess who got banned? Yep, the one who complained. She took her revenge by pointing out to her class (on literary hoaxes, no less) how easy it was to manipulate pages by editing entries on various trees to show that their names came from Vulcan derivatives. Holy Mr. Spock, Batman! She changed those changes back, but only after leaving them in place long enough that students could see that no one fixed the misinformation.

When Wikipedia, noble as it might be in its first principles, empowered anyone with a bit of determination and something resembling a fact to write or edit articles, it started us down a dark road. The presumption has been—and remains—that the wisdom of crowds will overwhelm strong, even malicious, falsehood with the bright lamp of truth. It's a swell theory. Alas, in practice the outcome can be something else. My guess is that there aren't three teachers in America who can't produce, at a moment's notice, half a dozen horror stories of wildly misinformed student papers whose writers had relied chiefly or wholly on Wikipedia as their source. At the same time, there are probably an equally small number who have not begun the class prep on a new topic— a writer, a scientist, a painter, or a historical figure—without consulting that same source. But the difference is that they don't, indeed can't, *trust* that material. It's fine as a starting point, but everything needs to be corroborated externally, since no fact can be warranted to be accurate. This situation did not obtain when one went to the library and consulted the *Encyclopedia Britannica*.

On the other hand, when one wished to know all the guitarists not named Richards who have been members of the Rolling Stones, *Britannica* was not helpful. And therein lies our dilemma: we want what Wikipedia has to offer, but we can never be sure about it.

So then, can we use Wikipedia? Should we? Yes, and maybe, in that order. But warily, always warily. The site actually offers some self-correcting mechanisms, but hardly anyone bothers to use them. First, the editors frequently note that a fact cannot be corroborated or needs a citation, meaning that no reputable source has been found. If that's not a red flag, it's at least an orange one. They're telling you that swimming at this beach is not safe. Whenever you see a message like that, do not put that information in permanent memory. Second, since founder Jimmy Wales believes in sources and citations, you should make use of them. Nearly every important fact that doesn't carry a warning has a superscript (that little numeral above the line of text); if you have any doubts at all or are simply curious, click on the number and be taken down to the bottom of the article, where the citation sometimes leads you to further clarity, or at least to the source, so you can judge for yourself. Then you can pop back up to the article and resume reading. That's not too much work to protect ourselves from lousy intel, is it? The problem with Everyone's Encyclopedia isn't that it is untrue, but rather that we can never be sure that it *is* true.

And therein, dear friends, lies the issue that we've been building toward throughout the book: the problem of trust.

Caveat lector. Let the reader beware (it just sounds better in Latin). We begin our reading lives as innocents: we want the truth and believe that writers share that desire. Much of our early training reinforces that impulse; after all, our school textbooks must be true, or else how can we be tested on their contents? I have had multiple people tell me that they arrived at adulthood (like my friend at the beginning) convinced that the contents of non-fiction books and articles must be true. Yeah, me too. But over the years we get our eyes blackened by writers and broadcasters who are not playing by the rules we hope obtain, and we get . . . what? Not cynical exactly, but wary, casting a doubtful eye on all we see. Okay, maybe cynical, just a little bit. But that's no way to live. There are those who get stuck at this phase and either give up on all information or soldier on, disbelieving everything. (This is the strategy Russian hackers employed in the 2016 election: put out so much bad information that those who saw enough of it would reject all information as hopelessly corrupt. Imagine their delight when some of their wackier inventions took flight with some sectors of the electorate.) For most of us, though, going through the world in angry disbelief is just plain unwholesome. Far better for us to develop strategies, whether the sources are online, print, broadcast, or radio waves from space, that let us separate the news from the noise. Those strategies include asking questions, considering sources, reading carefully, and generally using our brains. If we can do that, we will discover that there is far less noise than we had thought, and far more healthy grain in the fields of information. And that discovery will be very good news indeed.

It's April 23, by the way, Roy Orbison's birthday. Same as Shakespeare's death, only in 1936 instead of 1616.

16

Social (Media) Disease

IN A SPECIAL CIRCLE of Hell (size yet to be determined) that Dante forgot to elaborate in *The Inferno*, this one reserved for deliberate misinformers, there will be a corporate division where Facebook, Twitter, Reddit, Snapchat, and their social media ilk will form a digital daisy chain as they gnaw on one another's binary brains. Are these tech giants maliciously feeding us false information? No. Do they permit it, or even encourage it by their very structure? Absolutely. Don't they have a moral responsibility to stop it? How quaint. Have you forgotten already that ones and zeros have no ethics, no commitment to truth, justice, and the American way? Well, don't forget again. And while you're at it, add to the amorality of mere integers that of the companies built upon them.

Still, one or another of them gets hauled before some congressional committee every month or two, or about the time the Houses of the Holy get tired of not balancing the budget. Those hearings usually manifest a curious mix of contrition (Oh, Congresswoman, we're so sorry this transgression happened after we failed to predict it) and defiance mixed with pity (Senator, I'm not sure I can explain this to someone whose first car didn't have a radio). The mood on all sides is exasperation, with lawmakers miffed that this *thing*—whatever it is this time and however little it resembles last time—keeps happening, and the moneymakers that some of their interrogators have never turned on a computer. To be fair, many of the lawmakers have no idea what questions to ask or even what devices and software are involved, while the tech stars are just as mystified by notions of corporate responsibility. As a result, they bristle and sneer at each other for a few hours and go their own ways. Predictably, nothing comes of all the bluster, and in a little while, some other young billionaire gets his turn in the not-very-hot seat.

Social media are a breeding ground for a host of ills. Each one no doubt has elements particular to it, but for our purposes, let's stick to the generic problems. Individual issues resolve themselves when platforms sink beneath the waves of innovation, as they inevitably do. MySpace, anyone? Waiting for the demise of corporations, however, is inadequate on a policy level; actions born of bad faith continue to proliferate. Too many items shared are misleading, overblown, false, or breathless in ways designed to draw eyes (and shares). A recent item—article would be too strong a word—on the online news site Huffington Post bore the headline "Kellyanne Shreds Jim Acosta." If you opened the link you found a short account by Amy Russo of a tit-for-tat between CNN White House reporter Acosta and White House spokesperson-at-large Kellyanne Conway over President Trump's impending address to the nation on border security. Acosta asked Conway if she could, given Trump's history, guarantee that he would tell the truth (which, in the event, he did not). Conway shot back to ask if Acosta would, and would swear to it "so help you God. Am I allowed to mention God to you?" At this point she had lost the issue entirely and was merely making a personal attack. Acosta, used to the give-and-take, declared that she was the one with an "alternative facts" problem, referencing her most notorious phrase used after the inauguration-attendance kerfuffle in 2017. Exasperated, she called him "such a smartass" and went on to say that no one liked him. People listening to the exchange would all agree that one of them was being more than a little foolish, although which one would likely depend on the listener's political affiliation. What all should be able to agree on is that no one "shredded" anyone.

So why the headline? Because *shredded* is a clickbait term. It catches attention and causes people to read and share the contents. Or often, to simply share without reading. As long as it gets shared. Ones and zeros, right? The social media equivalent of "all publicity is good publicity" would be "all traffic is good traffic." In fact, traffic that stirs the pot, that angers and incites readers or viewers, is all good because it generates what? More traffic.

The Conway-Acosta dustup points up another deleterious feature of social media: it's the land of knee-jerk reactions. Without actually counting, I would guess that somewhere south of half of the comments had *anything* to do with the contents of the article. So, on precisely what were they based? On how the respondent feels about Kellyanne Conway, Jim Acosta, Donald Trump, the media, the administration, every Republican who ever lived, ditto every Democrat, take your pick. If the exchange between the principals was childish, it couldn't compete with the comment stream. Nor is this uncommon. The percentage of commenters on any link who actually read the content being shared is remarkably low. A goodly chunk of comments on *any* topic display a noteworthy ignorance of their specific subject, that is, whatever the link *linked* to. In general, comment streams on any sensitive subject—politics, climate change, evolution, the New England Patriots—constitute a thousand points of darkness. In a well-run universe, commenters would have to pass a short quiz on the piece at hand before posting. Of course, we don't live in a well-run world; ours is managed by humans.

For my money, the worst feature of social media is how easy they are to manipulate. This problem isn't *by* design, exactly, but rather *of* design. The root of this evil lurks at the very base of the platform: the *algorithm*. An algorithm, simply put, is a series of instructions, generally in mathematics and computing, for performing a specific task. You will sometimes see analogies between algorithms and recipes, although a recipe can be varied (how large is a pinch of salt, anyway?), a computer algorithm, not so much. Every social media platform that I know of lives and dies with popularity and traffic volume. Since they charge no user fees, and since making money is entirely the point of business, these businesses make their money via advertising. And how much money changes hands depends entirely on how many eyeballs the platform can attract. Believe me, it's just as unappetizing as it sounds.

Everything about Facebook, for instance, is designed to attract members in droves and to keep them as engaged as possible for as long as possible. The platform rewards popularity. And strives to create it. By its very design, having only a few friends will result in a thin stream of posts to read and engage with. If everyone cleaved to the actual friends and family members (remember, not all of either group will be users themselves), the average number of Facebook friends would fall somewhere between twenty and forty. And that situation will not make Facebook money. Having more friends will make your social (media) life more rewarding. For the platform. And if more is good, then lots and lots must be even better, right? So it ceaselessly throws friend "suggestions" at the user, many of them a friend of one or more of your friends. Quite a few of them, however, will have no discernible connection to anyone you know. Like that's a problem! Facebook can find you new friends. Most of those suggestions are "friends" once (or maybe twice) removed; that is, they are present just out of view as friends of one of your friends or even as friends of one of their friends. The presumption is that you and your friends have interests in common, so you and their friends will also have shared interests. In the real world, as we know, you may have nothing in common. You may have once had your friend as a student, and she has sought you out based on a fondness for a particular class or for you, while *her* friend lived two doors down from her between third and fifth grades. The likelihood that she and you both like fly-fishing and the Montreal Canadiens is minimal. For all you know, she's a Maple Leafs fan. Oh, the humanity!

The other way social media expand your world, whether you feel expansive or not, is by finding you corporate buddies. If you look on, say, L.L.Bean for a dog leash, that search becomes known to your device through the miracle of *cookies*, which are small bits of data sent by the website and stored on your very own computer or device. How sweet. The result of those cookies is that your electronic possession in turn possesses information about you, which it shares with . . . just about anything. That's why you begin seeing ads for L.L.Bean on your solitaire app. That same cookie causes Facebook (again, just for instance) to conclude that you

(a) like shopping at Bean's, even if that's your first time ever, and (b) just might own a dog. That's why your News Feed suddenly discovers an outfitter in Maine and some brand of dog food that probably isn't yours but that they're sure you'll like. This sort of thing goes on with women's clothiers and Midwestern universities and Hawaiian resorts and pretty much every sort of enterprise you can imagine—and a few that are unimaginable. All because websites leave little reminders for themselves on your machines. You were warned: everyone always said cookies were bad for you.

Now, all these things (and no doubt some others that elude me) that Facebook does with your profile and your behavior on the application occur because someone wrote a program—an algorithm—telling their computer system to treat your information in exactly that way. Let me know if that makes you sleep better at night.

Virology

The world of social media is fraught with peril. One of the big ones is that it will make you sick. Oh, you think not? Then why do memes "go viral"? Because some undefined magic (dark or light magic, it matters not) causes lots of people to suddenly become frantic to see that meme, that article, that tweet. The language is that of epidemics, which is no accident; the goal is for the item to infect as many people as possible.

Remember the Conway-Acosta nastiness? And the headline about her shredding him? "Shredded" is just one word that commands esteem in the sport of fishing for eyeballs. Almost each one is a superlative or extravagant version of some other, milder option to describe the same thing. "Greatest" is popular. "Iconic" is a sure-fire winner, to judge from its frequency. No one can compile a full list, because new candidates pop up all the time. Let's just say you know them when you see them. And sometimes look anyway, against your better judgment. Just lately, I saw this headline in Slate: "Judge Obliterates Trump's Census Shenanigans and Dares the Supreme Court to Reverse Him." Wow! "Obliterates" and "shenanigans" in the same come-on. Can't get more viral-hopeful than that. Here's what's going on with such inflation. The goal for pretty much any item on social media is to "go viral," meaning that it finds not merely an audience but one that shares the item like mad, moving out in larger and larger concentric circles until almost no connected person on earth can escape the cat video or argument between unreasonable people or talented child playing music in her bedroom or whatever it is. Even if *it* turns out to be Kellyanne Conway and Jim Acosta telling each other, "I know you are but what am I?" like a couple of petulant middle schoolers. That posting garnered more than seven thousand comments almost immediately, and for every commenter, there are scores or hundreds or even thousands of readers who aren't moved to join the mayhem.

In their excellent book *The Misinformation Age: How False Beliefs Spread* (2019), Cailin O'Connor and James Owen Weatherall detail how the most-shared item during the 2016 election cycle was a story on the so-called ETF News website (endingthefed.com) about Pope Francis endorsing Donald Trump for president. This bit of patent nonsense was shared or liked on Facebook more than 960,000 times. The website was run by a twenty-four-year-old Romanian, Ovidiu Drubota, who for reasons of his own had decided that he needed Trump to win. Drubota almost never originated stories; instead, he fished in the troubled waters of the extreme right wing, where, as with the extreme left, conspiracy theories and fake news grow large. He was successful. According to BuzzFeed's Craig Silverman, ETF News produced five of the top twenty most-shared political items in the three months prior to the election, including this one, the runaway champion. All wildly popular. And wildly false. Various sources split on how many readers will have read the piece, but the conservative average seems to be around ten per share, which would mean that nearly ten million distinct persons would have read that the pope was interesting himself in American politics. By contrast, the most-shared mainstream item was a column by Paul Waldman of the *Washington Post*, "The History of Trump's Corruption Is Mind-Boggling. So Why Is Clinton the Supposedly Corrupt One?" It trailed the papal hoax by slightly more than one hundred thousand views.

It bears saying that sharing and approving are two separate things. I remember seeing this shared by two different lefty friends outraged that such hoaxes were walking abroad in daylight. Such Facebook traffic makes it difficult to say with any accuracy what, if any, influence the bogus story exerted on the election, but most experts who look into these matters tend to agree that the number is not zero. We know that in general readers are confirmed in their opinions (in agreement or opposition) rather than swayed by the work of columnists. But columnists and opinion pieces are known quantities; a reader first encounters Paul Waldman only once. What effect unknown sources may have is, well, unknown.

This contagion model of social media takes us back to the

importance of getting everyone connected to everyone else, to acquire more friends, more followers, more others to follow. In this model, every connection becomes a possible disease vector. Multiple connections help: if one friend doesn't share something, you may have some others who will. Each of your friends forms a vector between you and every one of her friends (as well as between each pair of her friends, the number of possible combinations of which quickly becomes staggering). You in turn become the prime vector for all of those connections and each one of your friends then becomes another and so on out well past you as a private entity. In fact, the elegance of this system is that you can help with the spread of this system while remaining a private entity. No soapbox required.

So then, why a contagion? Because of what can be spread. Falsehood. Disinformation. Toxins in the body politic. A system so reliant on networks of users is relatively easy to subvert. All it really takes is wicked intent, one legitimate social media identity, and an amplification system. Here's what gaming the system looks like. During the 2016 presidential election, we now know, Russian hackers (not to be confused with Macedonian teenagers, although they may have worked in concert) sought to affect the outcome of the top race. While they weren't necessarily in love with Donald Trump, they, probably because of Vladimir Putin, certainly hated Hillary Clinton. She had been a thorn in Russia's diplomatic side for years, first as a US senator and then as secretary of state. The problem: in the weeks before the election, Clinton's poll numbers suggested there was no way she could lose the election. So they went for the next best thing: destabilize public opinion around the election and thereby delegitimize Clinton's authority once in office. But a funny thing happened on the way to the forum. Things started to look less certain. Some of that was because of Clinton's own missteps, some because of Trump's performance at his massive rallies, and some because of FBI director James Comey's bumbling return to questions about the Democratic candidate's private email server. That concern proved meaningless, since the emails on aide Huma Abedin's home computer were almost entirely those already revealed during the FBI's first investigation of the matter. The election narrative flipped again, and the Russians suddenly thought, hey, this guy just might have a chance. As a consequence, they upped the pace of their disinformation campaign, if not the basic design. From the outset, the plan was to plant untruths and exaggerated almost-truths, chiefly about Clinton, in the public consciousness via social media, mostly Twitter and Facebook. Along the way, they also planted a few negative stories about Trump; what's the point of a destabilization campaign if you don't weaken whoever wins the election? Even so, a vast majority of the effort was aimed at the Democratic contender. When she showed polling weakness, the plan went into overdrive.

About this whole endeavor, the one thing we still do not know (and may never) is the identity, in keeping with our disease vector model, of Patient Zero, the person who sparked this outbreak with its awful consequences. It could be the head of the Internet Research Agency, a shady outfit based in St. Petersburg and devoted to promoting Russian interests by means fair or foul. Mostly foul. Or it could be someone a step or three higher in Russian circles of influence. As ever, with contemporary Russia—and a good deal of evidence in this instance—we generally can be pretty sure if not who Patient Zero is, at least who sponsored him in the first place. Putin and his minions, of course, denied that almost before it was asserted. Whatever the case, the IRA (which sounds nearly as ominous as the full name does innocuous) has vigorously pursued a pro-Putin agenda regarding Syria, Ukraine, the United States, and the Russian opposition.

What we do know, on the other hand, is the amplification system. That was comprised of a small army of hackers and bogus-content creators along with a larger army of bots. A *bot* is simply another name for a *web robot* (cyber rule number one: never use two or three syllables when one can suffice), a piece of software designed to perform a simple task. The sort of task usually given as an example is *web spidering*, or metaphorically scurrying around the World Wide Web collecting and storing information. Humans, being large and clunky, would take vastly more time to perform the same tasks, and bots never get tired or bored. Another task to which bots are ideally suited, however, is to show up as virtual cheerleaders for anything their master likes or attackers of anything their master dislikes. They accomplish such tasks by being networked into, um, *botnets*. Simply put (the only way I can understand it), a botnet is a series of linked computers with each machine running one or more bots.

Yeah, but who owns that many computers?

We do. You and I. You know about viruses and malware attacks because they make your computer go crazy or seize up until a ransom is paid. The really insidious actor, it turns out, is simply living inside your hardware awaiting orders. These bots can reside not in ten or twenty computers but ten or twenty thousand. Or million.

But back to the amplification system. What was publicly known, because it was broadcast, was the original disinformation campaign, orchestrated on television network RT (formerly

Russia Today) and radio-web news agency Sputnik. Both are either funded directly by the Russian government (RT) or established by the government and funded by a subsidiary, Rossiya Segodnya (Sputnik). Independent and unbiased news sources they are not. These two pushed narratives about Clinton's corruption, about her physical and mental health issues, including claims that she had had two strokes, and about her cozy relationship with Islamist extremists. These false stories were spread by a cadre of *internet trolls*, chiefly from Russia as nearly as can be told. Their job, as with any internet troll, was to insert the stories or insinuations about them into political discussions, web chats, and blogs, in part as a distraction and in part to poison the well of political discourse. From there, the aforementioned legion of bots, or botnet, provided likes and shares to make it seem that the story really had legs, which some of them then grew. Once a tall tale appeared to gain a foothold in the public consciousness, some actual people bought in. Seeing their friends relate these tales in actual English (rather than whatever that patois native to the Russian troll is), others would find it more palatable. And so on. Thus do wacko ideas and narratives spread from the fringe to the mainstream.

One aspect of Russian interference that only came fully into view in late 2018 and early 2019 is the way that hackers insinuated their way into social media discussions of nearly every political stripe. As Professor Cailin O'Connor of the University of California at Irvine explained to NPR's Shankar Vedantam, "They made Black Lives Matter groups. They made gun rights groups. They made LGBTQ groups. They made animal lovers groups, weirdly." The goal wasn't to make more friends but to more effectively spread misinformation and confusion. O'Connor goes on to explain that the hackers were building a basis of shared trust by posing as like-minded people with any group they targeted, then using that trust to sow poison. What makes this practice so insidious is that trust is the foundation of learning. Vedantam, NPR's beat reporter on social science research, notes that we learn from persons we trust: teachers, parents, friends, proven news providers. In violating that trust, the hackers were successful in turning a greater number of disparate groups against one another. Contrary to earlier reports, they did not just target the Right, although that was the area of greatest effort. And reward. For maximum destabilization, mistrust and paranoia need footholds in many communities, among many tribes.

But not all of the deception is coming from Russia. As an example closer to home, the completely unhinged Pizzagate conspiracy theory is an all-American whopper. If by all-American we include overt racists and neo-Nazis. The story of child prostitution, pizza, Democratic bigwigs, and a nonexistent basement originated with an October 30, 2016 tweet, allegedly from a Jewish lawyer but actually from a white supremacist Twitter account, claiming that important Dems, with Hillary at the center of it all, were running a child sex ring. In a marvel of economy, the tweet managed to bring in pedophilia, Clinton, John Podesta, and Huma Abedin within the 140-character limit. You might think such a wild story could never take hold in the week and a half between that initial tweet and the election on November 8. You would be wrong. The fringier elements of the right wing went wild over this one, including Alex Jones and his InfoWars conspiracy-peddling website. Before long, it was getting play among the almost-respectable sources (depending on how you feel about former national security advisor General Michael Flynn and his son, Michael G.

Flynn). Professor Jonathan Albright of Elon University has noted that a disproportionate number of retweets of this story came from the Czech Republic, Cyprus, and Vietnam, and that a great many retweets were the work of bots. Did this story alter the election outcome? Very unlikely. This nightmare tale was so improbable that the only people taken in by it were those already confirmed in their hatred of Hillary Clinton, and they were never voting for her anyway. Anyone whose sanity was still intact at Halloween 2016 was not likely to buy such a wagonload of crap.

Lest you think that this kind of effort is the sole province of outlanders and outliers, consider an attempt made during the 2017 Alabama special Senate election. Two attempts, actually. By Democrats. In a December 19, 2018 *New York Times* story, Scott Shane and Alan Blinder reported that, according to an internal report, a group of Democratic operatives conducted a microscopic (four hundred followers by one estimate) false-flag operation suggesting that Republican candidate Roy Moore was being boosted by Russian botnet activity. One participant, Jonathon Morgan of the cyber-consulting firm New Knowledge, said he was unaware of the false-flag effort but that the project on his part was to experiment with techniques used by Russians during the 2016 election. He describes it as a research project to "find out how these kind of campaigns operated," a description at odds with the internal report, which said that the goal was to enrage and energize Democrats and depress Republican turnout. If that was the goal, it was an abject failure, given the tiny size of the effort.

The second attempt, nastier and more concerted, was the subject of a January 7, 2019 article by the same two reporters. This one posed as a conservative Baptist group, Dry Alabama, which backed Moore because it believed he would support a statewide ban on alcohol. The goal appears to have been to drive a bourbon-and-beer wedge between various Republican factions. An Alabama progressive activist, Matt Osborne, made no apologies for the ruse, saying that he believed firmly that Republicans were pulling this sort of stunt based on the success of the Russian interference the year prior, and to "unilaterally" decline to join in the fun would be to fight "with one hand tied behind your back." "There is a moral imperative to do this; to do whatever it takes." Reasonable people may doubt a moral imperative for a manifestly immoral action, and thus far, no evidence of such meddling has been found, partly because, as reporter Shane observes, he only found out because someone in the organization told him, and if groups remain tight-lipped, their misconduct will stay out of sight.

What the examples of 2016 and 2017 demonstrate, however much or little the deceptions succeeded, is that the election-meddling ship has sailed. Admittedly, neither of the homegrown misinformation campaigns was mainstream. None of the participants in the Alabama election mischief was working within the Democratic party machinery, and the Republican party cannot be held responsible for the alt-Right. But that day is coming, if for no other reason than it has always been here. Attempts by one party to subvert the efforts of the other by any means necessary has a long, inglorious history, including voter suppression in the Deep South and elsewhere, Nixon's dirty tricks campaign that gave us Watergate, and Chicago election meddling in 1960 and beyond. Anyone who thinks that history won't be repeated in the cyber-future is in denial about human nature. We must henceforth doubt any source we don't absolutely know to be genuine, whether New York lawyer or Alabama prohibitionist, either from past experience or by vetting the source ourselves. We can, you know. Vet sources. A few keystrokes in a browser search often suffice to establish or demolish authenticity. Sometimes, a bit more labor and time must be invested. Occasionally, only technology experts can ferret out the truth. The real question is not how much work is needed, but how much is democracy worth to you?

Special
Circumstances

17

The Criminal Element

Bad-Faith Writing

MY BASIC PHILOSOPHY INVOLVES the presumption that the human specimen is almost unlimited in its capacity for good. In apprehension, as one of our betters put it, how like a god. Able to reach upward to saintly behavior. Inclined toward both mistakes and the ability to learn from them. Given the right circumstances, willing without whining, almost without thinking, to sacrifice itself for others. Seemingly born with an instinct for right conduct. Loving the Good from earliest childhood. Which brings me to the problem.

Why is this quasi-divine vessel so often a scuzzbucket?

As much as I would like to believe that writers are at least a little above the average on the truth-and-goodness scale (having some stake in that verdict), there are no goodness fairies who brush the Tribe O'Scribe with magic dust. Writers are just as nasty, venal, brutish, and badly behaved as the rest of humanity.

And I'm not talking about the garden-variety oafishness, the poet who writes like an angel but is a monster at home, the conference star who backstabs friends and colleagues, the novelist whose books drip wisdom yet who knows nothing of himself and scatters desolation in his wake. In this case, I'm thinking about those who will say anything to make a buck, who trade truthfulness for manipulation, who willingly deceive. Part of the social contract readers make with writers of "true" prose is that the prose will be, um, true.

Seems simple enough, doesn't it?

You new in town? You may recall that way, way back at the beginning, I mentioned poison pills, those acts of bad faith that taint the entire landscape with their toxins. Fakery and flummery. Propaganda and malicious falsehood. Hoaxes and forgeries. Faked sources and phony experts. Bogus data and misapplied statistics. Crimes against truth of all sorts. They've been around for a while. Like, forever. This is where we meet them. Gird your loins.

Hoaxes

THE THING ABOUT WRITERS is that someone is always trying to foist something off on the rest of us. There have been hoaxes for as long as there has been writing, maybe longer. There may have been multiple poet-singers traipsing around the Peloponnese singing of Troy and Ithaca, each one claiming to be the true Homer. Who could tell? It wasn't like his face was on a bubblegum card. But Homer existed before writing as we think of it—there is a single mention in *The Iliad* of writing, and it probably indicated letters of a long-dead script being scraped into wet clay tablets—so no one could record the Homeric wars for posterity.

But we do know that literary fraud came along with written publication. Early on, there were no rules about theft of intellectual property. Chaucer could steal from Boccaccio, Shakespeare from Holinshed, and there was no law to be brought down on their heads. Enterprising writers of the eighteenth century, knowing that readers preferred old work to new fads, even if the old work never existed before last week, invented "legendary" poets from the dim Celtic past. Modern hoaxers have "found," "discovered," or "unearthed" ancient manuscripts and lost juvenilia, all of it wholly created by contemporaries, usually the finders themselves. Melissa McCarthy was nominated for her turn to serious films when she played forger Lee Israel in 2018's *Can You Ever Forgive Me?* Israel, whose career as a biographer had stalled, is believed to have forged more than four hundred letters purported to be by famous writers, some for direct sale, others to replace letters she stole from library archives. Clearly, the literary world has always had its criminal element.

Most of these examples involve fiction (both prose fiction and narrative poetry) in one way or another, but nonfiction also gets in on the fun. History is replete with examples of fraud, reporters taking shortcuts to fame by fabricating stories, and writers who make up or alter facts to make their work come out the way they would like.

Let's begin with the broad category of fraud, which we can break down into two major divisions, forgeries and hoaxes. Forgeries, for our purposes, are those works meant to mimic the writing of another person. Hoaxes are any writing that attempts to present something as true that is untrue. The most notorious forgery of the twentieth century may well be Clifford Irving's *Autobiography of Howard Hughes* (1972, although it was stopped before publication). Unless it's *The Education of Little Tree* (1976) by "Forrest" Carter. Or possibly Cleone Knox's *The Diary of a Young Lady of Fashion in the Year 1764–1765* (1925). Or the enormously anti-Semitic *The Protocols of the Elders of Zion* (1903). Or . . . never mind, just know that there are plenty of contenders. A common thread of the titles here is the matter of authorship. No authors have been conclusively identified for the *Protocols*, a work claiming to be the record of a Zionist plot to take over the world. We do know that it originated in Imperial Russia, a place rife with anti-Semitic impulses and rhetoric, and that it has become a sort of bible for virtually every group that thinks it has a beef with Jews. Forrest Carter, who claimed to be Cherokee and that *The Education of Little Tree* was his autobiography, turned out to be Asa Carter, a Ku Klux Klan leader and speechwriter for segregationist Alabama governor George Wallace. Knox, who authored the racy "memoirs" of an imaginary lady of fashion, was in reality Magdalen King-Hall, a nineteen-year-old daughter of a British admiral. And Irving, who really was who he claimed to be, falsely asserted that the elusive inventor-magnate-film-director had called him to ask that Irving ghost his personal story.

These inventions were eventually unmasked as the forgeries they are, but it wasn't always easy. Irving thought he could get away with his stunt because Hughes was so lost in his paranoid fantasies that he wouldn't notice, but it turned out that a vastly wealthy recluse, however deranged, has people to think for him. And their complaints unmasked the fraud for what it was and slammed the brakes on McGraw-Hill's plans. Knox/King-Hall's "diary" had historical inconsistencies, such as a character reading an actual novel, Horace Walpole's *The Castle of Otranto*, two months before it was published. Her book, however, was already a bestseller, which led to her being caught out: point enough eyes at a fraud, and someone will inevitably notice that certain details are chronologically impossible. You never know when some reader may turn out to be a Walpole fanatic, but give it enough time and such a coincidence becomes almost an inevitability. The *Protocols* probably began life as a parody of what some Russian imagined a Zionist congress was getting up to behind closed doors, and from there it became a pastiche of various documents, most but not all written with strong anti-Jewish sentiment. It is so extreme in its claims—really, Jews, a tiny percentage of the Western world's population, taking over that world?—that no reasonable person could take it seriously. Which explains why it has been so popular with Nazis and their latter-day ilk. The most difficult case was Carter/Little Tree, who was shown to actually be a white racist with no discernible ties to the Cherokee Nation, but that did not occur until 1991, fifteen years after publication and twelve after Asa Carter's death. By then the book, with its themes of simple living, concern for the environment, and Native American mysticism, had become a success with the public. Aside from the *Protocols*, none of these books would have had a problem had they been marketed as fiction. On the other hand, they might also have been less compelling; who wants to read a fictional autobiography of Howard Hughes? That question, however, raises the issue of what McGraw-Hill, Irving's planned publisher, was thinking, given the unlikelihood of the publicity-averse Hughes actually wanting his life story out in public. And in fact, Carter had already published the novel *The Rebel Outlaw: Josey Wales* (1972), which was the basis for the Clint Eastwood movie in 1976, and would publish a second Josey Wales novel and a third book of fiction before his death. Proving that exposure as a forger need not prove fatal, Irving emerged from seventeen months in prison to go on writing numerous novels and a memoir of his hoax, called *The Hoax* (1981), while King-Hall would go on to write many novels for adults and juveniles. You just can't keep a good man, or woman, down.

In contrast to forgeries, hoaxes are not exercises in mimicry. Rather, they are straight-up attempts to mislead. One of the more outrageous efforts of recent times was James Frey's *A Million Little Pieces* (2003). The book purports to be a memoir of Frey's addiction and recovery, consisting chiefly of his stint in an expensive rehab facility paid for by his parents. It is filled with harrowing events, including multiple root canals without anesthesia and the death of his girlfriend, Lilly. As with several of the forgers, Frey was undone by success. The book was picked up the Oprah Book Club in 2005, turning it into an even larger smash than it had been. And that fame, alas, sealed his fate. A website called The Smoking Gun, which specializes in the unsavory business of plastering the legal misfortunes of celebrities on electronic screens, couldn't find a mug shot from any of the places Frey said he had been arrested. That failure led to further investigations, and soon it turned out that they couldn't verify much of anything the book said had happened in real life. Soon others were engaged on a succession of fruitless searches for corroborating evidence. And all that failure led to a second visit, in January 2006, to Oprah's sofa. This one was a lot less cordial than the first, a one-hour woodshedding of not just the author but his editor, Nan Talese, pulled in from the wings to receive her own hiding. Oprah was incandescent, and if you can honk off America's queen of empathy, you've really done something. Some early reviews had questioned the veracity of the "true" story, along with attacking the book's style in at least one case, but they had been shouted down by the book's supporters. In the aftermath of all this inquiring, it subsequently came out that his second "memoir," *My Friend Leonard* (2005), was also largely fabricated.

So why didn't he simply market the thing as a novel? Ah, that. You see, he did. And got nowhere with it. Even Random House, his eventual publisher, turned it down as a work of fiction. We demand a higher degree of aesthetic control from our fiction than we do nonfiction, since any wobbles in the latter can be excused due to the exigencies of truth-telling. Fact can trump art. Don't feel too bad for Frey, though; he has since turned his efforts to the world of make-believe and produced bestselling novels, including the Young Adult hit (as part of the pseudonymous writing collective Pittacus Lore) *I Am Number Four* (2010), which was made into a DreamWorks film the following year. This may or may not strike one as just, depending on what one thinks of his initial effort, but nearly everyone can concur that he got off lightly with a few tears of shame on a studio couch.

What can the ordinary reader do in these situations? Very little, sadly. Most of us don't have the wherewithal to track down falsehoods at this level. We won't be getting any calls from Howard Hughes's truth team. Nor can we disprove the existence of a certain eighteenth-century lady, recordkeeping being what it was three hundred years ago. So some of this must fall to experts, even when those experts, in the form of publishers' editorial departments, let us down. But here's one thing we might be able to do, one question we could ask, and it might be okay for some fancy editors, too: just this, does it sound too good to be true? If it does, there's a better-than-even chance that it is exactly that, too good to be true. Seriously, the most determined recluse in America reaches out by phone to someone he's never met about revealing the secrets of his life? Come on! Or a racy memoir by a young lady who never appears in any source in her own time suddenly appears precisely two hundred years after its composition?

I'm not saying to reject every book with a dodgy-sounding origin story. We wouldn't want to lose *The Boys in the Boat*, would we? And that one sounds so much like a miracle that it alerts our Spidey-sense. At the same time, the book is so careful in its research, so well documented, that it soon allays any fears we might initially harbor. Still, for every one of those, there's a Hughes autobiography, a long-lost manuscript, a hard-luck story by a kid from the slums of Winnetka. So not rejection, but wariness. Ask that origin story to back up its claims with solid information, clear documentation, simple facts.

Faked News

The first Pulitzer Prize ever returned occurred in 1981, when the *Washington Post* gave up the award given to Janet Cooke, a twenty-six-year-old reporter, for her story on "Jimmy," an eight-year-old heroin addict. The story was a powerhouse, a terrible tale of deprivation and depravity where pushers stole childhoods. The problem? Jimmy didn't exist. She later claimed that he was a composite, but even then, certain details—that he only attended math classes (what elementary school in the early eighties changed classes?) or that dealers provided him with free heroin for three years (not exactly a genius business model)—seemed false. The tragedy of Janet Cooke's reporting was that there were so many truly hideous stories in the heroin epidemic of the 1980s, so many ruined lives, stolen childhoods, that had she simply taken the time she could have found a real story worthy of that lost Pulitzer.

Cooke was not the first nor the last reporter to have an approximate sense of truth. In 2003, Jayson Blair was fired from the *New York Times* for fabrication and plagiarism in a large number of articles. He had seemed like a rising star in the *Times* newsroom until questions began to be asked. An investigation ensued, resulting in a major front-page article and the dismissal of Blair, who swept two editors out of office in his wake.

For sheer criminality and longevity in journalism, though, it would be hard to top Stephen Glass. A rising star at *The New Republic*, he published forty-one articles over a three-year period. By the magazine's later reckoning, twenty-seven of those were based on fabricated evidence. His articles had the sort of vivid detail that editors die for, and his withering attacks on his targets were becoming legendary. Except that they weren't true. Consider, for instance, the piece that brought him down, a May 18, 1998 article, "Hack Heaven." In it, Glass detailed the hack by a fifteen-year-old cybergenius, Ian Restil, of a major software player, Jukt Micronics, resulting in the publication of every employee's salary and other salacious details including nude photographs. Instead of pressing charges, the company hired young Ian, an action made easier because the kid had his own agent. A teenage hacker with his own Jerry Maguire. Stop me when any of this sounds fishy. It evidently didn't to the editors at *TNR*. Adam Penenberg of Forbes's digital unit, then called Forbes Digital Tool and now known as the less awkward Forbes.com, on the other hand, scented a rat if not a cod. Which of the many improbabilities of the article emitted the strongest aroma? Not the brainiac and not the "super-agent to super-nerds." It was the major software company no one had ever heard of. He and his colleagues subjected "Jukt Micronics" to every sort of online search they could imagine. Zilch. The only hit in the Nexis-Lexis database was Glass's story itself. Which in a fairly short time fell apart completely. Every single element of the story was fictional, including Glass's notes for the piece. And soon the majority of his work turned out to be fraudulent in whole or part. Mostly whole. His brilliant career was toast. He was twenty-five years old.

Almost nothing here is surprising. Three years is a long time to sustain a career of journalistic fraud, especially since fraudsters often become more brazen with repeated success, as seems to have been true in this case. It turns out, however, that this was not quite the end of the story. As late as 2015, according to the *Los Angeles Times*, Glass retracted portions of an article from 1998's *Harper's*, and the magazine retracted the entire article, although it remains available in the online archives. Some of the follow-up has been less positive. After the fall, Glass earned a JD degree from Georgetown Law and passed the bar exam in California, but the Committee of Bar Examiners refused to certify him, citing not his fabrications but his plagiarism (yes, he was guilty of that as well) as grounds for failing the moral fitness standard. Still, he remained unbowed. Never one to shy from self-promotion, Glass published a thinly veiled novel, *The Fabulist*, in 2003 about a character named "Stephen Glass," but with "Aaron" rather than his given "Randall" as the middle name, so we know it's not all true. Good to see he learned humility.

Not all the fallout from the Glass case was negative, though. Penenberg's article went a long way toward burnishing the credentials of online journalism generally, and he later became a professor of journalism at New York University.

False Data

AS WE HAVE SEEN, some writers have a fraught relationship with facts. This data-challenged condition is perhaps nowhere more prevalent than in economics, and perhaps no single practitioner of the dismal science suffers from it more than Heritage Foundation fellow Stephen Moore. For decades Moore has advocated supply-side economics as the answer to everything. Cut taxes in a bad economy. Cut taxes in a good economy. Then cut them again for good measure. Turn business loose and everyone will benefit. Except that . . . they haven't. Time after time, tax cuts have not, in the words of Moore and like-minded thinkers, paid for themselves. He advocated for the George W. Bush tax cuts in the early 2000s. The resulting shortfall failed to pay for the Iraq and Afghan wars, as promised, and resulted in a multitrillion-dollar deficit. The maneuver did not work for his father or for his father's old boss, Ronald Reagan, who offset the losses of his tax cuts by implementing other new taxes. When the Clinton administration instituted new taxes to whittle down the national debt in the 1990s, Moore predicted the end of the financial world. Instead, Bill Clinton ended his time in office with a budget surplus, something that hadn't been seen in years.

Nor has it been only tax cuts that drive Mr. Moore's car. He has been a devoted if contrarian fan of the Federal Reserve's interest policies. For decades, the Federal Reserve has managed inflation by cutting the rates at which it lends to banks during recessions (which do not typically show inflationary pressures), while inching rates higher as needed during boom times in order to keep the economy from overheating. Moore, virtually alone among economists and economic critics, has argued that this is all backward, that rates should be increased during lean times to stop nonexistent inflation in its tracks, and cut during good times because the economy likes speeding up. Why? you may ask. It just so happens that during his life as a pundit, incoming Democratic administrations—those of Bill Clinton and Barack Obama—have come into office during recessionary times, while the two Republican Bush administrations and the Trump administration have inherited very healthy economies. Raising interest rates at those moments of recession would almost surely further cripple the struggling economies, while cutting rates would turbocharge the booming economies, at least in the short run. Or so actual practicing economists tell us. There is virtually no economist of any political stripe who agrees with Moore, and history utterly refutes his dubious claims. Still, he persists in them, as any wrongheaded person has a right to do.

Where he crosses the line is when he marshals false facts in support of his claims. In print. Repeatedly. In July 2014, he placed an opinion piece in the *Kansas City Star* attacking a recent column by Nobel-winning economist Paul Krugman, who had pointed out that the Kansas tax cuts of 2012, advised by Moore and implemented by Governor Sam Brownback and the Republican legislature, had demolished the state budget without providing any of the promised jobs gains. In other words, this Great Kansas Experiment had proved a demonstrable failure. Ultimately, it led to Brownback's career ending in as much ignominy as is possible without major moral debacles. In his column, which tried to switch the subject to other places where low taxes had worked, he used facts he said were from the current five-year period. They turned out to be from an earlier period, 2007 to 2012, which encompassed the Great Recession, which did not hit all states equally.

Even then, he misquoted the numbers, claiming that "no-tax Texas" had gained more than a million jobs in the period, that low-tax Florida had gained "hundreds of thousands of jobs," while high-tax California and New York had lost hundreds of thousands. In reality, according to the Bureau of Labor Statistics, the gold standard in these matters and what Moore implied was his source, Texas gained fewer than 500,000 jobs, California did indeed lose big, just under half a million, but so did Florida, while New York experienced a very modest gain of 75,900. The losses in California and Florida are likely attributable to the housing collapse, the chief driver of the recession, which hit those states especially hard. To recap, then, Moore first misrepresented the period for which his figures were valid, and then, even when correcting to the appropriate period, produced false numbers. That is bad-faith writing with a vengeance. Nor did his *Kansas City Star* misadventure dissuade him from fact-free analysis. In September 2018, he wrote a *Wall Street Journal* opinion piece, "The Corporate Tax Cut Is Paying for Itself," in which he concluded that "faster-than-expected growth has produced a revenue windfall." His timing could have been better: when the fiscal year ended twelve days later, corporate tax revenue was down 31 percent, the largest one-year decline aside from the Great Recession itself.

The person who has benefited most in economic terms from Stephen Moore's economic theory is Stephen Moore. He keeps selling books coauthored with Arthur B. Laffer, the guru of supply-side thinking; continues to get plum speaking gigs; and, having done all he could to destroy Sam Brownback's career, advised presidential candidate Donald Trump during his 2016 campaign. Then on March 22, 2019, for reasons best known to himself, President Trump nominated Stephen Moore to an open seat on the very Federal Reserve he has spent so many years misunderstanding. Ultimately, his candidacy was undone not by his truth-averse economic writings but by a series of pieces in *National Review* in the early years of this century in which he denigrated women. He withdrew from consideration, but not without penning an op-ed denouncing the unfairness of it all. Some Republican senators, at least, breathed a sigh of relief at being spared the spectacle of voting against their president or for someone who would destroy the economy to achieve political ends.

Or consider the more directly harmful case of Andrew Wakefield, the now-disgraced English physician. Although his training was as a surgeon, he seems to have become obsessed with measles as a possible explanation for . . . something. His first foray into epidemiological mayhem occurred in 1993 when he suggested that the disease itself might be responsible for Crohn's disease, an inflammatory bowel illness. That theory was found to be not viable by subsequent studies. Still, the exposure put him on the map, and he was contacted by a woman who believed her son's autism was caused by the measles-mumps-rubella (MMR) vaccine. He conducted a study on twelve children, eight of whose parents stated that their children had developed autistic characteristics shortly after being vaccinated. The article, with Wakefield as lead author, appeared in the highly respected British medical journal *The Lancet* in 1998. Although no causality was alleged in the paper itself, Wakefield made numerous appearances in which he did suggest causality and call for suspension of MMR vaccinations. His findings caused a worldwide stir and led to several studies, all of which refuted the alleged connection. To arrive at his findings, he ignored data that conflicted with his thesis, claimed that none of the children had previously exhibited symptoms when at least five had already been noted to have developmental or neurological issues, worked at the behest of attorneys of the parents in the study who were looking for pretexts for lawsuits, and committed multiple ethical and professional misdeeds. The article was ultimately retracted by the journal and its findings renounced by ten of his twelve coauthors. He was stripped of his medical license in the UK and driven from the profession. A more thoroughgoing denunciation is hard to fathom.

Even so, the damage was done. His fraud had accomplished one thing: it provided a simple answer for desperate parents. And because the answer was so simple, so clean, no amount of rebuttal could undo that harm. The "establishment" (by which, presumably, was meant responsible physicians and researchers) was out to get him. Other researchers had financial motives—even after his clear grasping after gain was exposed. And so on. In the early days, Wakefield contributed to the confusion by planting counterarguments against his accusers. Nothing he did, however, could erase the facts, but no amount of facts could sway the antivaxxers, as they came to be known. Nor could the undeniable potential damage sometimes inflicted by this "common" childhood disease, including many documented cases of blindness and death over the decades. Since the anti-vaxxer movement got rolling, there have been numerous measles outbreaks in various spots around the United States—Americans have a propensity for buying into scientific and medical conspiracy theories—with foreseeable consequences. Most children will come through measles just fine, else my generation and those before would have been wiped out. But not all do. Especially at risk are those with compromised immune systems whose only defense is "herd immunity," the situation that previously obtained wherein so many people are inoculated that a disease can't take hold. And for those kids, especially, the consequences can be devastating.

So what can an ordinary reader do when stories grounded in such outright fraud appear? Not much. If you're like me, medical journal articles are about as readable as Sanskrit. What we must do instead is keep an open mind, not accepting the initial pronouncement, especially if it sounds too good to be true, too glib or pat, as this one did. Wait for the professional response. In this case, that response came faster than usual in scientific matters, so we could have seen hints early on that maybe Wakefield and company were not entirely reliable sources. When those rebuttals and studies that fail to validate findings reach publication, we cannot simply write them off because all large groups are evil, or doctors are on the take from drug companies, or whatever reason is on offer. We discussed this earlier in our considerations of climate science; deniers charge researchers with lining their pockets (forgetting that grants are typically entailed so that moneys have to go to specified uses, none of which is personal enrichment) while ignoring the massive financial motives of extractive energy companies that typically underwrite the war against climate science. In this case, however, there is one thing a civilian might have done to cast doubt on Wakefield's "findings": we might just ask ourselves how many valid medical studies have sample sizes of one dozen cases. And therein lies a useful strategy for spotting possible fraud in technical fields: **Watch for anomalies and oddities in the data**.

As awful as Andrew Wakefield's misdeeds and their outcomes may be, he's a rank amateur. If you want to see the damage the pros can do, look at Big Tobacco and Big Energy; now *those* people know how to commit scientific fraud. According to O'Connor and Weatherall's *The Misinformation Age*, the science connecting smoking and lung cancer was settled as early as 1953. That will surprise people who were alive in the fifties and sixties, since what they heard was that there was controversy among scientists. (If you want the full version of this hideous plot, see Naomi Oreskes and Erik M. Conway's 2010 *Merchants of Doubt: How a Handful of Scientists Obscured the Truth on Issues from Tobacco Smoke to Global Warming* [Bloomsbury].) Among the scientists who knew the truth were those working for the tobacco companies, so it isn't as if R. J. Reynolds et al. were caught off guard. Quite the opposite: knowing the truth, combined with seeing smoking rates drop in 1953–1954 in the wake of major articles about the lung cancer link, sent them into a frenzy. On its face, the science was irrefutable, so something had to be done about that.

Their solution: sow confusion. They cherry-picked data from other studies, such as links between asbestos and lung cancer (true, but ultimately not mutually exclusive with the smoking-cancer connection), misapplied other data, called into question the real science, and hired a few unscrupulous scientists of their very own, and set about creating controversy where none existed. Industry leaders published a major article spinning out confusion in hundreds of newspapers and developed pamphlets that were distributed to doctors' offices. *Doctors' offices.* The smoke-blowing, as it were, succeeded, and after the two-year decline, smoking rates started up again in 1955 and continued that trend for the next twenty years despite the surgeon general's warning in 1964.

Ordinary people will look at this and think, this is the most immoral corporate thing ever. All that conclusion tells us is that ordinary people are not leaders of energy extraction companies, who looked at the same story and thought, what a great idea! The tobacco template proved ideal for fighting the growing science on climate change. Why not, since the starting point was so similar? As reported in a *Scientific American* article from 2015, Exxon-before-Mobil understood from its own studies that burning fossil fuels was causing global warming as early as 1977, and it buried that knowledge for almost forty years. Deep-sixing those studies, though, would be insufficient, since the independent science was bound to start appearing soon. Nor could reputable expertise be found that could successfully refute the data, which was overwhelming. Never willing to be a victim of mere reality, the oily branch of American corporate life found an alternative: *How about disreputable expertise?* Refuting arguments was not required. All that was really needed was to drag the name of science through the mud. Not climate science, mind you, but all science on the subject. If a small but vocal cadre of scientists, never mind whether their credentials lie in the field in question, spread bewilderment, that would be a great help. Their job isn't to be right but only to make noise. There was just one problem.

Where do you find such a group? Cadres-R-Us?

Pretty much, yeah. A group of hard-right physicists, alumni of the Manhattan Project and NASA, fierce anticommunists all who saw government regulation as the first step down the socialist primrose path. This crowd—Fred Seitz, Robert Jastrow,

Fred Singer, and Bill Nierenberg—were wide-ranging "experts" for hire. Didn't matter what the scientific topic was, they could be relied on to cloud the beaker with misapplied data and bogus numbers, along with just enough reasonable-sounding-bites to make it seem as if they might know something. Over the years, they moved from hot topic to hotter, spreading a fog across the current state of knowledge about tobacco, acid rain, the danger of pesticides, and global warming. As Oreskes and Conway note, the playbook was always the same: "discredit the science, disseminate false information, spread confusion, and promote doubt."

These peddlers of suspicion were aided by one of the more generous regulatory impulses of the federal government they so mistrusted, the Fairness Doctrine. Enacted by the Federal Communications Commission in 1949, the doctrine states that broadcast stations must offer equal time to both sides of a controversial issue and do so in a way that did not tilt the scales unfairly in either direction. The presumption was that participants in such controversies were honorable and in possession of reasonable arguments. See how this Ship of Fairness might run aground? And it did. Before long, certainly by the smoking "controversy" of the mid-fifties, one side had discovered that if you approached the matter cynically, you could, if not win, keep the other side from winning. And as we have seen, Big Tobacco observed no boundaries of fairness or honesty in its fight with truth, nor would the contrarians in subsequent national issues. There were two major problems with the Fairness Doctrine. First, it was founded on a faulty premise that in every controversy there are two equally valid viewpoints. Sometimes, however, the facts are so overwhelming in favor of one side that there really is no equivalent opposition view, only one based on commercial considerations, which are rarely reliant on science or fact. The second error was that in its very wording it promoted, some might say demanded, false equivalencies. Presenting two sides of an issue as if equal when they are manifestly unequal—97 percent of those who actually study climate science concur that human activity is chiefly responsible for the rise we are seeing in global temperatures, and of the others, there is no guarantee whether they are all opposed or merely undecided—gives the deniers a forum even if they have no data to back them up or, as has happened in recent years, they seize on an outlying data point (in this case, the relatively stable North Atlantic temperature since 1998, a fact that has been well accounted for) as a way to throw dust in viewers' eyes. Although the Fairness Doctrine was revoked in 1987, most news outlets still more or less follow it, if only to silence the faux outrage of the losing side in controversies. That practice has had a deleterious effect on the state of knowledge and explains why American views on many topics are so at odds with the rest of the developed world.

It seems pretty clear that even though the original merchants of doubt have died off, there will always be plenty of contrarians willing to lie for money. Is there something we can do to protect ourselves? Yes. Maybe. I don't know. There are, at least, some things we can try.

☞ CHECK CREDENTIALS. And by that, I mean make sure the "expert" is actually an expert in the field at hand. I have earned the right to be called "Dr. Foster," but you absolutely don't want me removing your gallbladder (do people still have those?). So it is with a "scientist" from the XYZ Foundation. What is his area of science, and how qualified is he to discourse on this topic? Here is an instance where the internet is actually your friend. Credentials are pretty easy to check; I've done it twenty or thirty times on this chapter alone, and in most cases it was easy not only to find the information but to check it against at least one other source.

- CHECK THE CLAIMS. This is harder when you watch or listen to a live program than it is with print sources, since claims can whiz by at the speed of lies. But it can be done. If nothing else, hang onto one claim and check that. Most times, the segment you're watching will show up online and you can watch-and-check at your leisure. See if independent sources can confirm the claims or if they only exist in the closed loop of the speaker's think tank.

- FOLLOW THE MONEY (1). Here's one thing you can always bank on: in any controversy, somebody profits. Identify that party and most of the time you will also identify the most dubious argument. Who stood to gain in the Big Tobacco case (hint: its first name is "Big")? When *Reader's Digest* published "Cancer by the Carton" in 1952, tobacco companies stood to lose everything. Their propaganda full-court press was a foreseeable, if dastardly, response. But we should probably have seen through it before we did. With acid rain from coal, who benefited financially? Not the trout in Lake Sunapee. And the long money in the climate change "debate" all rests on the side of the extractive energy business.

- FOLLOW THE MONEY (2). This ties back into our first item. While you're checking credentials, find out who's paying the freight for this expert. This may take a little work. You'll never find some tag that says, "Bought and paid for by Charles and David Koch," the brothers who head a leading extractive company. That would be a tad obvious. But they finance various hard-right foundations and think tanks, including the Heritage Foundation, the Cato Institute, and their very own Americans for Prosperity. They have every right to do so and every right to protect their interests, of course, but that doesn't mean we have to take the word of their hirelings.

✏ CHECK THE LOGIC. One of the truly peculiar elements of the climate debate is a rhetorical turn by deniers that goes something like this: "The scientists who work on climate change receive millions of dollars in grants, so they have a financial interest in finding that the earth is warming. Without those dollars, they'd be out of business." Sounds almost reasonable. Unless you think. First of all, those "millions" are scattered among hundreds, possibly thousands of scientists, meaning that no one gets some enormous pile of cash. Secondly, most of the money is entailed: equipment costs, travel costs, salaries for scientists and their grad students and support personnel. It can't be spent on things (or persons) other than what it is entailed for. And accounting is fairly rigorous, so absent some major fraud (which nowadays is usually discovered sooner rather than later), that money does not wind up in the pocket of the lead researcher. And finally and most laughably, do you really think scientists didn't get grants before global warming? Or that they couldn't find another area of study also (I won't say equally) worthy of their time and effort and somebody's grant money? Meanwhile, the folks paying for this "expert" to lay his charges stand to rake in their billions as long as the situation remains as is.

This is an extreme instance, but if you watch for nonsensical arguments, you will find that they are pretty common. Bogus arguments often require a leap of logic or even a leap *from* logic in order to make a point. Speakers will sometimes give themselves away by speeding up at the questionable spot in their discussion. Not always, but it can be a sign. More to the point, observe your own reaction. If an assertion or a justification causes you to tip your head to the side or knit your brow in confusion, the difficulty probably isn't you.

As much as it pains me to say so, we've barely skimmed the surface of bad-faith writing and communication. These will suffice to give you an idea of what's wrong in the world of writing. The damage these bad apples do is incalculable. Health cures and disease prevention slowed by decades, hordes of victims condemned to avoidable death, irreversible damage visited on the environment and communities, legislative stasis where action is desperately needed. Worse, in some ways, they pollute the whole information barrel. Because they don't believe what they say, they don't worry about being disbelieved. If they aren't, that's almost as good as if they are, since it calls into question all others who would profess as purveyors of truth or expertise or merely experience: "Maybe yours is also a hoax; we can't believe you, either; maybe your facts and data are just as corrupt." The thing about fraudsters is, they win either way. They achieve notoriety, which is what some of them seek, or they debase the entire conversation. Their mere presence is a contamination. The ancients knew how to deal with such corruption in the social body, but we're more resistant to the wanton slaughter of bullocks. It does seem, however, as if some sort of purgation is in order.

Come to think of it, as I wrote this chapter, one or two Dantean punishments did commend themselves. One involves hornets—lots of them—and eyeballs. Seems fitting for those who would blind us with falsehood. The second? Trust me, you don't want to know.

Conclusion

Looking for Certainty in an Uncertain Time

IT SHOULD BE CLEAR by now that not every writer has readers' best interests at heart. Some want to push an agenda, some simply to sow discord or confusion, and a significant few to perpetuate a hoax or commit fraud. None of this is new. My Chatterton friend from the Wikipedia discussion teaches a course in forgeries and literary hoaxes; her reading list begins in the eighteenth century, right around the time of mass printing of texts. Such things were undertaken before that, of course, but hand-copying out phony "ancient" texts, for instance, was a massive undertaking. Those other crimes against truth began in earnest around the same time. To combat such mischief requires, as we have discussed, defensive measures. Those I have offered thus far have been more or less mechanical: more research, better fact-checking, clearer thinking, more muscular analysis. Pure nuts-and-bolts stuff. All of those measures can prove helpful, and all are fairly earthbound.

But let's consider an airier option: readers need to make greater use of their imaginations. Now, imagination is not fantasy, and good for that. We have entirely too many fantastic readings at present, too many pronouncements based on random statements violently manipulated and ending with phrases like "straight to Auschwitz," or "straight to the killing fields" referring to genocides in Nazi Germany and Cambodia, respectively. Instead, let's learn to practice *imaginative reading*, which is to say, let's become active cocreators of meaning. We already do that when reading "creative" texts, novels and stories and poems and so on, but we become curiously passive when we get to nonfiction. Why? It probably goes back to early exposure to school textbooks, which were best dealt with (and intended to be so) by passively accepting the information in preparation for the next quiz, the next test. My Ohio History (once required in the state where I grew up) did not encourage or reward invention on the part of seventh-grade readers. Or even questions. Those were asked by the editors at the ends of chapters. The message was clear: sit still, glean as much information as possible, don't think too much. Which is the lesson we learned.

But what if the lesson was wrong? What if there is a more active role for us? What would that role look like? And how might we benefit? How, for that matter, would we begin?

For starters, we should bring the same critical faculties to reading nonfiction that we use for our reading of "imaginative" writing. We want to develop those same habits of seeing connections that we use with novels and poems: how is this situation like others we've seen? What does it mean that people in this narrative reacted as they did? The writer will have one interpretation, but is that the only one? Are there possibilities he hasn't seen? How are these old murders like newer ones? How does this new information on, say, geologic formations alter my understanding of the ground I walk upon? The connections we seek can be multiple:

within the text in the way one part connects to another, between this text and others, between the events or situations in this book and the world outside books, the world of our own experiences.

We do not come to our reading as empty vessels waiting to be filled with knowledge. True, sometimes, as in the case of McPhee's *Annals of the Former World*, we may know precious little on a subject, but that is not to say that we know nothing about anything. Part of imagination is bringing what we know to bear on this new information. Knowledge is fairly mechanical. Understanding how to apply that cache of information in a fresh situation is not mechanical; it involves instinct and vision and what we might call "touch," the sense that this is an appropriate place to insinuate that knowledge into a book or article. Be forewarned, it won't always work out as planned, but that's okay. We make predictions as we read, assuming that information X will help explain something in the book we're reading. Sometimes, however, we find out two pages or ten pages or fifty pages later that X didn't fit the situation at all, that in fact it only misled us. That's okay, though. There's no test, no penalty for incorrect guesses. Besides, we already make such assumptions, so this approach only makes manifest something that we do unconsciously all the time.

I mentioned earlier that the Osage murders described by David Grann in *Killers of the Flower Moon* seem to bear some connection to more recent disappearances of Native American people, mainly women, in the American West. That continuity over nearly a century suggests something seriously wrong with relations between mainstream and Native communities, or within those communities, some terrible problem that didn't end with the conclusion of the Indian Wars. In making such connections, in imaginatively filling in the gaps, we make our reading belong to us; no one in the world will have exactly *that* understanding but us.

When I read *The Boys in the Boat*, the hardscrabble upbringing, the physical and social challenges, and the privations of the boys who would man the oars of that celebrated shell made me think of my immediate family and others I knew who had grown up in the Appalachian foothills of southeast Ohio, men and women shaped by struggle and hard labor from early childhood, by learning to plow a straight furrow behind horses at ages that adolescents elsewhere were learning to drive cars, by experiencing the Great Depression in the poorest counties of a generally prosperous state. I didn't know anyone who suffered the horrors that Joe Rantz did in his growing up, but I knew plenty who had gone through great hardship on their way to adulthood, and I saw how they turned out. No one in the world will have precisely that reading of Daniel James Brown's book, because no one would plug in the same figures, the same experiences, although I am certain many other readers substitute similar situations. This reading, though, is mine. You can't have it. And probably wouldn't want it.

Imaginative reading can serve us in another way besides making our understanding richer. It can help protect us against bad-faith writing. If we bring everything we have to bear on reading, if we apply what we already know, ask the questions that the little voice in the back of our head is asking *us* as we read, we stand a better chance of not being duped. When we listen to that voice, honestly and without preconceived notion, we generally know if something feels right or not. Most of the literary hoaxes foisted on publishers and readers have come about because someone's *will to believe* was stronger than their native judiciousness, their hope or greed or ambition overcame their best thinking. Had they not silenced that little voice—that may sound a little like Jiminy Cricket, slightly squeaky and a bit of a scold but a good soul for all that—they might have been spared the embarrassment of being the victim of a writerly con. We can never eliminate devious or misleading writing, nor can we ever completely avoid being taken in, but we can begin to take steps in that direction. Reading, as I have said elsewhere, is a full-contact activity: we have to bring the whole of our being to it if we are to do it properly.

I mentioned in the chapter on personal forms of nonfiction that, although we may not always think of it as such, nonfiction is a branch of literature. As far back as Horace in 19 B.C.E., his *Ars Poetica* tells us that the purpose of poetry is to "delight and instruct." Is this any less true of nonfiction? The instruction part is clear enough, but we ask for a bit of delight with that earnest intent. At the very least, if "delight" sounds too high-flown, we should be able to expect that nonfiction works will avoid being boring, that they will entertain. We should insist on it. Too often, we consider works of nonfiction as mere conveyances of information, but such thinking does a disservice to both them and us. True, there are many works of pedestrian nonfiction, but the same can be said of novels, short stories, verse dramas, haiku, sonnets, epics, tragedies, comedies, movies, and every other form of literature. The vast majority of writing, as with all human endeavors, is by definition ordinary, average, pedestrian. Perhaps that's just as well; it might prove too exhausting if every work were a masterpiece. In any case, that is the general condition in which we mortals operate. Sometimes, however, labors rise above the mediocre. And even far above. The results can be sublime.

The Books in the Book

I HAVE SPENT A lot of time slinging names and titles at you, and you have been really good sports about it. But I figure you don't really want to slog back through all those pages to find a book you want to check out further. Sound about right? So, here's the list, brought to you by the best of my limited abilities. I have limited the list to those I actually discuss, if only for a couple of sentences. There are quite a few others that only make cameo appearances and so would merely clutter this list; for those, please check the index.

Newspapers also make appearances here, especially the *New York Times, Washington Post, USA Today,* the *Dayton Daily News,* and the *Lansing State Journal.* I hope, despite signs to the contrary, that daily papers will continue to play a significant role in the cultural life of our country. So, too, with magazines, whose numbers have dwindled precipitously in my lifetime, disastrously during my adulthood. There are only a handful of general interest magazines left, yet those—*The New Yorker, The Atlantic, The New Republic, Harper's, Vanity Fair* among them—remain an important home for serious, muscular journalism. Periodicals have long been the lifeblood of our national discussion, places for more than sound bites and snarky one-liners. If they should vanish, I fear for the republic.

Agee, James, *Let Us Now Praise Famous Men* (1941)

Ambrose, Stephen E., *Undaunted Courage: Meriwether Lewis, Thomas Jefferson, and the Opening of the American West* (1996)

Augustine, *Confessions* (C.E. 397–400)

Barnes, Julian, *Levels of Life* (2013), *Nothing to Be Frightened Of* (2008)

Boo, Katherine, *Behind the Beautiful Forevers* (2012)

Brooks, David, *The Road to Character* (2015)

Brown, Daniel James, *The Boys in the Boat: Nine Americans and Their Epic Quest for Gold at the 1936 Berlin Olympics* (2013)

Chernow, Ron, *Alexander Hamilton* (2004)

Coates, Ta-Nehisi, *Between the World and Me* (2015)

Comey, James, *A Higher Loyalty: Truth, Lies, and Leadership* (2018)

Davidson, Cathy N., *Now You See It: How the Brain Science of Attention Will Transform the Way We Live, Work, and Learn* (2011)

Didion, Joan, *The White Album* (1979); *The Year of Magical Thinking* (2005)

Dillard, Annie, *Pilgrim at Tinker Creek* (1974)

Franklin, Benjamin, *The Autobiography of Benjamin Franklin* (1793)

Frey, James, *A Million Little Pieces* (2003)

Gladwell, Malcolm, *Blink: The Power of Thinking without Thinking* (2005); *The Tipping Point: How Little Things Can Make a Big Difference* (2000)

Grann, David, *Killers of the Flower Moon* (2017)

Hanna-Attisha, Mona, M.D., *What the Eyes Don't See* (2018)

Hemingway, Ernest, *Death in the Afternoon* (1932); *A Moveable Feast* (1964)

Hillenbrand, Laura, *Seabiscuit: An American Legend* (2001)

Hitchens, Christopher, *God Is Not Great* (2007)

Lawrence, D. H., "Reflections on the Death of a Porcupine" (1925)

Lerner, Ben, *The Hatred of Poetry* (2016)

Maddox, Brenda, *Nora: A Biography of Nora Joyce* (1988)

McCullough, David, *1776* (2005)

McPhee, John, *Annals of the Former World* (1998)

Newman, John Henry, *The Idea of a University* (1852, 1858); *Apologia Pro Vita Sua* (1864)

Oates, Joyce Carol, *A Widow's Story* (2011)

Obama, Barack, *Dreams from My Father* (2004); *The Audacity of Hope* (2006)

O'Connor, Cailin, and James Owen Weatherall, *The Misinformation Age: How False Beliefs Spread* (2019)

Oreskes, Naomi, and Erik M. Conway, *Merchants of Doubt* (2010)

Orwell, George, "Shooting an Elephant" (1936)

Pollan, Michael, *How to Change Your Mind* (2018)

Powers, Ron, *Tom and Huck Don't Live Here Anymore* (2001)

Robinson, Marilynne, "Save Our Public Universities," *Harper's* (March 2016)

Sedaris, David, *Holidays on Ice* (1997)

Shetterly, Margot Lee, *Hidden Figures: The American Dream and the Untold Story of the Black Women Mathematicians Who Helped Win the Space Race* (2016)

Specter, Michael, *Denialism: How Irrational Thinking Hinders Scientific Progress, Harms the Planet, and Threatens Our Lives* (2009)

Thompson, Hunter S., *Fear and Loathing in Las Vegas* (1971)

Thoreau, Henry David, *Walden* (1854); *A Week on the Concord and Merrimack Rivers* (1849)

Townshend, Pete, *Who I Am* (2012)

Tyler, Steven, *Does the Noise in My Head Bother You?* (2011)

Tyson, Neil deGrasse, *Astrophysics for People in a Hurry* (2017)

Wolfe, Tom, *The Electric Kool-Aid Acid Test* (1968)

Wolff, Michael, *Fire and Fury: Inside the Trump White House* (2018)

Woodward, Bob, and Carl Bernstein, *All the President's Men* (1974)

Woodward, Bob, *Fear: Trump in the White House* (2018)

Woolf, Virginia, *A Room of One's Own* (1929)

Young, Neil, *Waging Heavy Peace: A Hippie Dream* (2012)

Zapruder, Matthew, *Why Poetry?* (2017)

Thomas C. Foster is the *New York Times* bestselling author of *How to Read Literature Like a Professor, How to Read Novels Like a Professor,* and *Twenty-Five Books that Shaped America.* He is professor of English at the University of Michigan, Flint, where he teaches classes in contemporary fiction, drama, and poetry as well as creative writing and composition. He has written several books on twentieth-century British and Irish literature and lives in East Lansing, Michigan.

ALSO BY THOMAS C. FOSTER

READING THE SILVER SCREEN
A FILM LOVER'S GUIDE TO DECODING THE ART FORM THAT MOVES

From the *New York Times* bestselling author of *How to Read Literature Like a Professor* comes an indispensable analysis of our most celebrated medium, film. Using the investigative approach readers love in *How to Read Literature Like a Professor*, Foster examines this grammar of film through various classic and current movies both foreign and domestic, with special recourse to the "AFI 100 Years-100 Movies" lists. The categories are idiosyncratic yet revealing.

In *Reading the Silver Screen*, readers will gain the expertise and confidence to glean all they can from the movies they love.

HOW TO READ POETRY LIKE A PROFESSOR
A QUIPPY AND SONOROUS GUIDE TO VERSE

"*How to Read Poetry Like a Professor* is not unlike that freshman English class that everyone vies to enroll in—entertaining and informative without being intimidating. The curriculum is on point, and in the end, you'll have the tools to truly 'get' poetry, with all its manifest themes and variations." —*BookPage*

No literary form is as admired and feared as poetry. Admired for its lengthy pedigree—a line of poets extending back to a time before recorded history—and a ubiquitous presence in virtually all cultures, poetry is also revered for its great beauty and the powerful emotions it evokes. But the form has also instilled trepidation in its many admirers mainly because of a lack of familiarity and knowledge.

With *How to Read Poetry Like a Professor*, readers can rediscover poetry and reap its many rewards.

HarperCollins*Publishers* | HARPER PERENNIAL
DISCOVER GREAT AUTHORS, EXCLUSIVE OFFERS, AND MORE AT HC.COM.